ALSO BY JEFF CARROLL

Sam Rice: A Biography of the Washington Senators Hall of Famer

PERFECT
RIVALS

PERFECT

RIVALS

*Notre Dame, Miami, and the Battle
for the Soul of College Football*

JEFF CARROLL

BALLANTINE BOOKS • NEW YORK

ESPN
BOOKS

Published in the United States by ESPN Books, an imprint of ESPN, Inc., New York,
and Ballantine Books, an imprint of The Random House Publishing Group,
a division of Random House, Inc., New York.

BALLANTINE and colophon are registered trademarks of Random House, Inc.
The ESPN Books name and logo are registered trademarks of ESPN, Inc.

Library of Congress Cataloging-in-Publication Data
Carroll, Jeff.
Perfect rivals : Notre Dame, Miami, and the battle for the soul of college football /
Jeff Carroll.
p. cm.
Includes bibliographical references.
ISBN 978-0-345-51710-4 (hardcover : alk. paper)
eBook ISBN 978-0-345-52315-0
1. Notre Dame Fighting Irish (Football team)—History. 2. University of Notre Dame—
Football—History. 3. Miami Hurricanes ·(Football team)—History. 4. University of
Miami—Football—History. 5. Sports rivalries—United States. I. Title.
GV958.N6C37 2010
796.332'63—dc22   2010021378

Printed in the United States of America on acid-free paper

www.ballantinebooks.com
www.espnbooks.com

2 4 6 8 9 7 5 3 1

First Edition

Design by R. Bull

For Tom Wilcox, who sent the most encouraging text message
I have ever received: "Catholics vs. Convicts? That's a great idea!"
May a copy find its way to the other side and into his hands.

CONTENTS

PERFECT
RIVALS

Who Started It?

Of all the questions that would spring from the most heated college football rivalry of the 1980s, this is one that lingers. The inquiry usually arises in reference to the famed dustup in the tunnel on October 15, 1988, when History's Team, the University of Notre Dame, finally informed the Team of the Decade, the University of Miami Hurricanes, that it was not surrendering the neighborhood without a fight. Despite the seemingly obvious differences, the programs had more in common than they, or anyone else, thought at the time. Both programs had been defined largely and for a long time by their quarterbacks, and now the Hurricanes were starting a midwestern Catholic, Steve Walsh, who seemed like the perfect fit for the Irish, while Notre Dame was starting a black South Carolinian, Tony Rice, who was the kind of southerner the Hurricanes rarely let get away. In the early twentieth century, Notre Dame had built its program on the strength of working-class sons of immigrants, cast-asides, and a renegade coach who happened to be a genius. Likewise, Miami's burgeoning dynasty had featured three-star recruits with hardscrabble backgrounds and something to prove. Both head coaches, Jimmy Johnson of Miami and Lou Holtz of Notre Dame, had arrived from programs in turmoil.

With so much in common, perhaps the programs should have considered themselves kindred organizations. But by 1988 they decidedly did not, and had the bloodied knuckles to prove it.

So who started it?

Would you believe *a leprechaun?*

Not in 1988, not in the tunnel, but four years earlier, in the same stadium.

In 1984, first-year Miami head coach Jimmy Johnson brought his defending national championship team into South Bend, where the Hurricanes easily dispensed of their hosts, the Fighting Irish. But even as his team rolled by almost three touchdowns, Johnson did not enjoy the afternoon. He was frustrated by the lack of a police presence to keep the Hurricanes sideline free of unwelcome loiterers. He was tired of Notre Dame marching band members wandering past their boundaries into Miami's space. But most of all, he was of a mind to punt Notre Dame's leprechaun mascot all the way to the end of the rainbow.

"That obnoxious little student in the Irish getup kept running up to me and getting in my face," Johnson would later recall. "Anybody else might have knocked him on his ass. And I can't tell you it didn't cross my mind."

Johnson was too smart to be that brazen. Instead the Hurricanes, game firmly in hand, ran sideline plays designed to steamroll the energetic little guy.

———

Miami's offense, despite its best efforts, never did manage to run down the Irish leprechaun in the 1984 game. Instead, a year later, the Hurricanes would steamroll the Fighting Irish themselves. As they journeyed to Miami to conclude the 1985 season and head coach Gerry Faust's forgettable tenure—he had resigned earlier in the week to beat the firing squad—the Irish had dropped three of four to the Hurricanes, and none of the defeats had been close. In a series long dominated by Notre Dame, the tables began to turn in Faust's first year, 1981. After eight consecutive defeats to the Irish by double digits, the Hurricanes battered Notre Dame 37–15 in that season's final regular-season game. John Krimm, a cornerback on Faust's first team, remembers feeling "toyed with" by Miami quarterback Jim Kelly. Notre Dame managed to eke out a 16–14 victory over the 'Canes the following season, but losses by 20 and 18 points followed the next two years. And yet, frustrating as those games were, they were nothing compared to what awaited Notre Dame in the Orange Bowl on November 30, 1985.

"Before that game is played," says Frank Stams, a freshman fullback on the '85 Irish, "we go out an hour and fifteen minutes before the game. We go through our warm-ups like a well-schooled, well-disciplined team. We're doing everything the right way.

"Then I look over on the Miami side, and they're coming out of their locker room, and they don't even have their shirts on. Their belts are unbuckled. They're walking around bullshitting with people. Jimmy Johnson is bullshitting with people. You talk about swagger? I saw the swagger."

Doing color commentary on the game for CBS was former Notre Dame head coach Ara Parseghian. Notre Dame reveres its great coaches, and Parseghian is right there in the South Bend pantheon along with Knute Rockne, a mythic figure not just at Notre Dame but in American sports culture, and Frank Leahy, who built the Irish dynasty of the 1940s. By the time he shared an Orange Bowl booth with Brent Musburger for Faust's final game at Notre Dame, Parseghian had not coached a college football game at Notre Dame—or anywhere—for eleven years. When Miami was looking to revive its program in the late 1970s, it had actually made a preliminary inquiry to Parseghian, but the overture had not panned out. Parseghian instead turned out to be the rarest of birds in his profession: a coach who announced his retirement and then actually stayed retired. But just because you can take the coach out of Notre Dame doesn't mean you can take Notre Dame out of the coach, and as Miami's lead ballooned, Parseghian clearly sympathized with the Irish.

Or, as Jimmy Johnson would later put it, Parseghian had worn his "gold underwear" for the broadcast. In the fourth quarter, with the Hurricanes well on their way to a 58–7 victory, Parseghian's allegiance to the visitors became difficult for him to mask.

"It's time for Jimmy Johnson to show some compassion," he moaned.

The commentary by Parseghian and his booth mates cut straight to the heart of what annoyed Miami's players and coaches about Notre Dame: the idea that one of the most dominant programs in the country owed a collection of players who weren't as talented as Miami was—who didn't work nearly as hard as Miami did—some sort of deference.

"I was sitting at home, because I was a redshirt freshman," says Miami linebacker Bernard Clark, "and I heard them say, 'They're spitting in the face of the Four Horsemen.' I was, like, 'Who are the Four Horsemen? Who is Knute Rockne?' I really didn't know."

After the game, when Johnson heard about Parseghian's on-air laments, he was incensed. After all, Johnson noted, Parseghian himself was known to hang a whooping on an opponent from time to time. In 1966, Parseghian's eventual national champions hammered a hapless Duke squad 64–0. The year before, Notre Dame had clobbered Pittsburgh 69–13. In 1970, Notre Dame destroyed two military academies with long and storied football traditions, drubbing Army 51–10 and Navy 56–7.

"And even poor old Gerry Faust," Johnson would point out, "hung a 52–6 on Purdue in 1983.

"I guess I should have known," he added, "that nobody cries louder and more pitifully than a bully who's just had the shit stomped out of him."

Johnson understood Parseghian's devotion to Notre Dame and its role in his lack of objectivity, but beyond the call for "compassion" he was angry that the former coach's broadcast partners, Musburger and Pat Haden, were completely missing the boat with their explanations of what was happening on the field. Late in the fourth quarter, with the game already out of hand, Faust sent his punter out to kick from his own end zone. Johnson countered with his backup punt return unit. He would swear after the fact that there was no punt block called.

It didn't matter. Miami backup defensive tackle Bill Hawkins saw a gaping hole in the Notre Dame protection scheme and shot through it. He blocked the Notre Dame punt and a Hurricane fell on it for yet another touchdown.

"How can they be blocking punts when the game is completely out of hand?" Parseghian raged.

On one hand, Johnson understood the emotion. Faust's forced resignation had brought many people squarely over to his side, especially Parseghian, who knew more than anybody what kind of pressures the head coach of the Irish faced. And Faust was such a stand-up, kind man that no one with a beating heart wanted to see him go out this way—which was all fine by Johnson and the Hurricanes. In fact, the Miami coach had gone into the game fully expecting Notre Dame's players to rally around their departing coach. In an era before the Internet carried news around the country at lightning speed, the true tenor of the Notre Dame football team at that point, decidedly dour and interested in nothing more than getting its season-long nightmare over with, was something that Johnson had failed to perceive. Instead, the Notre Dame team his Hurricanes lined up against that day had quit on their coach well before they arrived in south Florida.

"I remember," recalls ND linebacker Wes Pritchett, "Michael Irvin was on that Miami team, and every pass he caught, whether it was a one-yard out or a twenty-yard touchdown, he did his little dance and rubbed our face in it."

Through the years, the Hurricanes would do plenty to contribute to their reputation as the bad boys of college football, so Johnson's shock and dismay at what he perceived was his program's unfair treatment by the media and the public was willfully disingenuous at worst and blissfully unaware at best. As the years went by, Johnson would reveal that it wasn't out of character for his teams to lay a beating on a hapless opponent out of sheer spite. Two years after breaking Notre Dame's spirit, for example, Johnson's Hurricanes would do the same to his own alma mater, Arkansas. That 51–7 victory was sweet revenge aimed at Arkansas head coach Frank Broyles, Johnson's college coach. Johnson felt that Broyles had embarrassed him during a job search years earlier, and he would later call Broyles "the first of three men I have written off in my life."

Nonetheless, looking back on the development of Miami's reputation as the unquestioned villain figure in college football, Johnson felt that no one played a bigger role than Parseghian that afternoon against Notre Dame. When the Hurricanes heard about Parseghian's emotional commentary, they stewed about the hypocrisy. "I don't like all that tradition stuff," Hurricanes running back Melvin Bratton said after the game. "I don't like Notre Dame. I hate them."

"We just pounded Gerry Faust into retirement," says Dan Sileo, a defensive lineman on the 1985 'Canes. "We beat the fuck out of them, and I remember the alumni guys coming up to us and saying, 'Hey, Notre Dame used to come in here under Ara Parseghian and beat us 77–7.' Ara Parseghian blasted Jimmy for it, but hey, bro, you used to come into the Orange Bowl and blow out Miami that way, and now you don't like it because it's Notre Dame? Tough shit.

"[Former Miami linebacker] Ted Hendricks would tell me, 'These fuckers would come in here and blow us out and not think twice about putting seventy on you,'" Sileo adds. "So when Miami was blowing them out, it was great. It was justice. It's called defending the 'U.'"

Notre Dame's players didn't feel that they had simply lost a football game or that their talent level didn't measure up to Miami's. They were left wondering if their entire operation was being left in the dust by the Hurricanes, who had their own way of "respecting the game": steamrolling over opponents and dancing on their graves.

"It was, like, 'What's the point of what we're doing?'" Stams says. "'Why can't we do it their way?' You grow up being disciplined and regimented in the game, but there's always an exception to the rule. Those guys were the exception. And yeah, you start scratching your head like 'Jesus, are we doing it the right way?'"

Even the coach they helped drive from a job respected the Hurricanes' aggressive style. "They were in the national championship picture at that time," says Faust. "In those days, how badly you beat a team affected the polls. So I didn't blame them one bit. That's football."

———

After the contest, the teams lined up for their customary postgame handshake. Among his Notre Dame teammates, Terry Andrysiak was not known as a locker room rabble-rouser. "He wouldn't say shit if he had a mouthful," Stams says.

But in the aftermath of the 51-point embarrassment, even the reserved backup quarterback had had just about enough. As the handshake lines moved along, Andrysiak spotted Johnson up ahead. Playing behind junior starter Steve Beuerlein, the quiet sophomore had gotten into the game only for fourth-quarter mop-up duty. But that didn't mean he hadn't taken the loss to heart any less than teammates who had suffered through nearly all sixty minutes of the epic humiliation.

When the paths of the backup quarterback and the winning coach finally crossed, Andrysiak took Johnson's hand and stared him straight in the eye.

"Coach," he began, "that was one of the most classless acts I've seen in my life. And in a few years, when you come to our place, we're going to kick your ass."

PART ONE

Collision Course

CHAPTER 1

A Monumental Task

"*Young man*, how long have you been playing football?"

Chuck Lanza looked up from his seat. Worn-out physically and emotionally from the whirlwind of the last week, particularly the last three days, he had allowed his posture to become relaxed and his mind to wander as he sat in a classroom with the rest of his Notre Dame football teammates. He had his feet propped up in front of him. He had been lazily examining his fingernails. "I was a little bit cocky at that point," Lanza says.

His new head coach, Lou Holtz, had noticed Lanza's demeanor. And he didn't like it.

Now the five-foot-ten, small-framed Holtz stood over the hulking offensive lineman. He wanted an answer to his question.

"I don't know," Lanza said. "Ten, eleven years?"

"Well," Holtz replied, "if you ever want to play another down, you will put your feet on the floor, sit up straight, and pay attention."

Message sent, message received, and not just by Lanza. Elsewhere in the modest auditorium, located in Notre Dame's Athletic and Convocation Center, wide receiver Tim Brown and quarterback Steve Beuerlein exchanged a knowing glance: This guy meant business. There was a long way to go—a very long way—but at least this seemed like a good start.

Holtz had loomed over the preceding few days, a span as difficult as any in Notre Dame's storied football history, as a distant figure. Some younger players, associating Holtz only with his previous employer, the University of Minnesota, knew little about him. While heeding his warning to sit still and shut up, they privately sat wondering where this guy, fresh out of the Twin Cities, got off taking such a tone with them. After all, most of them wouldn't have looked Minnesota's way had a scholarship come attached to a room assignment with the Dallas Cowboys cheerleaders. Upperclassmen, on the other hand, remembered him from his successful days at the University of Arkansas. Lanza, a southerner, had even been recruited by Holtz and had sat in his office in Fayetteville once upon a time. That had been a much more pleasant conversation.

Whatever impressions his new players had developed from recent news stories, prior knowledge, or tidbits circulating the grapevine, this was Holtz's first face-to-face encounter with the team he had just inherited. Understanding the odds he faced, he knew he had to make this initial meeting count. After all, the last few months under the previous head coach's regime hadn't been merely difficult, they had been toxic, bringing the proudest program in the land to the lowest moment in its history.

Faust had resigned just six days earlier, throwing the days preceding the last game of Notre Dame's season—that ill-fated trip to Miami—into chaos. Then came the weekend that wouldn't end. In fact, Faust had addressed his players just minutes before Holtz, in the same classroom in which they now sat at rapt attention. After a teary ten-minute farewell, Faust exited. About two minutes later, in walked Holtz.

In a private meeting with Faust during the week, Holtz had complimented his predecessor on his overall recruiting, but said he wished Faust had left him some more speed on the roster. That would have to come later. For now, the men gathered in the room for Holtz represented what he had to work with. Because Lanza had been the unlucky one sitting in the front row and giving in to his justifiable exhaustion, not to mention his somewhat less justifiable sense of exaggerated self-importance, he had borne the brunt of Holtz's stern message. But it had been meant for everyone.

"I want you to sit up straight!" Holtz barked. "Put your feet on the floor, keep your heads up, your eyes forward, and get ready to talk about winning football games."

———

When Dan Devine, a national champion coach in 1977 at Notre Dame, announced his retirement in 1980, the university's administration hired not one of the many able college coaches who would have jumped at America's most prestigious job, but instead Faust, who had never coached above the high school level. Not that Faust had been a run-of-the-mill high school football coach in his twenty-one years at Archbishop Moeller, just down the road in Cincinnati. He oversaw a veritable high school football empire, an empire he had built largely from scratch. Moeller's two-hundred-page game program brought in $30,000 in advertising revenue a year, and one unforgettable Friday evening Moeller outdrew baseball's Cincinnati Reds. At the time he left, Faust, also Moeller's athletic director, had been negotiating for Moeller to play a game in Japan.

On the field, Faust's last few seasons at the school were likely unmatched at that level anywhere, any time, before or since. In seventy-one games played from 1975 through 1980, his final season at Moeller, Faust's teams lost one game. They won five Ohio state titles and four mythical national titles. Working tirelessly on behalf of his players, Faust had sent three hundred of them on to college football scholarships, including fourteen to Notre Dame. The university powers that be had noticed.

Beyond all of that, Faust was considered by many to be about as nice a man as had ever walked the face of the earth. He was a proud Catholic who began every day with early-morning Mass, and a devoted husband who still wrote his wife, Marlene, thank-you notes. "His world is a hundred yards long," wrote biographer Denny Dressman, "with a goal post at one end and an altar at the other." In other words, he was a perfect fit for Notre Dame in the eyes of its administration, which still believed that Notre Dame didn't hire great coaches but rather *created* great coaches. A gifted football coach and motivator—Faust jetted around the country delivering motivational speeches to businesspeople in Moeller's off-season—and a prince of a man, Faust would never do anything to embarrass the image-obsessed school.

Off the field, at least. On the field, whatever else graced his résumé, he was still a high school coach. He had no preparation for the rigors and pressures of the job that greeted him in South Bend.

Faust's first batch of Irish players were skeptical of him from the time his hiring was announced, and he didn't do a tremendous job winning them over. The college players considered themselves grown men and wanted to be treated that way. They had serious doubts that a life-long high school coach would be able to relate to them, and Faust un-wittingly confirmed their suspicions, getting his players' contact information removed from the university's student directory. In today's celebrity athlete culture, the move would hardly be considered drastic: Most detail-oriented modern coaches, obsessed with maintaining a grip on every aspect of their programs, would consider it a necessary step to keep outside influences and distractions at arm's length. But in 1981 many Irish players felt the move was paternalistic and displayed a lack of respect and trust by the new head coach.

After a tough loss during Faust's first season, a few upperclassmen visited a popular downtown South Bend bar, Corby's Irish Pub, to drown their sorrows for a few hours. It was a pretty standard way for of-age Irish players to blow off some steam. But, according to Notre Dame linebacker Bob Crable, Faust "went ballistic." Yet again, Faust's players felt as if they were being treated like children.

Faust baffled his players by devoting much of an early team meeting to trivial changes to their uniforms: They felt they had spent an inordi-nate amount of time on the color of Notre Dame's game socks. The players, just a few weeks removed from giving national champion Georgia all it could handle in the Sugar Bowl, felt as though they had a good grasp on the time and effort required to be a successful college football team. Their new head coach, fresh off the high school sideline, was painfully proving that he did not.

"You had the sense right away that he was in over his head," says John Krimm, a first-stringer on Faust's first team. "I don't think he ap-preciated the physical and mental toll that, week in and week out, the season would take on a college player versus a high school player."

There were some triumphant moments during Faust's tenure, in-cluding a convincing victory over Louisiana State University (LSU) in his head coaching debut and an upset victory over No. 1–ranked Uni-versity of Pittsburgh a year later. But the disappointments were more frequent. Under Faust, the Irish lost four consecutive games to Air Force. They played to a 13–13 standstill in 1982 against an Oregon team that had lost its first six games of the season—and thirteen of its last fourteen dating back to the season before.

"We were a very depressed group of young men," says Mark Bavaro, an All-American tight end under Faust. "I couldn't wait to get the heck out of there. If the rules had allowed you to leave early back in those days, I would have tried like mad to get out of there."

———————

The beginning of the end for Faust came the Saturday before the Miami trip. In the final two minutes of the season's final game at Notre Dame Stadium, the Irish were driving against seventeenth-ranked LSU, trailing 10–7. Beuerlein hit Tim Brown in stride, a potential winning touchdown pass delivered right into the talented sophomore's hands. But Brown juggled the ball and Tigers defensive back Steve Rehage plucked it out of the air for the game-clinching interception.

Faust was shaking hands on the field with LSU coach Bill Arnsparger minutes later when an Irish assistant sprinted over to him and asked him to get to the locker room as soon as he could. When Faust arrived, Brown was inconsolable at his locker. Faust put his arm around the wide receiver and tried to assuage him.

"Timmy," Faust said, "you didn't lose that game. *I* lost that game."

Faust walked away and buried his head in his hands. Notre Dame sports information director Roger Valdiserri walked in, saw Faust in that condition, and was immediately convinced that the coach's resignation was imminent. He was correct. After seeing the way Brown was reacting to the defeat, Faust made his decision. He finally understood the degree to which his players were suffering because of the sideshow that had developed around his employment status.

Faust planned to get his resignation out of the way first thing on Monday of Miami week, but he couldn't reach longtime university president Theodore Hesburgh, who was attending a convention in Maryland. Since Faust felt obligated to inform Hesburgh first, the matter dragged into Tuesday.

That set up one of the more chaotic days in the history of the Notre Dame football program. On Tuesday morning, Faust finally reached Hesburgh in his Maryland hotel room and informed him of his decision. Hesburgh gave his blessing. Next, Faust walked over to the university's administration building—the structure topped by the famous golden dome—to speak with Father Edmund Joyce. Although Hesburgh was the university's president and Gene Corrigan its athletic director, Joyce wielded a tremendous amount of power when it came to the Irish football program. The two men met in the administrator's office.

"Gerry," said Joyce, "I was hoping you would do this." Joyce had been planning to fire Faust anyway.

"What's so noble about that?" says Steve Lawrence, a defensive back in Faust's final season and Holtz's first. "Everybody knows that you're not going to be there next season and you resign before the last game? Come on."

Faust gathered his assistant coaches next, racing against the clock before his usual Tuesday media teleconference. Then he blindsided the press by announcing the decision at the beginning of what was usually a routine chat about the upcoming game. Within minutes, the Notre Dame sports information staff was flooded with phone calls from national and regional media members who had not been on the phone for the initial bomb. A second press conference was scheduled for the evening to accommodate the second wave.

In his mission to distribute his news quickly that morning, however, Faust forgot a key constituency: his players. "I made a mistake," says Faust. "I didn't talk to the team. I wanted the game for the seniors and I didn't want to distract the kids from the real purpose of the last game, and that was for the seniors that were playing that year. I made a mistake by not sitting down and talking to the team and telling them why I was stepping down. I said nothing at all. We just went out and practiced that day. I didn't say anything to the team that whole week."

Before Notre Dame home games, Faust had taken golf cart joyrides around campus, mingling with fans and acting as an ambassador and greeter rather than a football coach. So when it came to their head coach, Notre Dame's players were used to coming in second place. As if they hadn't already been made to feel like an afterthought on the morning of his resignation, Faust supplied more reasons as the week went on. At his second press conference on Tuesday night, he tried to lighten the mood by jokingly lobbying for his next job.

"It's easy to contact me," Faust announced. "Just call Notre Dame. I need a fresh start."

Calls from suitors in the coaching world—mostly small colleges—and the business world began flooding in the next morning. Then, in his pregame interview with ESPN before the contest in Miami on Saturday, Faust again flaunted his availability. "I'm thankful that I had the opportunity to be at Notre Dame for five years," he said. "I don't regret it a bit. And by the way, I'm looking for a coaching job."

"He made light of the situation and he never considered, 'What about all these players that have been here?'" Lawrence says. "Or what about all the lives that have been affected while you've been here? Instead of being a little bit more modest, he's joking about it. He was just in a different place than everyone else, and the sad part about it is, he wasn't aware of it."

If their coach had already checked out, players figured, why shouldn't they? "I ran into three of their starters in Fort Lauderdale before the game," said Miami offensive lineman Barry Panfil. "They treated it like a minivacation. They were down here to have a good time."

While Faust was botching his exit, the Notre Dame hiring machine was springing into rapid action. In the grand scheme, Holtz's journey to his first team meeting had been arduous, a five-decade trudge. But the final leg was swift. The phone calls from South Bend to Minneapolis, where Holtz had just completed his second regular season at Minnesota, had come in the hours after Faust's resignation. The first one, to Minnesota athletic director Paul Giel, was made around four o'clock on Tuesday afternoon. As a courtesy, Notre Dame athletic director Gene Corrigan sought permission to speak to Holtz, and Giel granted it.

By the time Holtz went to bed that night, around midnight, it had been made clear to him that the Notre Dame job was his if he wanted it. Holtz said he would think things through overnight, but there never was much doubt which way he was leaning. His hiring was officially announced by dusk on Wednesday. The turnaround between Faust's resignation and Holtz's acceptance of the job the following morning had been less than twenty-four hours. Corrigan, who had begged Faust to step down during a shouting match at the coach's house a year before, was amused by media members who were surprised that he and the Notre Dame administration had sprung so quickly into action.

"Don't you think we have a list ready?" Corrigan asked. "If Digger [Notre Dame basketball coach Richard "Digger" Phelps] gets hit by a car today, there's a list in my drawer."

Notre Dame had acted decisively, largely because it knew exactly what it wanted this time around. When it became apparent that a coaching search was imminent, Corrigan had spoken with Parseghian, who had won national titles at the school in 1966 and 1973. Parseghian had been a head coach for fourteen years before he arrived in South Bend, he explained to Corrigan. And he had needed "every one" of them to prepare for the fishbowl that was the University of Notre Dame.

Holtz had dreamed about coaching the Fighting Irish since his days as a Catholic grade schooler in Ohio, when he claimed the nuns would lead the students every day in a rendition of the school's familiar "Victory March." Like a lot of Holtz's anecdotes, it is difficult to discern to what degree that tale was true and to what degree it was embellished, or even fabricated, in service to the narrative. But whether or not the seed had been planted that early and that theatrically, there is little doubt that Notre Dame looked like a destination job to him in late autumn 1985. Holtz's son Skip was already a student at Notre Dame, and Lou spoke openly about his interest in the job in South Bend as it became apparent Faust would not be back. Notre Dame, he had said, was the only place for which he would consider leaving Minnesota. He even claimed he had a "Notre Dame clause" in his Minnesota contract that would allow him to exit his post without penalty if the Notre Dame job ever opened. Later investigative reporting would reveal that this was a dubious claim, but it makes clear Holtz's desire to coach the Irish.

Holtz was introduced at a press conference late in the week, while the current team, under the guidance of Faust and his lame-duck staff, struggled to stay focused on the Hurricanes.

"The whole week, the coaches were in turmoil," says Mike Kovaleski. "You could just see panic and you could just sense fear, because they didn't know what was going to happen to them the following year. They didn't know where they were going to be. The whole team was just in complete turmoil and chaos and it was very frustrating to experience. The game was an afterthought."

But it still had to be played, and the Irish took the field in the Orange Bowl a bit like lambs heading to the slaughter. Meanwhile, all the way across the continent, in the Palm Springs, California home of University of Minnesota booster Don Knutson, Lou Holtz settled in for his first look at the team he was about to inherit. Armed with a Notre Dame media guide and a remote control, he tried his best to concentrate on his new team's game against Miami. But as the Hurricanes scored at will, that became difficult.

"No, no," he muttered as Miami added to its advantage. Occasionally, Holtz would even flip over to the rivalry game between Alabama and Auburn on a different channel. That game, after all, was far more competitive, the traditional Southeastern Conference rivals both firmly embedded among the top ten teams in the nation in that week's polls.

In late November of 1985, on the other hand, the Notre Dame–Miami matchup was anything but evenly matched. Even so, the game did contain some of the traditional elements of a rivalry: namely, that the teams played almost every year, and that they didn't like each other a great deal.

But while the Hurricanes largely held Notre Dame's past excellence in low regard, Holtz was keenly aware of the crush of history that would greet him in South Bend.

"I can't live up to all the expectations," he said as he watched Miami massacre the Irish. "I look at those records put up by Rockne, Leahy, and Parseghian and I swear to gosh it's a misprint. Nobody can win that many games."

Toward the end of the contest, one of the announcers pondered a brighter future for the Irish.

"Perhaps," said Ara Parseghian himself, "Notre Dame will rise from the ashes."

Holtz grinned as he repeated the sentence, placing his emphasis on the word *perhaps*. During his tenure in South Bend, Holtz would not often carry himself like an optimist. In fact, his signature trait, other than the sport's most famous lisp, would become his tendency to talk up his next opponent while at the same time speaking about his own team like it were a disheveled, disorganized, woefully overmatched mess about to rip apart at the seams. But only someone who was an optimist at heart could smile on this particular night, which marked rock bottom for Notre Dame, as if he were in on something the rest of the world was not.

———

The humiliating loss to the Hurricanes dropped Faust's record at Notre Dame to 30–26–1 and his team's 1985 season mark to 5–6. As difficult as the thrashing in Miami and all that had preceded it had been for the Irish, the next twenty-four hours would arguably be even worse. During the week of practice, the members of the coaching staff had tried to keep a cap on their emotions while knowing that they would all likely find themselves unemployed once Holtz arrived in South Bend. "There were just problems all around on that staff," says Chuck Killian, an offensive lineman under both Faust and Holtz. "There were guys that didn't even speak to each other." At the airport in Miami after the game, a lot of that latent tension finally surfaced.

The team was supposed to fly out of Miami on Sunday, late in the afternoon. Snow back home had grounded its chartered plane, however, and the Irish traveling party settled in for a long day of waiting. Evening became night, and night advanced past midnight and into the following day, with the Notre Dame football team still stranded and waiting. Because it was the wee hours of the morning at the end of Thanksgiving weekend, the airport was nearly empty, and the Irish spread out near their gate.

One group, consisting of predominantly white players, laughed and joked around. Another group, consisting of predominantly but not exclusively black players, did the same. A Notre Dame assistant coach, Rick Lantz, approached the group of predominantly black players and scolded them for having such a raucous good time after just being beaten so badly. Irish assistant coach Bishop Harris, who was black, took exception to Lantz's remarks. The players had worked hard all season, he said, and there was little they could do to change anything that had happened hours before. It was over. And besides, Harris pointed out, the other players were having a good time as well. Why single out one group over the other? Uninvolved witnesses cringed at what they interpreted as a dispute with racial undertones.

"I won't lie to you," said Allen Pinkett, star running back of the '85 Irish. "We had some racial tensions on those teams."

"It got really bad," says D'Juan Francisco, a freshman defensive back on the '85 team. "It got kind of tense, and that exchange happened in front of a lot of people. Everyone saw it."

The situation was eventually defused, but the night was relatively young, and the rest of the journey back to northern Indiana was far from smooth.

During the flight, the team plane bumped around in the most frightening turbulence that many of the players had ever experienced. "My best friend on the team was Tom Rehder," linebacker Mike Kovaleski says. "Tom was freaking out. He was this big guy, and he was grabbing my hand and my arm as he was going through this turbulence. He was literally scared—six foot eight, 290 pounds, and he was scared. Guys were getting sick. It was awful."

Finally, the lights on the runway at South Bend Airport became visible out the window through the clouds and the fog. Winter weather often made landing at the airport a tricky proposition. The plane began its descent.

"I thought we would crash into the runway," Pinkett said. "And that seemed fitting to me. Just go ahead and kill our ass."

Rather than try to land, however, the pilot pulled back. After another hour of turbulent flight, the plane finally landed safely on a runway in Chicago. The bus trip back to campus, usually about a ninety-minute ride, lasted three and a half hours because of the icy roads. The players were also made aware that the difficult trip, and the accompanying lack of sleep, would not be an acceptable excuse for missing morning classes. Some of them arrived at Notre Dame and essentially walked from the bus to an eight o'clock class.

Then it was on to Faust's good-bye.

"I just told them that I was very proud of them," Faust says. "I was happy that they were at Notre Dame because they belonged at Notre Dame. I told them I thought the future was bright and they had an excellent coach coming in. I said, 'I think you'll have some great teams.'

"People ask me if I would do it again if it ended up the same. No question about it, I'd do it again. Would I do things differently now? Yes, I would. I would do a lot of things differently."

With Faust's farewell out of the way, Holtz entered the room. Beyond setting the tone by demanding undivided attention, Holtz informed his players how the next few months were going to go. There would be five a.m. workouts—and not the kind of freewheeling, go-through-the-motions sessions they had become accustomed to under the old regime. These would be highly structured, impeccably organized, set-your-muscles-on-fire drills. "As a player, when you think about the season being over, you're looking forward to a little bit of a break," Kovaleski says. "We weren't gonna get one. And we didn't deserve it."

Having watched the loss two nights before, Holtz had listened as the CBS announcers, including two-time national champion Notre Dame coach Parseghian, sympathized with the downtrodden Irish. He also knew that the college football world was engaged in a full-on pity party—there might as well have been streamers and balloons—for the departing Faust. Of course, every great melodrama needs a villain, and in *The Tragedy of Gerard Anthony Faust*, that was Miami and its head coach, Jimmy Johnson. But Holtz would have none of it. There were toxins to purge, and one of the most poisonous ones of all was this creeping notion of victimhood.

"The reason that happened," he told the team, "is because you allowed it to happen. And if I had the chance, I'd do the same thing to you too."

In the last few seasons, the Hurricanes had been transforming college football. It was something that the University of Notre Dame Fighting Irish had done in the past, on multiple occasions in different eras. As Holtz stood in front of the classroom in late November 1985, he may have been the only person in the known universe who actually believed that Notre Dame football—this relic of the sport's glorious past that had been left behind as other teams surged headlong into the future—could join forces with Miami and do it again.

CHAPTER 2

The Pressure Mounts

New Orleans, occult capital of North America, is no stranger to odd sights, but this was way out there even for America's most haunted city.

Days before his team's Sugar Bowl contest against Tennessee that would conclude the 1985 season, Miami head coach Jimmy Johnson entered a hotel ballroom at breakfast time prepared for a typical prebowl pep rally. He was greeted with a standing ovation from more than two thousand Miami fans. Minutes later, the team's Ibis mascot pinned a royal blue cape around Johnson's neck before guiding him into a makeshift throne. Johnson was carried around the room while the mascot displayed a poster-size photo of the guest of honor to even more cheering.

Things had sure changed in just over one year.

Johnson may have been living in paradise, or at least as close to it as it got in the continental United States. But as his second season as the head coach at the University of Miami neared its conclusion his tenure had been anything but utopian. Which only made it that much sweeter that his team was on the doorstep of a national championship after demolishing Notre Dame.

The Hurricanes had won their first national title two years earlier under former head coach Howard Schnellenberger. Since then, not only had Johnson endured tough losses and staff dissension in his first year, his 'Canes had opened up his second year with a thud, falling in their opener to Florida State. But they had been on a roll ever since, and would enter their Sugar Bowl matchup against the University of Tennessee ranked second in the country by the Associated Press, behind only unbeaten Penn State.

In their poll, the coaches had Oklahoma ranked ahead of the

Hurricanes—a curious decision, considering that Johnson's squad had beaten the Sooners in Norman by two touchdowns in October. In an interview aired before the ABC broadcast of the Sugar Bowl, Johnson lobbied for votes.

"We would deserve to be No. 1," he proclaimed, hypothesizing a Miami victory. "I say this for one reason: what we have accomplished on the field."

If such talk seemed audacious on Johnson's part, he certainly wasn't the only person who considered the Vols—the Southeastern Conference champs, but ranked only eighth in the country—an afterthought. The first Sugar Bowl game had been played in 1935 and had been held, without interruption, every year since then. Never in the event's history had a team entered as a bigger favorite than Miami at 7½ points. "The atmosphere at the Sugar Bowl was very subdued for us because all the attention was on Miami," says Daryl Dickey, the Tennessee quarterback. "Everything everybody did was at Miami's practice. Our practices were very docile and quiet and we were basically left alone."

The focus on the 'Canes was not surprising, considering the wide disparity between what was at stake for each of the two teams. While Tennessee was essentially playing for pride, if Oklahoma defeated Penn State in the Orange Bowl, and the Hurricanes were able to dispatch the Volunteers in New Orleans as expected, there was little doubt that Johnson's team would capture at least a share of the national title. Many coaches had indicated that they would be willing to flip their vote if Miami was dominant enough, keeping alive the possibility of an undisputed national title for the 'Canes.

Unfortunately for Johnson, his experience did not measure up to his confidence. The Sugar Bowl was by far the biggest game he had ever prepared for, and December brought one misstep after another. Johnson knew X's and O's, particularly on defense. He certainly knew how to motivate players. However, the minute but vital details of preparation were escaping him. Johnson gave his players a full week off for final exam preparation—perhaps a principled maneuver but not a sacrifice his counterpart, his former boss Johnny Majors, was making in Knoxville. Johnson conceded a couple more extra practices to the Volunteers by giving his players a few extra days off around Christmas before reconvening for the trip to New Orleans. In all, Tennessee wrung a full week of practice more out of December than did the Hurricanes. Not only that, but the 'Canes' coaching staff took no steps to prepare its players for the noise levels it would be likely to face in an enclosed dome.

"If we had to do it over, we might do it differently," Johnson would lament later. "But what do you tell them? No vacation? Forget finals?"

———

That Miami was preparing for a national championship game while Notre Dame was at home, thinking about next year and bracing for life under Lou Holtz, showed just how far their respective paths had veered from long-established equilibrium.

Miami did not begin its football program until 1927. By that point, legendary Notre Dame coach Knute Rockne was at the height of his powers and Notre Dame's brand name in college football was firmly entrenched. Winning football was, of course, the biggest reason the Irish developed into an established American cultural phenomenon. But shrewd marketing had something to do with it as well, and Rockne drove that bus. While college football was largely a regional sport during his era, split into East and West factions, the Notre Dame coach established an intersectional rivalry against the University of Southern California that extended his school's reach. He brokered a national radio deal that brought the Fighting Irish into the living rooms of Catholics from Los Angeles to Manhattan every Saturday. Appropriate for a program that played its home contests in the shadow of the campus's famous glittering dome, every decision Notre Dame made concerning its football program in that era seemed to turn to gold.

The same could not be said for the University of Miami.

In 1940, for example, Miami had an opportunity to expand its reputation nationally, scheduling an intersectional game with UCLA. But the school instead chose to abide by the twisted principles of the pre-civil-rights Deep South, canceling the game rather than sharing a field with the Bruins' black star, Jackie Robinson. That helped guarantee Miami a few more years of irrelevance, and even a 9–1–1 record in 1945 did not earn the Hurricanes a spot in the season's final Associated Press poll.

Five years later, after more than two decades of trying to gain a foothold as a relevant program, the Hurricanes made their first big splash as a potential national power. Indirectly, Miami's sudden glory was tied to Notre Dame's national cachet. On October 7, 1950, Purdue had traveled to South Bend and upset the Irish 28–14 to end Notre Dame's thirty-nine-game unbeaten streak. A victory over Miami the next week for the Big Ten's Purdue seemed like little more than a formality. The Boilermakers had shut out the Hurricanes the year before, in Florida. "Purdue will slaughter Miami," predicted Jim Leonard, Villanova's head coach, after his team lost to the Hurricanes.

Instead, Miami scored all of its points in the second half of a 20–14 upset. For the first time, the city caught Hurricane fever. More than one hundred thousand fans showed up at the airport to greet the victors. Approximately thirty thousand of them burst through police barricades and crowded the runway. The team's plane had to circle the airport several times before it could land. Even fans unable to join in the live celebration found creative ways to indicate their support. At the Miami courthouse, prisoners housed in the building's upper floors created makeshift confetti from toilet paper and sent it fluttering through the bars toward the ground more than fifteen stories below.

Miami's victory reverberated from coast to coast. In California, a newspaper columnist wrote that he was now convinced that gamblers had infiltrated college football. It was the only reasonable explanation he could muster.

By the time Notre Dame visited five years later, on October 7, 1955, the first-ever meeting between the two schools, Miami had begun to establish itself as a budding southern power—but again the 'Canes would disrupt their own ascent.

On the other hand, Notre Dame's reputation as one of the premier programs in college football was well established. The school had already won seven national championships and collected four Heisman Trophies. Even so, the Irish weren't simply living off past glories. Though six years removed from their last consensus national championship, the shadow of legendary former head coach Frank Leahy still loomed large. Nobody in the game—not Michigan, not Army, not even Bud Wilkinson's mighty Oklahoma Sooners—could match Notre Dame's dominance under Leahy. And the Irish had not showed much decline since his retirement, finishing fourth in the country in 1954, the first season under replacement Terry Brennan.

A record crowd of 75,685 people crammed the Orange Bowl to watch one of the biggest games in the history of the Hurricanes program. Miami was ranked fifteenth coming in, the Irish fifth after shutting out their first two opponents. Besides being a first crack for the Miami program to measure itself against college football's most famous program, it was also an opportunity for the Hurricanes to begin to put behind them the troubling events that had derailed their considerable momentum a year earlier.

In late October 1954, the NCAA convened in New Orleans to mete out discipline to schools that had violated its principles. On the same day that the governing body handed down formal punishments to the legendarily scandal-ridden City College of New York basketball program, it put Miami on probation for providing athletes with transportation to and from campus at the start and end of the academic year and winter break, for illicitly bankrolling recruits' visits to campus, and for conducting illegal tryouts for prospective players. The penalties given CCNY were mostly symbolic: In the aftermath of a point-shaving scandal, the school had for all intents and purposes removed itself from big-time basketball. But Miami's program was riding a wave under head coach Andy Gustafson, and the probation, which came with a bowl ban, served to stop it cold. At the time of the punishment, the Hurricanes were 4–0 and very much in the running to qualify for a major postseason bowl.

In the third quarter against the Irish the following year, in front of that enormous Orange Bowl crowd, the Hurricanes advanced the ball to the Notre Dame seven-yard line, then called four running plays up the middle that advanced them only to the two-yard line. That sequence pretty much encapsulated Miami's evening. For its era, the 14–0 Notre Dame victory was a showcase of offensive creativity. Notre Dame, which had barely thrown the ball in victories over SMU and Indiana to begin the year, went to the air sixteen times. Paul Hornung, who would go on to become Notre Dame's fifth Heisman Trophy winner a year later, threw a pair of touchdown passes to account for all the game's scoring. Miami, meanwhile, completed a remarkable twelve of thirteen passes against the vaunted Irish defense for 138 yards, but couldn't dent the scoreboard.

After the 1955 season, the NCAA ruled that Miami had not sufficiently cleaned up its athletic program, and extended the postseason bans for its football, baseball, and basketball programs another year. Miami would continue to have some mild success under Gustafson. It beat a god-awful Notre Dame team in 1960 in the second-ever meeting of the two schools. And in 1965, Notre Dame's second season under Parseghian, the teams played to a 0–0 tie at the Orange Bowl in the final game of each of their regular seasons. That Irish visit to the Orange Bowl was certainly an event in Miami. Comedian, actor, and huge Hurricanes supporter Jackie Gleason attended the coin toss. Right before kickoff, the stadium lights were temporarily cut while fireworks exploded over the open end of the Orange Bowl. Adding to the pageantry, the public address system boomed a recording of a howling hurricane wind to accompany the pyrotechnics. The scoreless tie that followed the pregame theatrics was Notre Dame's first since its 1946 classic against No. 1–ranked Army at Yankee Stadium, and its first tie of any kind in twelve years.

As heartening as it had been to play the famed Fighting Irish to a draw, however, all the off-the-field troubles prevented the Miami program from completing its seemingly inevitable trajectory into the upper echelon of college football programs. By the 1970s, Notre Dame was back in the top ten and competing for national titles on a regular basis. Notre Dame–Miami was an annual series by that point, with the Hurricanes serving as a mere punching bag for Parseghian's and later Dan Devine's Irish in between their marquee games against teams like USC, Michigan, Purdue, and Michigan State. The eventual national champion Irish clobbered Miami 44–0 in 1973, 38–7 in 1974, and 32–9 in 1975.

As far as Miami was concerned, the games seemed to prove a sad truth: Theirs was a program that was incapable of sustaining any momentum.

In 1966, with the encouragement of university president Henry King Stanford and the scouting acumen of Tampa-area booster Ed Dick, Miami signed the South's first black football player, Ray Bellamy. The action helped staunch the exodus of talented black players from the

South to the midwestern powerhouses of the Big Ten. But Miami was never really able to cash in on its bold move; at one point during the seventies the program employed five head coaches in just six seasons. Before former NFL head coach Lou Saban arrived to finally breathe life—and money—into the failing program, many members of Miami's board of trustees had even considered pulling the plug permanently.

Miami had made plenty of bad decisions during its descent into decades of irrelevance. But even if the school had been more nimble in navigating its course, the dawn of the television age probably would have kept the Hurricanes and other programs of their ilk grounded. Frightened that television overexposure could cut into ticket sales and doom the sport financially, NCAA power brokers strictly limited the number of televised games from the beginning of the medium's emergence in the early 1950s. Whichever network owned the sport's broadcast rights at any given time did what it could to maximize its very limited schedule, broadcasting the only guaranteed ratings winners. As a result, schools like Michigan, Oklahoma, Alabama, Texas, and, of course, Notre Dame, were beamed into living rooms as often as the NCAA's restrictive policies allowed. Schools like Miami rarely appeared. In 1971, for example, schools in the Atlantic Coast Conference appeared on television twice, carried by just twenty-six affiliates. Southeastern Conference teams, by contrast, had seven television appearances, with the games carried by nearly 1,200 network affiliates.

Because television exposure was so closely tied to recruiting prowess, the setup kept a rigid power structure in place. The elite programs remained the elite programs year after year, and with no real scholarship limits in place, those elite programs were able to hoard top players. Schools would sign upward of sixty players a year and carry as many as 150 scholarship players on their rosters in a given season.

In 1973, however, the foundation that maintained college football's caste system began to crumble. Smaller schools used their numerical advantage in the NCAA to vote in strict scholarship limits. Beginning in 1975, schools could sign only thirty players a year and keep ninety-five scholarship players on their rosters. Coaches and administrators at the elite football schools were predictably infuriated—"I don't want Hofstra telling Texas how to play football," said Longhorns coach Darrell Royal—but for schools longing to compete with the big boys, the door had finally opened a crack.

As a man who had learned from college football royalty while coaching for Alabama's Paul "Bear" Bryant, new Miami coach Howard Schnellenberger had a tremendous appreciation for college football's heritage, even as he set his sights on upending it. When Schnellenberger, a Catholic, took his players to South Bend, he provided them with a guided tour of campus landmarks, like the famous Grotto. When Notre Dame's head coaching position opened after Devine's surprise retirement in 1980, Schnellenberger's name made it onto a few speculative lists. The same thing happened as the heat grew on Faust.

At various times in the 1970s, prior to Schnellenberger's arrival, the administration at the University of Miami had considered disbanding the football program. From dingy, outdated locker rooms to little fan and alumni support, the challenges appeared too great to overcome, and the work of overcoming them no longer seemed worth the trouble. "One of the great sins down there at the University of Miami was the perception of itself," Schnellenberger says. "There was no swagger. There was no confidence. There was no spirit."

Schnellenberger, arriving from the NFL, where he had been a Miami Dolphins assistant, made a determined effort to work around those issues, not against them. Through a series of deft maneuvers, most notably locking down the South Florida recruiting base, he finally started the program moving toward major status. So Schnellenberger was not happy to see his Hurricanes taking a backseat to anybody, including the Irish. And that was clearly what was happening on a trip to Tokyo, Japan, during his first season, a trip Schnellenberger had considered a potential distraction from the moment he spotted it on his new team's schedule.

The contract for the game had been arranged during Lou Saban's tenure and had the benefit of adding a couple hundred thousand desperately needed dollars to the Miami recruiting coffers. But taking the most anticipated game on the schedule out of the Orange Bowl, says Schnellenberger, was "about as derelict as you can be" when the ultimate goal was to build an elite program, and noted: "I thought it was a terrible, terrible move to move the marquee jewel in your crown and take that to Tokyo."

The "Mirage Bowl" had been the brainchild of a Japanese businessman who fell in love with the pageantry and atmosphere of college football during a trip to the United States, and the Notre Dame–Miami matchup was the third such game. It didn't take more than a day or two for Schnellenberger to realize that, during a week in which rain fell almost nonstop, his team had been assigned a practice field that turned into a mud pit when wet. Meanwhile, Notre Dame prepped on the game field, which retained its condition despite the downpour. "That chapped Howard in a big way," says Dave Stewart, an offensive lineman on Schnellenberger's early teams.

It wasn't the only thing that would unnerve Schnellenberger during a trying week overseas. Whereas in United States department stores valuables were kept under glass, Japanese merchants kept expensive items out in the open: Such was the level of trust between seller and potential buyers. Soon enough, several pieces of expensive gold jewelry disappeared after the Hurricanes visited the in-hotel shop. With everything he already had to worry about, rooting out the thieves on his roster was not an issue that Schnellenberger was particularly pleased to have to deal with. He also wasn't happy to see alcohol served at official social functions. Miami had given players very little preparation for the cultural differences they would experience in Japan, and now, trying to maintain control over the cast of characters that Saban had left behind, the staff was paying the price. Hours before the game, one unfortunate player hopped on a Tokyo bullet train out of curiosity, then didn't know how to make his way back. He missed most of the game, arriving just in time to join his teammates for the flight back to the United States.

"They were extremely dysfunctional," says Dean Masztak, Notre Dame's tight end. "They had no sense of team. We had these receptions for both schools at the hotel we stayed at. Some of their guys actually started fighting—fistfighting—in the lobby of the hotel. I don't know what was going on, but it created a heck of a ruckus."

Given all of that, the game went pretty much as expected, with Notre Dame blowing out the Hurricanes 40–15. During the game, the culture clash became comical as confused Japanese spectators cheered wildly when the ball soared high in the sky on punts but barely reacted during touchdowns and other big plays.

Less than a month earlier, after an epic upset of Penn State, Schnellenberger had held up a football in the locker room and proclaimed, "This is the day that people will know Miami has turned its program around." The Hurricanes then lost 30–0 to Alabama the next week before being drubbed by the Irish in Tokyo. The sport's traditional powers weren't quite ready to roll over for the 'Canes just yet.

————

Schnellenberger had been brought to Miami to revive a moribund program. Expectations were modest: string some winning records together if possible; pull off the occasional bowl victory; fill a few seats at the Orange Bowl; avoid the sort of embarrassments that would mar the trip to Tokyo. He was the only one who really believed that national titles were attainable, and certainly the only person who believed it could be done so quickly. Marking off a portion of Florida as the "State of Miami," Schnellenberger dedicated himself to locking down talent in the area. "The whole coaching staff, going back to the late forties and fifties— they were all graduates of the University of Pittsburgh," Schnellenberger says. "They thought that was where the best football players in the world played: Pennsylvania, Ohio, New Jersey, New York. They had been going up there and getting second-best players for too damned long. I felt if we could build a core with South Florida kids coming to the University of Miami in unison, that we could match up talentwise with anybody."

By 1983, just four years after the Tokyo trip, the strategy paid off with a 31–30 victory over Nebraska in the Orange Bowl and perhaps the most shocking college football national championship in decades. Schnellenberger had been asked to deliver stability; he had instead guided the program to the sport's pinnacle. "When we won our first national championship in 1983, Miami had the littlest weight room in the country," says Dan Sileo, a defensive lineman who played for both Schnellenberger and Johnson. "We had a bench, a squat rack, and some dumbbells. That was the weight program. But we loved it. The Texases and Ohio States, they had all that fancy stuff, [but] we'd go out and beat the shit out of them."

Johnson, in contrast to Schnellenberger's tenure-long honeymoon in Coral Gables, had come to Miami with a clear directive to continue the championship tradition that Schnellenberger had begun. Schnellenberger had proven that it could be done, and Johnson was required to build on his predecessor's momentum. "Unless he has nerves of steel and a hide of leather," Charles Whited wrote in the *Miami Herald*, "smilin' Jimmy Johnson probably will have moments to rue the day he ever left Stillwater, Oklahoma, where life remains fairly uncomplicated, being heavily into the production of feed and hogs."

The dream opportunity became a nightmare almost from the first meeting that Johnson held with his new staff, which he was forced to retain at least for his first season. "I really don't think I can work with you," Tom Olivadotti, Schnellenberger's defensive coordinator, announced even before the gathering was adjourned. "[The media's] pounding, hurt though it might, was a minor matter indeed compared to the pounding I took for not being Schnellenberger in the hallways and meeting rooms of the University of Miami football offices," Johnson said. Miami boosters and influential alumni were displeased that the position wasn't given to Olivadotti, and made their sentiments known. "My feeling," one of them told the *Miami Herald*, "is one of complete disappointment."

Even so, the staff that stayed pressed ahead, and fate rewarded their perseverance with a series of devastating losses to conclude the 1984 season.

In the second-to-last game of the regular season, in the Orange Bowl, the Hurricanes led Maryland 31–0 at halftime. Then, behind backup quarterback Frank Reich, the Terrapins outscored Johnson's 'Canes 42–9 in the second half to win 42–40. "All we had to do was make one play in the second half," Johnson lamented afterward. "Just one play. We let so many people down. It just makes me sick."

The fun was just beginning. A week later, to conclude Johnson's first season at Miami, the Hurricanes hosted Boston College. The defense was still reeling from the collapse the week before, but for most of the night the Bernie Kosar–directed offense covered for them. Only about thirty thousand fans had braved the rain to watch Heisman Trophy candidate Doug Flutie, BC's quarterback, face the beleaguered 'Canes defense, but that relatively small group would witness college football history.

With twenty-eight seconds remaining, Miami's Melvin Bratton scored on a run, his fourth touchdown of the game, to put the 'Canes ahead 45–41. In the press box, Fiesta Bowl representatives, planning to invite the Hurricanes, jumped out of their seats with joy. Barring a miracle, Miami was going to survive.

A short time later, with six seconds on the clock, BC's Flutie dropped back to pass from the Miami forty-eight and heaved the ball as far as he could into the misty South Florida evening. When it finally came down, receiver Gerard Phelan was waiting. Somehow, the football eluded the touch of several Miami defensive backs in the vicinity, instead landing in the Boston College receiver's hands for the touchdown. Final: BC 47, Miami 45.

That throw and catch constitute probably the most famous highlight clip in the history of the sport. But it was not the end of Johnson's first-season woes. A few weeks later, Miami fell to UCLA in the Fiesta Bowl, 39–37, to finish 8-4 in its national championship encore. Any goodwill Johnson had been extended upon his arrival—and there had not been much—had been squandered by the late-season collapse. Less than a decade before, the university had considered shutting down the program for good. Now, after a little taste of glory, perfection was the expectation.

"There was tension throughout the year," says Rich Dalrymple, whom Johnson hired out of tiny Otterbein College in Ohio to be his sports information director. "We had some bumps early, and then we had some near driving-off-the-cliff episodes late in the season. And whenever anything was going in the wrong direction, there were always people saying, 'Well, this wouldn't have happened with the previous guy.'"

"You could see some things going on," says offensive lineman Matt Patchan. "I even heard that there was fighting in the press box between the coaches. I don't know how much of it was true, but we heard about it."

In response, Johnson restructured his staff almost immediately after the season ended, surrounding himself with people he was more comfortable with for 1985. He was determined to avoid a repeat of the conclusion of his first season in Miami. By the time Notre Dame came to town, the Hurricanes had won nine consecutive games and were once again quietly stalking the national championship.

But while a second national title in three years beckoned after the thrashing of the Irish, so did the Big Easy. Miami kicker Greg Cox incited a brief altercation when he called a French Quarter street artist a "con man." Offensive guard Maurice Maddox was sent home after sleeping through a morning team meeting.

"We partied too much," said linebacker Winston Moss. "I mean, we were on Bourbon Street. We had never seen anything like that. We thought we were going to handle Tennessee easy that year, so we went out every night and had a good time."

———

Miami's allotment of tickets for the Sugar Bowl was 12,500, and they sold all of them.

"They must have sold them in Knoxville," forty-year Associated Press veteran Austin Wilson would joke after the game.

It was true that the Louisiana Superdome was packed with Tennessee fans, 90 percent by some accounts. Of the 12,500 tickets Miami had sold, more than three thousand had somehow ended up in the hands of Tennessee fans. One New Orleans travel agency booked one thousand Sugar Bowl trips: More than nine hundred were purchased by Volunteer backers. Orange-clad Tennessee fans vastly outnumbered Miami fans on Bourbon Street all week long, and they clogged the highway into town on game day, filling the air with jubilant renditions of "Rocky Top" while stopped in traffic.

And yet, for the first four minutes in the Superdome, the Hurricanes looked like the best team in the country, and no disparity in crowd support was going to slow them down. They stuffed the Volunteers on the opening drive of the game, then executed a beautiful fake punt a few moments later, with running back Melvin Bratton sprinting through an open field to inside the Tennessee twenty-yard line. On the next play, quarterback Vinny Testaverde placed a throw right over the shoulder of Michael Irvin in the end zone, one future NFL star connecting with another to give Miami a 7–0 advantage. The 'Canes appeared to be off and running.

They would not score again.

Tennessee brought constant pressure all night, blitzing on almost every down with up to nine players. With Volunteer fans filling the majority of the seats at the Superdome, the pre-snap noise level when the Hurricanes had the football was deafening. "That was the loudest game I've ever been in," Patchan says. "My son plays at Florida. I've been to the big games: the SEC Championship, the [BCS] national championship game. Nothing comes close to that game. Once we let them back into it, they didn't let up. It was like an airplane lifting off for three hours. We couldn't hear anything."

The Hurricanes linemen tried shorter splits in order to hear Testaverde better and neutralize the crowd noise. They were still no match for the Tennessee crowd.

"It was like playing next to a freight train," says Scott Provin, a Johnson-era Miami offensive lineman. "We couldn't hear anything. We just couldn't compete with that type of crowd noise, and everyone really struggled hearing Vinny make any kind of audibles whatsoever." Testaverde was sacked seven times and threw three interceptions. The Hurricanes, flustered by the noise, committed fifteen penalites for 120 yards. "You try and you try and you try," said Michael Irvin, "and nothing goes right."

Tennessee, more than a touchdown underdog coming in, rolled 35–7.

"Once we completed a pass and got our first touchdown, it was like the dam broke on them," says Tennessee quarterback Daryl Dickey. "Once we scored on them and tied the game, I don't think they ever had a chance offensively after that."

The "Sugar Vols" would long be remembered as one of the most beloved teams in Tennessee history. For Miami, on the other hand, a second straight season had ended with disappointment. And this one really hurt, because of what had slipped from the 'Canes' grasp. Oklahoma had beaten Penn State handily in the Orange Bowl, so a Miami victory would have meant a national title and redemption for Johnson's miserable first campaign the season before. To cap off a perfect week, Miami defensive lineman Greg Mark got into a fight with a Tennessee fan on Bourbon Street hours after the game, undergoing minor plastic surgery for facial lacerations administered by a jagged beer bottle.

Suddenly, the skepticism that greeted Johnson upon his arrival seemed well founded. Was the Oklahoma hayseed really in over his head? With a remarkable nucleus of players returning, year three, 1986, would be the real test.

CHAPTER 3

Boot Camp

In the week leading up to Lou Holtz's debut as the head coach at Notre Dame, the diminutive forty-nine-year-old, tired of trying to explain a fine point of special team play, strode out onto the practice turf to field a few punts himself.

The kick began its descent, and Holtz positioned himself. But instead of making a clean grab, the ball glanced hard off of one of his pinky fingers, shattering a bone.

Poetic justice, his players surely must have thought.

When Holtz had arrived in late November, he had promised pain in the off-season, and he had certainly delivered. Off-season workouts were like nothing Notre Dame's returning players had ever experienced. They were earlier, more regimented, and certainly more intense. "This is a great day to be alive," a peppy, clapping Holtz would remind his bleary-eyed players as they arrived. "Come on, it's noon in London."

"I never wanted people in the other team's locker room to say, 'We got beat, but they weren't very tough,'" says Holtz. "I wanted them to be in the whirlpool saying, 'We don't want to play those suckers again.'"

The weather in South Bend during the winter months can get as bad as almost anywhere in the country. While classmates slept away the especially brutal predawn hours, the Irish players trudged through a blanket of snow toward the weight room. "You go back and go to bed for an hour or so and wake up, and [you] think you've had the worst nightmare of your life," said Frank Stams.

"The crazy thing was, we enjoyed it," says Tim Brown. "Guys were throwing up and they were happy."

"Those workouts were an incredibly good idea," says offensive lineman Jim Baugus.

During a visit to a prominent Big Eight school, California native Mark Green, a prized running-back recruit, had been appalled at the partying and mischief he witnessed. At the time, he felt that Notre Dame seemed like a calmer, more studious alternative. And it was. In South Bend, however, in those first few months under Holtz, he looked around and felt as if he were back on that raucous recruiting visit, except this time the scene wasn't taking place at a fraternity or off-campus house party but in the weight room.

"I remember guys passing out and puking all over the place," Green says. "And it was, like, 'Hey, you're not as good as you thought you were, are you?' [Holtz] did something that we didn't realize until after we had left the university, and that was creating a common theme amongst all the players which gelled us and pulled us together and allowed us to work as a team. And that common theme was that we all hated him. Everyone was on the same page in that regard.

"We thought he was a jerk. We really did," Green continues. "He was hard on you. He pushed you, he got the maximum out of you, and he would very quickly replace you if he didn't feel you were playing up to your capabilities. You went out and you competed; you played hard all the time simply because you knew you were dealing with a crazy man."

———

On the surface, at least, the gulf between the Notre Dame and Miami programs grew that much wider when Notre Dame selected Holtz, a success at all of his college stops, to restore the program's wavering pride.

To begin with, Miami's trademark demonstrativeness—something Johnson didn't exactly discourage—was anathema to what Holtz considered one of his core values: that players go about their jobs on the field with enthusiasm, yes, even exuberance, but also that they leave the theatrics and celebration of self to others.

"If we had choreographed any dances," says George Streeter, a defensive back at Notre Dame, "I think our scholarships would have been changed to theater or something. That happened one time, early on, in practice. Braxston Banks did a little dance and Lou made a big example out of him. He said he would never, ever see the field again if he did that."

Holtz's principles were forged during a hardscrabble midwestern upbringing, a time when, he would later explain, "we needed a raise to be considered poor." He was born on January 6, 1937, in Follansbee, West Virginia. Steel was Follansbee's prime industry, and the Holtz family had settled there when Leo Holtz, Lou's grandfather, decided to leave the coal mines of Pennsylvania behind for the blast furnaces of northern West Virginia. Andrew and Anne Marie Holtz, Lou's parents, rented a two-room basement in Follansbee. There was no shower or bathtub in the dwelling. When any of the Holtzes could grab a few minutes of privacy, they bathed in the cellar's lone sink. Lou owned one pair of pants and one flannel shirt, which Anne Marie washed on weekends.

When he was nine years old, Lou took on a paper route to help out the family, bringing in six dollars a week. His father, meanwhile, found work wherever it was available, whether that meant pitching in at the local railroad, driving a bus or truck around town, or something else.

Soon after the Japanese bombed Pearl Harbor on December 7, 1941, bringing the United States into World War II, Andrew Holtz and all of his brothers enlisted in the Navy to assist the cause. Eventually, Lou Holtz would grow to have complicated feelings about his father, particularly after Andrew Holtz's separation from Anne Marie while Lou was off to college. But the traits revealed after Andrew's four years in the service were not open to interpretation.

When Andrew Holtz returned home in 1945, he spoke little of his travails fighting for the future of western civilization. But decades later Lou would receive a phone call from one of his father's former shipmates. The man had kept a journal—illicitly, as official military policy banned the exercise—of his experiences in the war, and he was ready to share it. In its pages, long after his father's death, Lou Holtz learned that Andrew Holtz had been smack dab in the middle of two of the pivotal events of the war: Midway and Saipan. These were Allied victories that had changed the course of history, yet while he was alive, Holtz's father spoke nothing of them.

"Service," Lou Holtz said, "was just something Dad's generation did. You didn't brag about it or even talk about it. This sparked my lasting distaste for excessive celebrations and 'Look at me' exploits, whether by athletes, politicians, or businesspeople."

With Andrew Holtz away at war, Anne Marie moved her children out of Follansbee to East Liverpool, Ohio, where they stayed with her parents. During that time, Lou first became involved with football, joining the seventh- and eighth-grade team coached by his teenage uncle Lou Tychonievich. Holtz was in fifth grade, so he had to make up for the disparity in size, speed, and strength with toughness and smarts. In high school, he was an undersized blocking back on his team's single-wing offense. He may have been physically overmatched, but he was a sponge when it came to absorbing instruction about the sport, to the point that he could coach teammates who played other positions through their responsibilities. He wasn't afraid to sacrifice his own body in service of some method learning, either.

"One time in practice he played noseguard over me because he wanted to know about the position," recalled Don Chadwick, one of Holtz's East Liverpool teammates. "We had a 280-pound guy playing next to me who double-teamed Lou with me. We plowed him into a puddle. We almost drowned him."

Holtz's coach, Wade Watts, noticed his superior knowledge of and feel for the game. Mostly, however, he noticed Holtz's passion, and suggested that he go to college so that he could become a coach someday. "He was great for us in the locker room, on the bus," Watts said. "There was something about him." With less than $200 that he had been saving to buy a car, Holtz paid for a semester at Kent State University, hitchhiking from East Liverpool to Kent every day and back.

A mediocre high school student who had finished in the bottom half of his class, Holtz would need to work tirelessly to secure success in college. And in a community where people had to work very hard to keep their business their own, some townspeople awaited his imminent failure with relish. During his freshman year at Kent State, while wandering the aisles of a local grocery store, Holtz happened to overhear a pair of local busybodies judging Anne Marie Holtz harshly for working so hard to put her undeserving son through college.

"She took a night job and everything," one of the women said to her companion. "It's such a waste."

The incident motivated Holtz to plow through, nose always to the grindstone, his first semester at college. The following summer, he ran into one of his high school coaches and shared his own coaching aspirations with him. The coach, Frank Smouse, offered Holtz a job in the fall coaching the Ravenna High School freshman team. Under the young coach's guidance, the ninth graders went undefeated.

Although he weighed just 165 pounds, Holtz decided the next autumn to go out for the Kent State football team, figuring that the experience would help boost his understanding of the game to prepare him for a career as a coach. Some of Holtz's teammates, even close friends and fraternity brothers, didn't think that he'd make it through his first training camp. They were wrong. Although Holtz was hardly a standout at the college level, or even a starter, he was eventually granted a partial scholarship to reward his effort and know-how. When Holtz tore some knee cartilage the spring before what would have been his third season on the football team and fifth year in school at Kent, his playing career ended. But the injury turned out to be a blessing in disguise. Instead of biding his time as a backup linebacker for another season, Holtz was granted a head start on his future career, coaching the freshman team and spending his Saturdays doing some advance scouting for the varsity.

So began his journey, and as with any successful coaching career, a certain amount of luck factored in. The knee injury at Kent State, as it turned out, had been an omen. Even the bad breaks always worked out for Holtz in the long run. After three years as the offensive and defensive backfield coach at William & Mary College in Williamsburg, Virginia, he was one of two finalists to replace departing coach Milt Drewer. He was disappointed when recently fired Southern California coach Marv Levy was hired instead, but, looking back, he felt that getting that job at age twenty-six would have been a career-killer. "I wasn't ready to be a head coach," Holtz said. "Not even close. If I had been hired, I would have failed."

At South Carolina, another stop on the journey, Holtz suffered a steep demotion when Coach Marvin Bass, who had hired Holtz to be his defensive coordinator, resigned in the spring before what would have been Holtz's first season. The demotion came with a 27 percent pay cut—not easy for a young married couple trying to raise three small children—and the new coach reassigned Holtz to serve as an academic adviser to the team. Holtz was also assigned to do advance scouting during the season, a job he had also performed as a Kent State graduate assistant.

While hitting the road to watch some of the best programs in the Southeast, Holtz noticed a common thread connecting the top coaches. Guys like Paul "Bear" Bryant of Alabama and Charlie McClendon of LSU might have run completely different systems on the surface, but buttressing it all was a foundation of rock-solid fundamentals. The lesson wasn't glamorous or particularly profound, but it stuck.

It was reinforced throughout the course of the 1968 football season when Holtz took a job on the staff of Ohio State legend Woody Hayes. Even though Ohio was home to Holtz, and Columbus something of a dream destination, he almost didn't take the job coaching the Buckeyes' secondary. Sitting at the same time on an offer from Georgia Tech, Holtz was warned repeatedly about working for the volatile Hayes. In the end, Holtz took the job, and in Ohio State's first game of the year, against SMU, Holtz's defensive backs intercepted quarterback Chuck Hixson six times.

As anticipated, Holtz had to endure the worst of Hayes: flung film projectors, near physical assaults on his assistant coaches. At the team hotel in Pasadena, California, where the Buckeyes had traveled to face USC in the Rose Bowl for the national championship, Hayes exploded at Holtz in front of a lobby full of wives, fans, and reporters. But with Hayes, assistants and players learned to take the good with the bad— and to take Hayes's actions with a grain of salt. Before Holtz had ever coached a game at Ohio State, Hayes warned him to take a firing seriously only if it was put into writing. Otherwise, Hayes was probably just blowing off steam. At the same time, Holtz received an up-close validation from one of the greatest coaches of the era of what he had witnessed on those scouting trips to the Deep South a couple years before. Hayes was a perfectionist's perfectionist, obsessing over blocking and tackling fundamentals.

Holtz knew his place as one of Hayes's underlings, but he also clung to his own ambitions.

"Lou grabbed me after the season," says Rex Kern, the sophomore starting quarterback for the Buckeyes, "and he said, 'Rex, I want you to come into my office. I'm gonna give you the keys to success.' And he said, 'You need to jot down all of your goals.' He said, 'Write down the one hundred things you want to do in your life and just start checking them off.' You could tell that Lou had the swagger and he had the enthusiasm and that he would go on to greatness."

Holtz was referring to a list of 108 goals for his life that he had written out a few years before, while sitting in occupational limbo in Columbia, South Carolina.

"It looks like you've left something off," his wife Beth had said when he proudly showed her the list that evening. "If it were me, at the top of the first page, in big letters, I'd write, GET A JOB!"

By the time the 1968 Buckeyes put the exclamation point on their national championship season with a 27–16 victory over USC, finding a job was no longer an issue for Holtz. William & Mary, where he had finished second to Marv Levy a few years earlier, contacted him and offered him the head coaching job that Levy had just vacated. At age twenty-eight, Holtz and Beth had given his coaching career five years to see if anything promising was developing. Otherwise, at age thirty-three, he would go back to school and work toward either a law degree or a history doctorate. William & Mary hired Holtz when he was thirty-two. Holtz guided W&M to the only bowl appearance in school history, the 1970 Tangerine Bowl.

"He was very much in charge," says Joseph Montgomery, a center whom Holtz recruited. "Someone asked me once, 'Gosh, he's not really very big.' He was very big to me. If you had him in your face, he seemed very big."

In some ways, Holtz at William & Mary was a fully formed, if younger, version of the head coach that he would become. Montgomery recalls doing a double take one evening while watching ESPN's college football studio show, which Holtz cohosts, as his old coach rattled off a parable using his fist and a bucket of water as props. Holtz, who to this day has never met a cornball metaphor he didn't love, had used the same story to convey a message to his William & Mary team four decades earlier.

Being so young in his first head coaching job, however, Holtz was bound to make a few mistakes. His biggest one was trying too hard to emulate his old Ohio State boss, Woody Hayes. Most of the time it worked. "He knew what buttons to push about insecurities and things like that," says Montgomery. "Once he got you there, he made you earn it all over again. He might have been tough, but he was so positive about what you could accomplish." Holtz's calculated outbursts backfired, however, when he made his exit from William & Mary after the 1971 season. That team had started the year with four consecutive victories but struggled down the stretch. After a loss to Temple in the second-to-last game, Holtz thundered to his team, "I don't know where I'm gonna be next year. But it's not gonna be here."

It was a motivational tactic, pure and simple, meant to rattle his men out of their comfort zone and get them playing up to par again with a shot at a conference title remaining in the season's final contest. Holtz had no real intention of leaving. Instead, the players folded, losing again to drop below .500 for the third consecutive season under Holtz. When indeed circumstances came together to take him to North Carolina State after the season, it left his players with a sick feeling in the pit of their stomachs. In reality, Holtz's move had nothing to do with his players or their performance at the end of the 1971 season: Lou and Beth Holtz loved the colonial atmosphere in Williamsburg, Virginia. But under a new president, William & Mary decided to deemphasize intercollegiate athletics. As an ambitious young coach, Holtz wanted no part of it. "He couldn't come in and tell us, 'Hey, guys, they're going to jack your program down,'" says Montgomery. "You can see why he couldn't do that." But the brains of twenty-year-olds don't always operate logically, and when Holtz left, all that his players knew was that their coach had threatened to abandon them, then followed through when their play had not picked up. Even after decades had passed, Holtz would express his regret to former William & Mary players about the way things had ended.

The situation Holtz inherited in Raleigh very closely paralleled the one he would step into at Notre Dame more than a decade later. The Wolfpack were coming off of three consecutive three-victory seasons, but the returning players were talented and eager to turn things around. They were probably even more malleable than the group of frustrated malcontents that greeted him in South Bend. North Carolina State finished seventeenth in the country Holtz's first year, sixteenth his second year, and ninth in his third season in Raleigh.

Then, after his fourth season at North Carolina State, Holtz made perhaps the biggest blunder of his career—one that just about anybody would have made. In 1976, the New York Jets offered Holtz their head coaching job. Still under forty years old, Holtz felt that the offer to coach at the game's highest level in the nation's largest media market was too much to walk away from. And he was still young enough to get his career back on track if it turned out to be the wrong move.

And did it ever.

Holtz's tenure with the Jets would last less than one season. After three victories and the realization that the pro game was not for him, he resigned in early December to become the head coach at the University of Arkansas.

In 1976, Arkansas had gone 5-5-1 and missed the postseason. In 1977, Holtz's first year, the Razorbacks went 11-1 and clobbered Oklahoma in the Orange Bowl. Many Arkansans still feel that the Razorbacks deserved the national championship that year (it went instead to Ara Parseghian's Notre Dame Fighting Irish). Perhaps Holtz had been an abject failure as an NFL coach, but a year away had not cost Holtz the magic touch when it came to coaching in college. Lou Holtz was the master of the turnaround. He had done it at North Carolina State, and now he had done it at Arkansas.

Then there was Minnesota. As recently as the 1960s, the Gophers had been a national football powerhouse, but by the time Holtz had arrived in 1984, it was a program in disrepair. The Gophers had won just one game the previous season. They had not been to a postseason bowl since 1977. Then, in Holtz's first spring, forty-two thousand fans showed up to watch the Gophers scrimmage. "He told us if we listened to him and did the things he told us to do, we would win," says former Minnesota wide receiver Dwayne McMullen. "And that turned out to be true." Unlike some of his creative counterparts in the coaching profession in the mid-1980s, including Jimmy Johnson at Miami, Holtz was hardly an innovator. While Miami was modeling its system on the professional ranks, Holtz sometimes seemed to be modeling his instructions on grainy footage of eras gone by. He instructed his receivers, for example, to line up in three-point stances, an anachronism by that point. "You had to have the right split, the right yardage, the right depth," McMullen says. "Our motto was that the little things counted. He was very much a perfectionist."

By year two, Holtz had Minnesota back in the postseason: The Gophers would play in the Independence Bowl in Louisiana on December 21. But their head coach would not be accompanying them. He had work to do in South Bend, and not a whole lot of time in which to do it.

———

When Holtz accepted the Notre Dame job, he sensed that the place was different from some of his other coaching stops. Just a few weeks into his first recruiting venture, he found out how different it really was.

In the winter of 1986, Holtz traveled from South Bend to Woodruff, South Carolina, to see about a recruit. He made the journey even though Tony Rice, quarterback of the powerhouse Woodruff High School Wolverines, seemed like the longest of long shots for the Irish.

Rice was born on September 5, 1967, to a teenage mother who decided that she was too young, immature, and unstable to give her son adequate care. Instead, he was taken in by his grandmother, Mary Rice, seventeen miles down the road. From a very early age, there were plenty of characteristics that marked Rice as unlikely to wear the blue and gold. For one, he was raised a Southern Baptist. Even while Rice was growing up, Notre Dame's student body wasn't 100 percent Catholic, but at a school that wears its denomination proudly on its sleeve, self-selection ensured that a high percentage of Catholics would always be among the people enrolled at Notre Dame. A black Southern Baptist from South Carolina, a state that previous Irish coaches had barely touched in recruiting, didn't exactly fit the Notre Dame profile.

Rice and his grandmother lived in a house in Woodruff until he was thirteen years old. Then Mary Rice decided that she was tired of letting her pride obscure her good judgment. She sold the house and moved into public housing in town: the projects. The projects that Rice grew up in, however, were much different from the gang-infested, violence-plagued high-rises that dotted many urban areas, like Miami.

"I don't think anyone owned a gun," Rice says. "Your neighbors knew you. You slept with your door open. People were always welcome to come in. There was no crime. The only crime that happened was one time someone ran over a dog."

The living situation wasn't the only thing affected by the depressed financial situation of the Rice household. When he entered junior high school, Rice wanted to join the school band. "I was always banging on things," he recalls. But he couldn't afford drums, so he elected to play football instead.

By his senior season at Woodruff, Rice was one of the most sought-after quarterback recruits in America, at least by programs that ran a system that could utilize his skill set. While he lacked the pinpoint accuracy of the traditional drop-back college quarterback, Rice made up for his deficiencies in other ways. He was lightning fast, especially for his position, and had the natural strength of a linebacker, so he was difficult to bring down. The key for Rice was his superior leg strength. In one instance, he filled up the mechanical leg-press machine with all the available weight in the Woodruff weight room. When that wasn't enough, a teammate hopped on top of the stack. Rice kept pumping the weight, teammate and all, up and down in a steady rhythm. Besides starting at quarterback from his freshman season onward, he served as his high school team's punter and placekicker. Rice also had a cannon for an arm. He might not have been able to thread a pass through a needle, but he wouldn't have to if he could lob it seventy-plus yards through the air. So dominant was he at the high school level that his head coach at Woodruff, a veteran who had led the program since the 1960s, reconfigured his entire playbook around Rice's skills. There were twenty-one plays in the book, and about twenty of them were some variation of a run-pass option for the quarterback, with a fullback counter or two mixed in to keep defenses honest.

By the summer before his senior season at Woodruff, Rice was trying to whittle down the long line of suitors vying for his future services. He was impressed with North Carolina coach Danny Ford and by the restaurant he ate at during his visit to Chapel Hill, an experience, he told a local newspaper, that made him feel "nasty rich." He was flabbergasted when the University of Alabama's president wrote him a personalized letter. He visited Pittsburgh, but his mother and grandmother both laughed at the idea of him living so far away from home. However, that didn't stop a coach at a school even farther away, Lou Holtz of the University of Minnesota, from recruiting Rice.

When Holtz was hired later that fall at Notre Dame, he continued his pursuit. During his visit to the Rice home, he immediately warmed up the room. In fact, after a few minutes, he settled into Mary Rice's favorite easy chair. Tony Rice was shocked when his grandmother let the transgression slide without so much as a word.

"She fell in love with him," Rice says. "She said, 'You're going to follow that little man.' He won her heart."

As a result, Holtz won Rice's pledge, against all odds, to sign with Notre Dame. It was a major early recruiting victory for the new coaching regime in South Bend. But Holtz would soon come to understand that, unlike at some of his other coaching stops, earning the players' commitment was only half the battle at Notre Dame.

Soon after Holtz returned to campus, he received word from the school's admissions department that Notre Dame could not accept Rice as a student. The news was difficult on many levels. First, Holtz had led Rice to believe that acceptance to Notre Dame wouldn't be an issue. Second, in doing so, he had violated one of the first edicts laid out to him during his phone interview with Notre Dame vice president Edmund Joyce.

"The head football coach has nothing to do with admissions," Father Joyce had told him.

Hat in hand, Holtz visited Joyce, hoping he could earn a one-time exception. In between the time Rice accepted the scholarship and Holtz was informed that admissions had rejected him, other schools recruiting Rice had moved on to their next targets. Despite his talent, the young quarterback was trapped in limbo.

For Holtz, this wasn't an easy sell. Rice's academic record was poor, and not just for an elite academic institution like Notre Dame: In fact, Rice would not have qualified to play anywhere in the country in 1986 as a freshman. Rice sported a 2.65 cumulative high school grade point average—not Harvard level but good enough for most schools—but a 640 Cumulative Scholastic Aptitude Test score, which was below the NCAA's newly enacted freshman eligibility requirements. "I enjoyed playing ball down on the corner, but I didn't like to study," Rice said of his Woodruff days.

Rice had a recourse. Under Proposition 48, athletes who failed to meet the NCAA's standards could attend school as freshmen but could not participate in their sport. If they succeeded academically, they would gain full eligibility, although they would be granted three years, not four. Opponents of the controversial legislation felt that the use of a sliding scale was both arbitrary—by making large distinctions between small increments in a student's standardized test score—as well as discriminatory against socially and economically disadvantaged athletes like Rice, who tended to struggle on standardized tests even when they were successful in the classroom.

"I do okay in math, but the verbal, some of those words I never even saw before," Rice told his local newspaper. "I know I can do the work in college. Some people just can't take those tests, but it doesn't mean they can't go to college."

Holtz felt Rice was a nice kid and a hard worker as well as a gifted athlete and natural leader. Convincing Joyce was another matter.

"This is not acceptable," the university vice president told his new head coach. But in the end Joyce made an exception and overruled the admissions office on Rice's application. As he and Holtz ended their tense discussion, Joyce left no doubt as to where he stood, lest the gesture be misinterpreted.

"I just want you to know one thing," he said. "This will never, ever happen again."

————

The first test of the effectiveness of Notre Dame's off-season gauntlet would come in South Bend against Michigan. And what a test it would be. Coach Bo Schembechler's Wolverines were coming off of a one-loss season in 1985 that ended with a glorious one-two punch, a defeat of archenemy Ohio State to close the regular season, followed by a Fiesta Bowl victory over Nebraska. Unranked at the start of the season, Michigan had risen to No. 2 in both major polls after the strong finish. And there was plenty of talent returning. Little running back Jamie Morris had already led Michigan in rushing for two consecutive seasons, standing up to the weekly physical toll the Big Ten exacted despite his five-foot-seven height. Quarterback Jim Harbaugh was an experienced veteran on a path to the first round in the next spring's NFL Draft.

But it wasn't Michigan's skill that frightened Holtz.

It was the Wolverines' size.

When Michigan had the ball, 246-pound Notre Dame defensive tackle Robert Banks would have to surrender sixty pounds to six-foot-seven-inch, 306-pound Wolverines offensive lineman John Elliott. Notre Dame's nose tackle, Mike Griffin, was outweighed by a full forty-three pounds by his most frequent combatant, Michigan's John Vitale. On average, Notre Dame's defensive linemen weighed thirty pounds less than their Michigan counterparts.

That wasn't the only handicap the Irish were facing in game one of the Lou Holtz era. Holtz preferred a mobile quarterback who could run the option and even shed a linebacker when necessary. His quarterback at Minnesota, Rickey Foggie, had fit that description. So did the backup on the 1985 Notre Dame team, Terry Andrysiak, who was now a junior, as well as Rice, the freshman academic casualty. The returning starter, Steve Beuerlein, on the other hand, did not. Beuerlein was a traditional pocket passer, and one with NFL talent. He just wasn't the kind of quarterback that Holtz would have handpicked to run his system.

When Holtz was hired, there was a concern for Beuerlein—concern that Holtz recognized and attempted to allay. In his first meeting with his new players—the one when Chuck Lanza was instructed to put his feet on the floor and sit up straight or else—Holtz also singled Beuerlein out.

"I thought he was gonna tell me, 'Thanks for your contributions to Notre Dame, you can stay on the team, but you're not gonna play,'" says Beuerlein, who had thrown thirty-seven interceptions and just thirteen touchdown passes up to that point in his college career. "But he told me in that meeting, 'You are gonna be my quarterback at Notre Dame.' He said there were a bunch of reasons for it, but basically he said, 'You are a drop-back quarterback, so because of that I'm gonna throw the ball more than I'm comfortable doing.'"

Holtz also told Beuerlein that, as his quarterback, he could expect some shoddy treatment at practice. In fact, in the Thursday practice before the season opener, Holtz threw his quarterback off the field before the practice really began. His sin? An offensive lineman jumped offside during a warm-up drill. Holtz wanted to send a message to Beuerlein about the degree to which he was accountable for the entire offense. But against Michigan the coach would let bygones be bygones and make good on his promise to let his quarterback wing it a little. Beuerlein would throw thirty-three passes in the game, completing twenty-one of them for 263 yards. But at the end of the game, it would be a couple of his misfires that would loom largest.

After five seasons of Faust, including the humiliation at Miami that remained the most vivid memory in the minds of the Irish, Notre Dame fans were in a frenzy about the unveiling of the new coach's program. Wearing a snug navy suit and a pair of oversize glasses, Holtz spoke at the Friday night pep rally on campus, telling an energetic student body, "I didn't come here to be a legend." They weren't hearing it. Seconds later, as the words *national championship* came from his mouth, Holtz was drowned out by the roar of the crowd. Less than twenty-four hours later, after a single half against the Wolverines, he would already look like a guy who could deliver what he said he would: change.

First, though: the hype.

The beginning of a new coaching era at Notre Dame was certainly not something that escaped the television network hyperbole machine. The ABC broadcast of the game began with the audio of actor Pat O'Brien, in the role of Notre Dame coaching legend Knute Rockne, delivering the famous "Win one for the Gipper" speech from the sanitized Hollywood biopic of Rockne from the 1940s. After that, announcer Keith Jackson went through the roll call of Notre Dame coaching luminaries, their black-and-white mug shots rolling by as the school's famous fight song played softly in the background.

"I think Lou realizes that he's come into, at least early on, a can't-lose situation," Jackson said after the pregame portion of the broadcast finally went live. "He's playing a very tough football team today, and if his team just has a respectable showing, I think he'll be pleased and I think the partisans of Notre Dame will be very pleased."

After Jackson's introduction, which he concluded by saying a Notre Dame victory over the Wolverines would be "the upset of the decade," ABC aired a sitdown interview with Holtz conducted by studio host Jim Lampley. The new coach did nothing to temper the enormous expectations in South Bend.

"To come here and not succeed I think would be very damaging to me mentally," Holtz said. "I don't feel pressure. I feel responsibility. If we can't be successful here, I'll have wished I'd never come."

Rather than trying to match the third-ranked team in the country straight-up, Holtz unleashed a barrage of creative, even gimmicky formations to keep the Michigan defense off balance. Shovel passes. Bootlegs. Reverses. An occasional wishbone formation, even with the lead-footed Beuerlein running the huddle.

It worked for a couple of reasons. First, this being the season opener, the Irish had a lot of extra time to absorb extra playbook material and run it efficiently. Schembechler and his Michigan staff, meanwhile, had no opportunity to scout the new Notre Dame. Adjustments were being made on the fly, while the Irish played the role of aggressor. Second, despite the Wolverines' overall talent advantage, Notre Dame had a great equalizer in Brown. No matter what wild formation Holtz called for his offense, the speedster from Texas was in the middle of things, carrying the ball twelve times in his new hybrid role.

At halftime, Notre Dame led 14–10. The Wolverines surged ahead in the third quarter, but a Beuerlein two-yard jump pass to tight end Joel Williams cut the deficit to 24–20. Unfortunately for Notre Dame, usually reliable kicker John Carney yanked the extra point wide left, a costly mistake and a harbinger of things to come.

As the afternoon wore on, the Irish continued to outgain the Wolverines. But they also continued to self-destruct at important times. In the third quarter, fullback Pernell Taylor fumbled away a possession inside the Michigan twenty-yard line. "Everyone in this stadium," said Jackson's ABC broadcast partner at one point, "has to be wondering if Notre Dame will fold now like they did last year against Miami, or if they have character."

In the fourth quarter, Beuerlein connected with tight end Williams on what appeared to be an eight-yard touchdown pass in the back of the end zone to give the Irish a late lead. But the back judge, sprinting into position, ruled Williams had not gotten one foot in bounds. It was a stellar catch by Williams, who nabbed the ball as a Michigan defensive back-dove at his feet, then remained nimble enough to dance along the back of the end zone. "There is no question," says Williams. "No doubt. That foot was down. Watch it."

The one replay angle available at the time made it impossible to tell whether Williams's right foot, obscured by the Michigan defender, came down behind the end zone before he was able to bring both feet down in play. Afterward, the story out of the Notre Dame camp was that a Michigan ballboy had told a Notre Dame ballboy, both of whom were standing behind that end zone, that Williams had caught the ball in bounds. As if that settled it. Regardless, Carney put his twenty-five yard attempt through the uprights to cut the Michigan lead to 24–23. Had he not missed the earlier extra point, the game would have been tied.

It was the second time that a Notre Dame drive had failed to penetrate the end zone after advancing to the eight-yard line. Minutes earlier, a Beuerlein pass into the end zone had been intercepted by Michigan defensive back David Arnold.

Because the stakes were more defined late in the game, those plays stood out. But Notre Dame errors were by no means confined to the final two quarters. In the first half, for example, Irish receiver Reggie Ward had run the ball to the Michigan nine-yard line before fumbling it away. Another receiver, Alvin Miller, dropped a perfectly thrown Beuerlein pass deep inside Michigan territory in the waning seconds of the second quarter. A catch would have meant a chip-shot field goal and probably a 17–10 advantage.

"Michigan just couldn't stop us," says Notre Dame offensive tackle Byron Spruell. "That's what we'd come off to the sidelines saying: 'They're not stopping us, guys. We have a powerhouse of a team.'"

Despite all the wasted chances, the Irish would still have a chance to pull off the upset as the clock wound down.

With thirteen seconds to play, following a Michigan fumble, the Irish advanced the ball to the Wolverines' twenty-eight. Here was a chance for Carney to redeem himself. In his career, the kicker had nailed fifteen of sixteen tries from between forty and forty-nine yards. This one measured forty-five yards. Six years earlier, Notre Dame's Harry Oliver had beaten Schembechler's Wolverines with a fifty-one yarder as time expired. Now it looked as if another Irish kicker would ruin Michigan's day and put an early, perhaps devastating crimp in the team's national championship hopes. The ball was snapped and held perfectly by Dan Sorensen, and the Notre Dame kicker thought he got every inch of it as his right foot swept through. "When I kicked that ball," Carney would say, "I could have sworn I had enough power on it to send it into the tunnel."

"The upset of the decade," as ABC's Jackson had deemed a potential

Notre Dame victory, seemed imminent as the ball exploded off Carney's reliable foot. But then physics interfered. After climbing normally on its ascent, the ball's awkward rotation pulled it out of its straight line to the goalposts and it began hooking wildly. By the time it nose-dived into the turf, the kick was wide left and well short. Holtz, a holy terror at times during the winter and through fall practice as he prepared his squad for this moment, this coming-out, hooked his left arm around his kicker's shoulders as he walked off the field, then empathetically patted him three times on top of his bowed helmet.

"After it's over," Carney said, "you start putting all the pieces together. Lou Holtz's first game. National coverage. Michigan. Had a chance to be a part of history, and blew it."

Notre Dame Stadium sat in stunned silence as the Michigan offense took the field to run the final few seconds off the game clock. Over the previous five years, Irish fans had sat through the same kinds of near misses, only to find themselves inevitably heartbroken when the final gun sounded. But these fans saw things through a new lens. Yes, the Irish had made some very costly, boneheaded mistakes, but they had also outgained the Wolverines 455 yards to 393. Yes, Carney had missed an extra point and the game winner, but he had come through before; given the opportunity, he would come through again. Instead of jeering the Irish for letting victory slip through their grasp, nearly sixty thousand fans began cheering wildly as Notre Dame's players headed toward the tunnel to the locker room.

The media, which had pounced on every stumble the two years prior, was positively glowing in its early reviews of Holtz's program.

"Prayers are appreciated, but no longer necessary," wrote the *Chicago Tribune*'s Bernie Lincicome, a writer who wasn't afraid to pull out the long knives when necessary. "Notre Dame is going to be okay. Seldom has a loss offered such great rewards."

"Notre Dame," Rick Telander wrote in *Sports Illustrated*, "finally has itself a real college coach who can draw up real college plays."

The 1986 schedule offered a one-year respite from the Miami series—nice timing for a program that had a lot of work to do, a lot of confidence to restore, before it was truly ready to test itself against the gold standard again. But if the Irish could play Michigan to the wire—

if they could mostly outplay a team with realistic national championship aspirations—surely they could beat just about anybody. "From that point forward," Beuerlein says, "we believed we could play with anybody. That game was kind of a validation that we were ready, that we had a plan, and that we could do it."

CHAPTER 4

Ethnic Interaction

Soon after Johnson took the job at Miami, he ran into Walter High-smith, a local high school coach and the father of one of his best play-ers, Alonzo Highsmith. Johnson was still receiving a cold reception from the Miami fan base and asked the elder Highsmith why that might be the case.

"People are concerned that you're going to recruit too many black players," said Highsmith. "That's kind of your reputation. And I think a lot of people probably don't want that."

"I'll guarantee you this," Johnson said, "I'm not going to keep count of how many black players I recruit. I'm going to recruit the best foot-ball players."

———

For a generation of football fans raised on his comedic banter on NFL pregame shows, and perhaps at least vaguely aware of his Jimmy Buffett lifestyle in the Florida Keys, it's probably difficult to fathom Jimmy Johnson, the fierce competitor. But "believe me," says Greg Cote, who covered Johnson's Miami teams for the *Miami Herald*, "if you were around Jimmy Johnson in the fall of 1985, this was not a laid-back guy. This was a guy who you didn't want to be around after a tough loss."

The competitive gene was always strong in the otherwise fun-loving coach. Early in Johnson's coaching career, during a stint as Iowa State's defensive coordinator, he excitedly woke up his wife, Linda Kay, around midnight. The big news? He had upended the reigning shuffleboard champion down at the Ames Elks Club. The Iowa State staff at the time was packed with southerners, including Tennessee-bred head coach

Johnny Majors. For kicks, Majors decided one winter day to reserve a tennis court at a local park, requesting that the park district flood it ahead of time so the southern boys could try a little ice skating. Majors figured a good time would be had by all, with everyone equally inept on skates. Instead, while the other coaches crashed around the ice all afternoon, suffering injuries numbed only by the large quantity of adult beverages consumed prior to the skate, Johnson glided around the court like a National Hockey League veteran. Only afterward did he reveal that he had taken ice-skating lessons in anticipation of the event.

Johnson was born in Port Arthur, Texas, in 1942, and first learned to compete in neighborhood street football contests. "The hardest hitters then were two black kids we called Baby Joe and I.E.," Johnson would later recall. "And when they knocked you out of bounds—off the grassy median of a boulevard where we played—your head was likely to hit the curb or the pavement." Socializing with the guys from the neighborhood, along with the blacks and Mexicans who worked alongside him at a local dairy, would turn out to be tremendous preparation for the racial and cultural stew that is the city of Miami.

"Ethnic interaction," Johnson wrote in his autobiography, *Turning the Thing Around*, "was so normal to me that I didn't actively think about it."

That wasn't the only way that echoes of Port Arthur continued to ring through his coaching career. If Johnson seemed to find some of the hell-raisers he coached—both at Miami and later with the notoriously rowdy Super Bowl champion Dallas Cowboys—a little more endearing than did the general public, there was good reason: He identified with them. Port Arthur was home to a large number of solid, safe, middle-class neighborhoods, the type that C. W. and Allene Johnson settled into after moving across the Arkansas border. At the same time, the town had a dark, exciting underbelly: the port docks on the Gulf of Mexico. The port hosted lots of merchant sailors, in town for a night, maybe two, with time on their hands and little to do. Up sprouted black-market casinos, roughneck taverns, and a healthy selection of whorehouses. Johnson and his best friend in high school, Jimmy Maxfield, simply couldn't keep themselves away.

In contrast to Notre Dame's Holtz, grades were not much of an issue for the exceedingly bright Johnson. So he had little difficulty balancing his studies with a little mischief on the side. Through some of Maxfield's father's business connections, the pair were able to talk their way into the saloons and whorehouses, downing a few beers as they watched the sailors and scantily clad women walk up and down the stairs. Maxfield even parlayed the adventures into a stream of income, charging gawkers from school a quarter to tour the joints. On other evenings, Johnson, Maxfield, and other adventurous boys from Thomas Jefferson High would cross over the nearby state border into Louisiana, where the drinking age was just eighteen, an age for which most of them could pass.

As a teenager, Johnson may have not been serious about a lot of things, but he was certainly serious about football. The coach at Thomas Jefferson was Clarence "Buckshot" Underwood, a Texas coaching legend who had trained under Paul "Bear" Bryant when the Bear had been a young up-and-comer at the University of Kentucky. Johnson developed into an all-state linebacker, no small feat in a talent-rich state like Texas. But even though all the major Texas universities came calling, Johnson had been raised a transplanted Razorback, and when Arkansas extended a scholarship offer, any recruiting war for his services ended then and there.

A standout at the next level as well, Johnson didn't give much thought to coaching until late in his college career. Instead, he found that his psychology courses held his interest, and decided that after graduation he would pursue a master's in the subject so he could work as an industrial psychologist, paid by corporations to make sure working conditions kept employees happy and productive.

During Johnson's senior season, however, a group of coaches from nearby Louisiana Tech came to Fayetteville to learn the Razorbacks' innovative 3–4 scheme, the "Arkansas Monster Slide Defense." Johnson was summoned to draw it up on the blackboard, and he proved to be a natural at making it all understandable. The Louisiana Tech coaches didn't forget. A few months later, when the program's defensive coordinator took a health-related leave of absence, Tech head coach Joe Aillet called Johnson to see if he wouldn't mind filling in for a year. He accepted the offer and quickly found coaching to be his calling.

Like many ambitious young coaches, including Lou Holtz, Johnson spent a good portion of his twenties playing geographic hopscotch. He spent a season as a graduate assistant back at Arkansas, then served as the defensive coordinator and study hall watchman at a high school in Mississippi. Picayune went winless that season, but Johnson was hardly deterred. He jumped from there to Wichita State, where he coached the defensive line, and then on to Majors's staff at Iowa State.

As much fun as he was having on his midwestern stops, and as much as Johnson was honing his coaching style and feeding his insatiable competitive desires, the opportunity to return to warmer climes was too enticing to pass up. So when Clemson offered him a job on its defensive staff, Johnson accepted, even though Iowa State offered to match the salary. However, that turned out to be the shortest stint of Johnson's career. He never coached a game at Clemson, leaving within a few weeks when Oklahoma offered to make him its defensive line coach, even as friends in the coaching world warned him that such a rapid jump could damage his reputation.

Whatever hit Johnson's reputation may have taken was neutralized by his performance on the Sooners staff. By 1970, Johnson's first season in Norman, he was experienced and confident enough to assert some of his own ideas about defense. That didn't always do many favors for his and defensive coordinator Larry Lacewell's relationship—the two old pals from their Wichita State days would go days without speaking over one philosophical spat or another—but it did wonders for the Sooners defense. The core of Johnson's philosophy was simple if unorthodox for the era: Defensive linemen in traditional schemes were too passive. He wanted them to attack as soon as the ball was snapped, rather than wait to read where the play was headed, then pursue. "It's more than a technical strategy," Johnson said. "It's a frame of mind that starts with the defensive line." In 1969, the year before Johnson arrived to coach the Oklahoma defensive line, the Sooners surrendered an ugly 287 points. In 1972, his last year, they gave up just 92 points all season. They shut out four opponents, including Penn State, whom they defeated 14–0 in the Sugar Bowl.

From Oklahoma, Johnson returned to his alma mater, Arkansas, where he served as his old coach Frank Broyles's defensive coordinator for four seasons. When Broyles decided to retire after the 1976 season, he strongly considered Johnson as a possible replacement. But then the Razorbacks lost their last four games, and instead Broyles decided to go outside the program. He hired Lou Holtz, and Holtz guided Arkansas to an 11–1 record in 1977 and to the brink of a national championship. But he did it without Johnson.

Still just thirty-three years old, Johnson instead left for Pittsburgh, where Jackie Sherrill had just been hired. By that point, it was only a matter of time before some school hired Johnson to head its program. He interviewed for the opening at Air Force, but decided it wasn't the right opportunity. When the Oklahoma State job opened after the 1978 season, Johnson decided to pursue it full bore.

The situation wasn't exactly ideal. Oklahoma State's brazen boosters were out of control in the mid-1970s, leaving the program on perpetual probation. "The only way some of these athletes can survive is if people like me give 'em money," notorious booster Jim Treat said at the time, "which I will continue to do. The NCAA has no power over me, only its member institutions, and Jim Treat's going to do what he damn well pleases." When Treat felt the North Central Oklahoma Business Development Association, a Cowboys booster club that had developed a large slush fund for Oklahoma State football players, was directly involving head coach Jim Stanley and his staff in its payoff scheme, he blew the whistle. "I'm not going to sit here and lie to you and say the money was spent on flowers for homecoming," club member Gip Duggan said. "[But] everybody speeds. So you should catch the flagrant ones. I'd say we were going maybe sixty-five mph, but Oklahoma is going eighty-five to ninety and Nebraska 110."

Stanley, who allegedly dispensed regular payouts to players from a stack of bills in his office, was fired, and Oklahoma State's coaching search zeroed in on the young defensive coordinator at Pitt. In conservative Oklahoma, school officials were thrilled when Johnson interviewed and his wife, Mary Kay, present during a portion of the process, played the role of the subservient, supportive spouse.

"I'll just keep making Jimmy as happy at home as I can," she told the selection committee. "I think that's the biggest contribution I can make."

"There was just something about that answer," one of the board members gushed later on.

Reality, though, was quite different. As a young coach with raging ambition, Johnson was the classic workaholic. "Am I a family man?" he pondered after he was officially hired at Oklahoma State. "I've got as much time for them as they do me, and that isn't much."

Years later, when he was the head coach of the Dallas Cowboys, Johnson sent his parents extra game tickets they had requested—along with an invoice requesting payment. He wasn't one to go the extra mile for family. Eventually, Johnson and Mary Kay would divorce: He simply didn't have the time for that kind of traditional home life. Johnson was consumed with the task of being a football coach, and answering for his long hours at the office just wasn't part of his makeup.

"He wasn't in any hurry to go anywhere," says Mel Campbell, who played for Johnson at Oklahoma State and followed that with a stint on his staff as a graduate assistant. "Football was his life. His family took a backseat back then, and he expected everybody else to make that choice too."

On the field, as opposed to the cutthroat wheeler and dealer who would take charge a decade later in Dallas, the Jimmy Johnson of 1979 was a nurturer, making it his No. 1 priority to get the downtrodden Oklahoma State Cowboys to believe in themselves again. The effects of constant NCAA investigation and probation had thinned the scholarship ranks significantly, and Johnson's first Oklahoma State team operated with a skeleton roster. Johnson encouraged walk-ons, purchasing soccer shoes for $3 apiece to suit up the dozens of players who had much more spirit than ability. "He was a human pep rally," said Pat Jones, a coach on Johnson's staff who eventually became his successor. Although he took great pride in his psychology degree from Arkansas, Johnson's methods weren't revolutionary. But because of the staff's youth, the energy level at practices and meeting rooms came across as sincere, not at all contrived.

"Instead of intimidation and growling at us, it was more peppy and enthusiastic," says Rick Antle, a defensive lineman. "You'd see him jogging up and down the field, maybe sometimes hopping and skipping. I loved going to practice. I thought the man walked on water."

Johnson installed the attacking defensive front that he had been championing for years, but it seemed a choice at least partly by necessity. In the Big Eight conference, it was going to be difficult, if not impossible, to compete with Nebraska and Oklahoma for the kind of blue-chip behemoths that ideally packed the line of scrimmage. Johnson and his staff didn't even try.

"There's just not enough of them," says Dave Wannstedt, Johnson's defensive coordinator at Oklahoma State, Miami, and later Dallas. "We knew that for us to win a championship and to play great defense, you had to have great defensive linemen.

"When we were at Oklahoma State, we knew we weren't going to recruit the top players," Wannstedt explains. "We couldn't get 'em away from Texas. We couldn't get 'em away from Oklahoma. So we had to recruit these linebackers that were oversized, tall kids and weren't quite fast enough to play linebacker, and then we converted them to defensive linemen. It was really a trend we started in the Oklahoma State days out of survival mode, and then we started getting some great results."

In 1983, Johnson's final season in Stillwater, the Cowboys surrendered just 162 points and defeated Baylor 24–14 in the Bluebonnet Bowl. Howard Schnellenberger resigned at Miami after winning the national championship that year. Johnson heard the news after completing a round of golf with some of his Oklahoma State assistants, and his interest was immediately piqued.

"I'd love to have that job," Johnson said as the group sat around the clubhouse after their rounds. "That's what I've always dreamed about in college coaching: being at a place where you've got the talent to win the national championship."

Soon after, Johnson met Miami athletic director Sam Jankovich at a coaching convention in Dallas and expressed his interest in the job. The two hit it off, and Johnson was hired. Miami was a city still celebrating after the Hurricanes' shocking ascent to the national crown the previous season. At the same time, it was a city still healing after long-latent tensions had erupted at the start of the decade.

———

There were multiple reasons for the emergence of the Miami program beginning in the late 1970s and culminating with the 1983 national championship. Howard Schnellenberger was the face of the renaissance and finished the task, but Hurricanes insiders are quick to credit his predecessor Lou Saban as well. College football's multipronged sea change in the 1970s played a big role, too, taking scholarships and television exposure out of the monopolistic control of a few traditional programs and distributing that wealth around the country.

But one enormous reason for the program's emergence was the changing demographics of the state of Florida itself. As much as the three major universities in the state—Florida, Florida State, and Miami—came to dominate college football in the latter two decades of the twentieth century, it was easy to forget that they had been also-rans for most of the sport's history. Florida joined the Southeastern Conference in the 1930s, yet didn't win a league championship until 1991. Florida State didn't play in a major New Year's Day bowl game until the end of the 1979 season, when it was trounced by Oklahoma.

In 1900, despite its large geographic size, Florida had one of the smallest state populations in America, sitting just 3 out of the 391 members of the United States House of Representatives. The southern portion was particularly sparse, home to just one out of twelve state residents. Growth came steadily for a few decades, then exploded after 1950. From that year to 1960, Florida experienced a 79 percent growth rate and remained one of the top five fastest-growing states for the rest of the century. Nowhere was that more evident than in the once almost-uninhabited south: South Florida doubled in population size between 1950 and 1960. When Schnellenberger took out a map in 1979 and demarcated the "State of Miami" recruiting territory, it was viewed—and rightfully so—as a masterstroke that altered the balance of power in college football. But it wasn't as if every previous coach in the university's history had failed to notice all the talent right under his feet. Schnellenberger had the good fortune to come on board as "the U's" backyard had reached a population level that could supply a self-sustaining college football powerhouse.

Well before the population growth of the latter half of the twentieth century, however, Miami and all of South Florida had been home to a significant black population. Consequently, post-slavery racial conflict often flared up in Miami. The city was officially incorporated in 1896, and two years later the United States armed forces stationed more than seven thousand white soldiers in Miami as part of the Spanish-

American War effort. In July of that same year, a black local refused to step aside on the sidewalk for two white women and he was beaten to within an inch of his life by some of the visiting soldiers, who then invaded the nearby black villages and destroyed whatever they could get their hands on. Later that month, a black cook named Sam Drummer was shot dead by a white soldier in midday when he accidentally brushed against a white woman while trying to navigate a narrow hallway. The crime, despite witnesses who had no difficulty pointing out the perpetrator, went completely unpunished. By the early part of the twentieth century, an unofficial racial boundary was drawn through the city. In fact, the Color Line Ordinance nearly became official city law in 1916, but the vote was tabled by the city council.

The Civil Rights Movement of the 1960s didn't end the racial tension. In fact, there were thirteen documented incidents of racially charged violence or disturbances during the 1970s, all of it leading up to a disturbing climax in 1980. The events began in December of the year before. A black insurance salesman named Arthur McDuffie, divorced with two children, was riding a borrowed motorcycle home to his sister's house, where he was staying after the divorce, from a friend's house at around one a.m. A police officer witnessed him perform a "wheelie" in an intersection, then turned on his lights and began pursuit. McDuffie, driving on an expired license, fled. Soon, McDuffie and a dozen police cars were involved in a hundred-mile-per-hour chase through the streets of the city. When he finally stopped, McDuffie was beaten by up to a dozen officers. His watch came off during the fight, and one officer shot it with his revolver for sport. Within three minutes, McDuffie was in a coma. Although the police tried to report it as a motorcycle accident, evidence at the scene and in the autopsy after McDuffie died four days later made it clear that he had been beaten to death.

A few months later, several of the officers were tried for the murder of McDuffie and other crimes related to the incident. They were all acquitted. At five in the evening, a few hours after the verdict, black residents began throwing rocks and bottles at white motorists driving down Sixty-second Street. At the same time, a rumor spread that a white man had fatally shot a black child. It was completely untrue but helped further ignite the fury. Soon after, several young white people in a car on their way home from the beach unknowingly drove into a riot zone. The windshield was shattered by a rock, which struck the driver square in the head. The man, eighteen-year-old Michael Kulp, swerved off the road and into two black residents, severing a ten-year-old girl's leg. A female riding in the car escaped as the mob descended, but brothers Michael and Jeffrey Kulp were stuck. Authors Marvin Dunn and Bruce Porter described what happened next in their book *The Miami Riot of 1980*:

> The Kulp brothers were beaten continuously by a variety of people for about fifteen to twenty minutes. They were punched, karate-kicked, and struck with rocks, bricks, bottles, and pieces of concrete, one of which weighed twenty-three pounds. At one point, someone picked up a yellow *Miami Herald* newspaper dispenser and brought it down on Jeffrey Kulp's head. They were shot several times with a revolver and run over by a green Cadillac, whose driver then came over and stabbed them with a screwdriver.

After the beating was over, one local man placed a red rose in Jeffrey Kulp's mouth. Jeffrey died a few weeks later in the hospital after nine surgeries. Michael Kulp somehow survived the attack but suffered lifelong injuries.

About an hour later, in the same area, a fourteen-year-old boy, a fifteen-year-old boy, and a twenty-one-year-old relative of one of them were beaten savagely to death. The violence continued for several days. By the time the rioting was finally quelled, eighteen people had died and the city suffered more than $100 million in property damage.

Although nothing on the scale of the 1980 riots, Miami continued to be troubled by racially charged incidents throughout the early 1980s. From the perspective of Jimmy Johnson, one thing was for sure: His new residence was no college town.

"You don't go there for the tradition," says Matt Patchan, an offensive lineman under both Schnellenberger and Johnson. "We didn't go sing our fight song to the crowd after the game. We had no on-campus stadium. Playing down there in Little Havana, it was like playing in a quasi–third world country. You could walk down the sidewalks in the city and hear eight to ten different languages being spoken."

The Hurricanes' locker room was perhaps the one place in Miami during that time period where blacks and whites as well as Hispanics from the city congregated en masse with common goals in mind. Schnellenberger's "State of Miami" concept was a terrific way to amass talent on the Hurricanes' roster, but in the wrong hands such an experiment could lead to an explosion of latent tension. Johnson, luckily, was the right person for the job. He may have been ridiculed as a hayseed who was in over his head when he was hired to come to the scarred city, but his upbringing in integrated Port Arthur gave him a strong and useful foundation. Johnson couldn't stop cliques based on common identities from forming within the larger group of players. Even at the height of the program's cohesiveness, black players and white players often sat at separate cafeteria tables; and as Miami began to draw in talent from other areas of the country, like Texas, cliques began to form based not on race but on geographic origin. But what Johnson could control, he did. He recognized, for example, that at away games, allowing the team to split themselves into two buses—one that played rap music and the other playing rock and roll—was a model for racial segregation. Instead, one bus carried offensive players and the other carried defensive players.

"What I think he was a master at," says Rich Dalrymple, Johnson's sports information director at Miami, "was understanding the personalities and the types of kids he had on the roster and really allowing their personalities to become a part of the mystique of the team and grow. A lot of them were kids from the city and kids who didn't come from the greatest family backgrounds, but he knew that this was their opportunity to make something of their lives, and he knew this was a chance to channel their hunger and their enthusiasm and make it part of something."

The Miami that everyone remembers from the 1980s—the boisterous crew that completely turned the page on the era of Bear Bryant and other such stoic, rule-by-fear coaching luminaries—was a product of Johnson's ability to coax the best out of everyone, from Miami street kids to Rust Belt imports. A fine line existed between exhibiting confidence and rubbing everyone's face in their greatness, and sometimes the Hurricanes under Johnson crossed that line. They probably crossed it in beating Notre Dame 58–7 in November of 1985, waking the sleeping giant. They would for sure—at least in the eyes of the public—at the end of the 1986 season. "The large majority of those guys—under Jimmy Johnson, at least—ended up getting their degrees and are now productive citizens and generally very nice guys," says Steve Kim, a blogger and freelance journalist who has written on Miami football history for several websites. "But since they did touchdown dances and wore fatigues one time, they were demonized."

Johnson, remarkably in tune with his diverse team in a fractured city, never much cared how it came off publicly.

"We were edgy guys, absolutely," says defensive lineman Dan Sileo. "Every time we went out there, it was like the Roman gladiators. But I mean, don't be such a tight rear end. It's college football. Coaches are making $4 million a year today. Let's not pretend that [the] hypocrisy that goes on in college football doesn't exist. What do you think is wrong with college football: Miami Hurricane guys saluting after getting a sack, or a coach making $4 million a year off kids that don't get paid? The hypocrisy—there it is in a nutshell."

CHAPTER 5

The Battle of Sun Devil Stadium

The Miami program drew a great deal of its strength from its burgeoning reputation as college football's renegade outsider. "They wanted to be both the team that crushed you and the team that was just mercilessly booed by opposing fans," says Greg Cote, who covered the Johnson years for the *Miami Herald*. "They drank that in." As far as the Hurricanes were concerned, no program represented college football's stodgy establishment more than Notre Dame. What most of the young 'Canes were not aware of, however, was just how closely the DNA of their upstart potential dynasty resembled that of the program they despised above all others.

If the men who had guided Notre Dame, both the university and the football program, through its formative days had been told that the South Bend school would one day represent the sport's old guard, no doubt they would have demanded at least three forms of proof—as soon as they stopped laughing long enough to speak.

Notre Dame at the turn of the century was a tiny institution of no more than a few hundred students, the majority of them enrolled not in the university program but in the associated school for high-school-age boys. In the late 1890s, a group of men from the University of Michigan, a few hours up the road, traveled down to tutor Notre Dame's men on the game of football. Predictably, the Ann Arborites put a hurting on their pupils: At the time, baseball was the primary sport played on the campus.

That would change soon enough. As early as 1905, after the team completed a disappointing 5–4 season, the *Scholastic* student magazine trumpeted the first known "return to glory" demand: "The time has come," the article declared, "when Notre Dame should take her old rank in the football world." Still, even as Notre Dame began to embrace football, the college football world was slow to embrace Notre Dame. Back in the mid-1890s, some of the major universities of the Midwest, including Michigan, Purdue, Wisconsin, and the University of Chicago, formed the Western Conference (later the Big Ten). The league's formation was an attempt by the universities to codify player eligibility requirements and curb some of the abuses that were marring college sports of the era. Notre Dame applied for admission on several occasions. Each time, it was rejected. The other universities simply did not view the South Bend school as any sort of peer, its religious-based curriculum and its open admissions policy to any boy willing to work his way through school acting as two major roadblocks.

The rejection by the local conference stung, but even more damaging was the members' collective decision not to schedule games against the Irish. In 1910, Michigan coach Fielding Yost canceled the annual game between the two schools on the eve of the competition, claiming that Notre Dame was suiting up ineligible players. Instead of facing schools with big regional followings and reputations, Notre Dame was forced to fill its schedule with undistinguished opponents like Adrian College, Morris Harvey, and Marquette. In 1913, Irish coach Jesse Harper came upon a solution: fan out nationally for more willing opponents. "I had to go some place," Harper explained, "where I could get some ball games." Kindred spirit Army, which had been similarly snubbed by some of its fellow schools in the East, was the first major program to agree to a game. The Irish victory in 1913 at West Point featured a deadly forward passing game that Army was completely unprepared for, and the Notre Dame shutout victory is considered one of the major turning points in the Notre Dame football program's development from ambitious upstart to national icon.

Under Schnellenberger and then Johnson, Miami was rightfully credited with spearheading a speed revolution in college football in the early and mid-1980s. But Knute Rockne, Harper's successor as head coach at Notre Dame, was a few decades ahead of them. "Rockne looked for speed, quickness, and guts," one of his former players said. "Most coaches in those days were impressed with size and went for big men." Although Notre Dame had mostly stayed out of the muck that had soiled college football's earliest days, Rockne had little issue with bringing in skilled football players who might be a little lacking in the classroom. In fact, he even derided local peers Northwestern and the University of Chicago as schools where, according to Murray Sperber's myth-busting history of Notre Dame's early days, *Shake Down the Thunder*, "faculty members were 'more interested in academics than athletics.'"

The rest of the story is pretty much committed to the collective cultural memory of college football fans everywhere. As the decades slipped by, Notre Dame claimed more national championships, more Heisman Trophy winners, more All-Americans, more fans, and more tall tales than any other program in America. As the football program's prestige grew under Rockne and subsequent Irish coaches like Elmer Layden, Frank Leahy, and Ara Parseghian, so did the academic prestige of the once maligned Catholic university. Far from being a renegade outsider, by midcentury Notre Dame had emerged as the de facto head of the college football establishment.

Yet, even then, there remained in its fan base a little bit of the spirit of the perpetual underdog, the outsider spunk that had helped Notre Dame through the growing pains of its trying early years. Early in 1986, Holtz was working hard to harness that fight and use it to his current team's advantage. Even in its most renegade incarnations, however, there is no record of Notre Dame players donning camouflage military fatigues as a show of solidarity and a means of intimidation. Maybe if Rockne had thought of it, though...

In its somehow equally heartbreaking and heartening loss to Michigan to begin the 1986 season, Notre Dame had paid dearly for a series of errors, from disarray on a Michigan kickoff to Pernell Taylor's ill-timed fumble to John Carney's extra-point miss. Clean up the mistakes, it seemed, and it would be smooth sailing.

If only it were that easy.

The next week, the Irish lost again, 20–15, to Michigan State. The Irish ran into the Spartans' Todd Krumm after he signaled for a fair catch on a kickoff, costing Notre Dame fifteen crucial yards and shortening the field for a Michigan State scoring drive. Punter Dan Sorensen had a punt partially blocked. Quick-kicking on third down, Beuerlein shanked one, gift-wrapping field position for the Spartans. The Irish could not seem to get out of their own way, although they were able to give Holtz his first victory a week later, a 41–9 blowout over Purdue. Starting center Chuck Lanza, the target of Holtz's unrestrained ire a few months before, dominated the line of scrimmage in the game, blasting holes in the Boilermakers defense as the Irish rolled up 276 rushing yards.

There were no Hurricanes on the schedule, but if there was a worthy surrogate for Miami, it was Alabama. The Irish traveled to Birmingham for the contest against the second-ranked and undefeated Crimson Tide on October 4, a week after the victory over Purdue. Technically a neutral-site game, the partisan Alabama crowd at Birmingham's Legion Field made it feel like anything but. The hostile crowd, however, was the least of Notre Dame's problems.

As had been the case with the Hurricanes the year before, the Crimson Tide had speed that the Irish simply could not match. And that wasn't true only on the perimeter. Alabama's most fearsome player was linebacker Cornelius Bennett, who stood at a hulking six foot four, weighed 235 pounds, but moved like a wide receiver. "That was Cornelius Bennett's field day," says Byron Spruell, Notre Dame's right tackle in Holtz's first year. "We could never locate him and he was all over the field. It was like there were three of him on the field." Bennett made his presence known early—and painfully. In the first quarter, Beuerlein faked a play-action handoff and began rolling to his right. Bennett wasn't fooled. The Irish quarterback never saw the All-American coming, although a Notre Dame offensive lineman scrambled to reach a free-rushing Bennett and mitigate the damage. No luck. Just as Beuerlein, still moving, began to lift his head and survey the field, Bennett crashed into him at full speed. Both of the quarterback's feet left the ground as the Alabama linebacker drove him into the artificial turf. "When I got up," Beuerlein said, "I saw mouths moving, but I heard no voices."

Although he would spend the evening in the hospital for observation, Beuerlein continued to play, sharing time with backup Terry Andrysiak. It was a nice display of toughness, if not youthful stupidity, but the tone had been set.

Again, special teams was a problem. And that was particularly galling for a head coach who, unlike some of his colleagues, understood the importance of that facet of the game. In a big game against Maryland during his North Carolina State tenure, Holtz had asked the television announcers to name his special-teams lineup instead of his offense or his defense before kickoff. Sufficiently motivated, the Wolfpack special teams played a big role in the victory that afternoon.

Against Alabama, Tim Brown, of all people, fumbled a punt deep in Crimson Tide territory. The Tide recovered and reached the end zone moments later. Sorensen's first punt was nearly blocked. His second one was returned sixty-six yards for a touchdown by Tide return man Greg Richardson, the first score of the game. The artificial turf at Legion Field only served to further accentuate Alabama's speed advantage, and when it was all over, the Irish were picking themselves up off the ground after a 28–10 loss that didn't really feel that close.

The following week, against Pitt, the Irish led 9–7 late. However, Sorensen's fourth-quarter punt was blocked by Pitt's Matt Bradley. A few moments later, with less than ninety seconds to play, Panthers kicker Jeff Van Horne booted a short field goal to put his team ahead 10–9. Beuerlein, who had recovered from the concussion the week before, drove the Notre Dame offense down the field in short order, setting up a thirty-eight-yard field goal try by Carney for the win.

This attempt, coming with fourteen seconds to play, would be the kicker's opportunity to redeem himself for the Michigan miss almost exactly a month before.

On this afternoon he had already connected from thirty-five, forty-eight, and twenty. When Carney's foot connected with the football, holder Sorensen immediately leaped from his crouch to celebrate what felt and looked like the game winner.

Then Sorensen, Carney, and the rest of the stadium watched as the ball sailed inches outside the right upright. No good. "The players are heartbroken," Holtz said, his team falling to 1–4, with three of the losses coming by a combined 7 points, two of them after last-minute field goal misses, "and my heart's broken for them."

Next up was Air Force, which should have been a respite after the grueling parade of top-twenty teams and national title contenders. But after the previous four seasons, Notre Dame's players would have been foolish to view it that way. Of all the marks against Faust, perhaps none stood out as much as his performance against the Falcons. The academy, its nonscholarship grinders pitted against Notre Dame's battalion of high school All-Americans, had defeated the Irish four times in a row heading into the 1986 contest.

This Air Force team was 5–1, and returning from the previous year was linebacker Terry Maki. In the Irish 21–15 loss in 1985, Maki had made an incredible thirty tackles, including nineteen unassisted stops. In a late play that could have been taken right off of the 1986 Notre Dame highlight reel, Maki blocked a potential game-winning Notre Dame field goal. The Falcons returned it seventy-seven yards for a touchdown.

When Holtz took over the Notre Dame program, he had pledged that the days of losing to Air Force and teams of its caliber were over. "It's one of the first things Holtz said when he came in there," said linebacker Ned Bolcar. "He said, 'Mark this down. Notre Dame will never lose to a military academy.'" And on this particular Saturday, the Irish made good on Holtz's promise. The gap in speed and athleticism was something that Faust's teams had been unable to take advantage of, but Holtz's team fully exploited it. Brown returned an early kickoff ninety-five yards. Cornerback George Streeter was a one-man wrecking crew on defense. Perhaps most illustrative of the talent differential, the slow-footed Beuerlein carried the ball ten times for thirty-seven yards. That included a one-yard improvisation for a touchdown, a sequence that would have left the quarterback dead and buried in the backfield against most Division I-A opponents.

The victory over Air Force started a three-game winning streak for the Irish, a sorely needed morale boost for a team that had been in the emotional dumps after the string of close early losses. That set up a showdown in South Bend between the suddenly surging Irish and the nation's second-ranked team, Penn State.

It wouldn't have been Notre Dame without a costly special-teams gaffe, in this case Tom Galloway's clipping penalty that wiped out Brown's ninety-seven yard touchdown return. But the Irish, newly fortified after three consecutive victories, marched onward against the Nittany Lions, a team on a collision course for a winner-take-all bowl bout against Jimmy Johnson's top-ranked Hurricanes.

Beuerlein, entrusted with the offense against all of Holtz's instincts regarding drop-back quarterbacks, played the game of his life, completing twenty-four of thirty-nine passes for 311 yards. Most important, in a game in which the Irish absolutely could not afford costly errors, he did not throw an interception.

With two and a half minutes to play, Beuerlein drove the offense all the way from their own twenty to a first down on the Penn State six-yard line with fifty-three seconds to play. For Notre Dame, trailing 24–19, this was a chance to purge all the stinging memories from the season's first few games. For the visiting Nittany Lions, a shot at the national championship hung in the balance.

Awakened from its daze, Penn State stiffened. The Irish lost yardage on first and second down, setting up a third-down play from the eighteen. Beuerlein's spiral to Williams in the back of the end zone was perfectly thrown, but the tight end could not hold on after cornerback Gary Wilkerson plowed into him. On fourth down, Notre Dame's final opportunity at the upset, none of the three receivers the Irish sent into the end zone could shake free of their Nittany Lion defenders. Instead, Beuerlein checked down to running back Mark Green, who was stopped at the six-yard line. Game over. Another heartbreaker.

By the time the Irish reached the final game of Holtz's tumultuous first season, their record stood at 4–6 and they were out of contention for any bowl invitation. It being an even-numbered year, however, the last week of the regular season meant a journey to Los Angeles to play longtime nemesis USC. A victory over the Trojans, who had failed to significantly build on a promising 4–0 start but still had performed well enough to earn an invite to the Citrus Bowl on New Year's Day, would at least leave the Notre Dame players who were coming back something positive to build on during another long off-season.

This time USC was the team in turmoil, much as the Irish had been when they had traveled to Miami the previous year. Unlike Gerry Faust, Southern Cal coach Ted Tollner had not yet resigned, but he was certainly under fire after a series of mediocre seasons. As it had in Faust's last year at Notre Dame, the speculation surrounding the head coach seemed to have infected the roster. The Rodney Peete-quarterbacked Trojans were talented but lacked the composure of a winning outfit. The week before they welcomed the Irish to the Coliseum, the Trojans had been blown out by crosstown rival UCLA, committing six unsportsmanlike penalties. Still, in the locker room before the game, Toll-ner reminded his team that victory over the Irish was well within its reach. "Notre Dame," Tollner said, "finds a way to lose games."

Only once during the season had Notre Dame been blown out, against Alabama, but for three quarters the Trojans took out some of their frus-trations. "USC runs that horse [the USC mascot] around so much when they score," Holtz said, "for a while I thought I was at the racetrack." So irked with his quarterback was Holtz after USC defensive back Louis Brock Jr. returned an interception fifty-nine yards for a touchdown that he replaced Beuerlein with Terry Andrysiak for a drive in the first half. But nothing Holtz and the Irish did seemed to work. In the final seconds of the first half, Irish defensive back Steve Lawrence leveled USC receiver Lonnie White, violently separating receiver from ball. Lawrence stood over White and barked gleefully as the receiver recovered his senses. On the next play, however, USC kicker John Shaffer came in and split the up-rights from sixty yards, a record by a Pac-10 conference team.

How discouraging was the evening for the Irish? The Parseghian Meter told that story. In Notre Dame's prior season finale, the old Irish coach turned CBS broadcaster raged against Miami coach Jimmy Johnson as the score spiraled out of control. Once again, as USC's lead ballooned, he had difficulty containing his emotions. "That's a South-ern California holding call!" he complained after an early flag against an Irish offensive lineman. "We ought to have more points on the board," Parseghian said when the time of possession in the first half fa-vored Notre Dame, although the scoreboard favored the Trojans. Parseghian quickly clarified himself: *Notre Dame* should."

By late in the third quarter, the score was 30–12 USC. The develop-ments were deflating for Irish fans who had spent the entire season watching the team fall valiantly in close battles against some of the nation's best teams. All along, the signs indicated that a breakthrough was forthcoming, and now this: an embarrassing showing on national television against a struggling rival. Even university vice president Edmund Joyce, the man who had spearheaded the hirings of both Faust and Holtz, had already closed the book on 1986 as USC took control. "Recently we haven't been as successful as we used to be," Joyce said during a halftime interview on CBS. "I was hoping that today our team might rise to the occasion, but USC looks a little too strong to me."

Following a touchdown by Todd Steele, however, Brown returned the ensuing kickoff into USC territory. And something seemed to awaken in the Irish. "I can't tell you why or how," Holtz said, "but they finally came to realize that they no longer wanted to be average." Notre Dame scored touchdowns on three consecutive drives in the third and fourth quarters, drawing to 37–35 with less than five minutes to play. The tiring Irish defense found reserves of energy when it counted, stuffing Peete on fourth down and inches inside its own five-yard line, then holding on third-and-short with about two minutes to play.

With less than five seconds remaining, running back Mark Green barreled to the USC one-yard line. In came John Carney to attempt the chip-shot field goal.

Three months before, Carney had been in a similar situation in Holtz's first game. With a chance to beat Michigan at Notre Dame Stadium, however, the kicker had missed badly, yanking a duck hook wide left.

A few weeks later he had missed again with a chance to beat Pitt.

This time, as the clock hit zeroes at the LA Coliseum, Carney didn't miss. The eighteen-yarder split the uprights, giving the Irish the 38–37 victory. Befitting a fan base that had suffered through afternoon after afternoon of close calls without a payoff, following the commercial break, the CBS cameras returned to the action after Carney had already kicked the game winner as Notre Dame's players mobbed one another. It was certainly a different scene from the one that had ended the previous season, the mugging at Miami. The players were almost entirely the same ones who had been embarrassed at the Orange Bowl. The big difference was, without a doubt, in the man running the Irish sideline.

"Seeing the transition from Coach Faust to Coach Holtz," says Ted Gradel, Carney's backup as Notre Dame's placekicker, "was an interesting insight into how organizations can be run and how different they can be under different leadership."

––––––

Unlike Notre Dame, Miami didn't schedule any military academies as regular-season punching bags. But the Hurricanes had clearly paid at least some attention to the fashion favored by Army combatants in the field.

"I used to show up to games, in fatigues, my fatigue pants," says defensive lineman Dan Sileo. "That's how the whole thing started for the Fiesta Bowl. I used to wear fatigue pants because my legs were so big, because they're really wide.

"So then somebody got the idea of starting to wear fatigues for games, and we were wearing 'em when we got off the plane in Scottsdale. It was a joke. It started as a joke. We were kind of goofing on ourselves, but because it was Penn State, everyone was so tight-assed about that game. I just kept saying to people, 'Lighten up. It's a college football game.'"

While the Hurricanes had cruised through their schedule largely unchallenged, the nation's only other unbeaten team, Penn State, squeaked by several opponents. Besides the near loss at Notre Dame, the Nittany Lions had defeated Cincinnati 23–17 and Maryland 17–15. Appropriate for a place nicknamed "Linebacker U," Penn State's heart and soul was linebacker Shane Conlan. Quarterback John Shaffer was 65–1 as a starter since middle school but had about as much chance of playing in the NFL the following season as his sixty-year-old coach, Joe Paterno. The Lions did have a talented backfield, with talented freshman Blair Thomas occasionally spelling one-thousand-yard rusher D. J. "Deke" Dozier. Talentwise, Penn State didn't appear to belong on the same field as the Hurricanes, but while other teams fell by the wayside, the Nittany Lions managed to stay unbeaten all year. When the regular season ended, they were the default No. 2 team in both the Associated Press and coaches polls.

Where many saw a potential mismatch, however, officials of the ambitious Fiesta Bowl saw opportunity.

By the mid-1980s the existing bowl hierarchy had been in place for many years, and the New Year's Day lineup was pretty much an accepted slice of Americana. The Rose, Orange, Sugar, and Cotton Bowls were considered the top tier, issuing the biggest payouts and signing agreements with the most prestigious conferences. In 1981, the Fiesta Bowl applied to the NCAA for a New Year's Day slot. It was considered a bold move, even a renegade maneuver. Fearing a lawsuit, the NCAA reluctantly granted the request, and the New Year's Eve lineup grew to five games.

Because of the conference tie-ins, the four traditional New Year's Day bowls still maintained a monopoly on the games that mattered, those that helped determine the national championship. But in 1986 the nation's two top-ranked teams were unaffiliated independents, freeing them up to head to a bowl of their choosing. The Miami administration endured a tremendous amount of pressure, including phone calls from the state's governor, to stay in-state and play in the Gator Bowl or the Citrus Bowl, two games also looking to raise their profile. But the Fiesta Bowl's corporate partnership with Sunkist, along with its relationship with NBC, gave it the freedom to both double its normal payout and move the game to prime time on January 2. In the end, it was a no-brainer for both schools. They would settle it on the field at Sun Devil Stadium in Tempe, Arizona. It was a matchup—one of the establishment powers taking on the party-crashers—that hardly needed any added hype. Thanks to the free-spirited Hurricanes, however, it would receive plenty of it.

Johnson beat his players to Arizona by several days, arriving early to tend to some media and logistical obligations. Back home in Coral Gables, away from their head coach's watchful eye, Hurricanes Alonzo Highsmith, Brian Blades, Vinny Testaverde, Melvin Bratton, and Jerome Brown found an Army-Navy Surplus store in Miami and went shopping. At an earlier practice Highsmith and Blades had been together when Highsmith, the team's fullback, turned to his teammate and declared, "Time to go to war!" When it came time to board the team plane to Phoenix, about two dozen Miami players were outfitted head to toe in full combat fatigues. With takeoff already set, it was too late for the coaches who had been left behind to send the players back to change, so they stepped off the plane for the Fiesta Bowl dressed that way.

Word traveled quickly. At a nearby banquet, an assistant to Miami athletic director Sam Jankovich whispered to him, "Did you hear what they did?"

"No, what?" asked Jankovich.

"They came off the plane wearing combat fatigues."

"Please tell me you're kidding," Jankovich said.

But the assistant wasn't kidding.

"If there is one thing that I could change in life," Jankovich would say years later, "it would be that our players never walked out of that plane with fatigues."

The combat gear would reappear during a week in which at least a handful of the Hurricanes seemed determined to validate every stereotype ever attached to them.

During the week, the Penn State and Miami players were scheduled to attend a steak fry together. It was planned as a friendly bowl week get-together, with some three thousand people showing up to mingle and watch players from both teams put on humorous skits. The 'Canes became angry almost the second they walked in. The Fiesta Bowl had distributed sweat suits to players from both teams upon their arrival in Arizona. But while Penn State's gear was done in its traditional colors, blue and white, Miami's players were given all-black sweat suits. To the Hurricanes, the implication was clear: Black was the traditional villain's color. It was one thing for the independent, story line–obsessed media to paint the matchup as some sort of clash of good versus evil, quite another entirely for the bowl personnel to participate in the narrative. The 'Canes had been instructed to wear the sweat suits to the steak fry, but when they showed up, the Nittany Lions were outfitted in suits and ties. When Penn State coach Joe Paterno took the stage to speak, he asked his players to stand up and show the crowd "what kind of guys we have at Penn State."

Now the Hurricanes were really fuming. Then came Penn State's skit. The Nittany Lions rolled onstage a garbage can labeled *Jimmy Johnson's Hairspray*. The 'Canes were offended: Only *they* could tease their coach, not some inferior squad from middle-of-nowhere Pennsylvania. Gregarious punter John Bruno then made an awkward joke about the team's racial unity: "We even let the black guys eat with us at the training table once a week."

Finally, it was time for Miami's skit. Instead of leading a performance, however, Jerome Brown walked up to the microphone and removed his sweat suit. Underneath were the camouflage army fatigues he had been wearing when he exited the team plane.

"Did the Japanese sit down and eat with Pearl Harbor before they bombed them?" Brown bellowed. "We're out of here."

Brown motioned to his teammates, many of whom had also zipped off their black sweat suits to reveal their fatigues. All-American linebacker George Mira Jr., Miami's tackles leader that season, was sitting next to Johnson. "What do you think, Coach?" he asked him. "You guys do what you need to do," Johnson said, and Mira stood up and walked out, as well.

For the rest of the week, the 'Canes popped off almost nonstop to reporters covering the bowl.

"You know what I think of John Shaffer and D. J. Dozier?" Brown said. "I think they're nothing. Shaffer thought he had a bad bowl game last year. That was nothing. After this game, he'll wish he'd graduated. The dude's about to star in a nightmare."

By the end of the week, the Hurricanes had even managed to offend the crew covering the game for NBC, which liked nothing more than some compelling theater to pump up the ratings. At what was supposed to be a mundane photo shoot planned for the network to take mug shots of all the players, Brown collected gaudy gold chains from several teammates, creating a community pile so that everyone could wear one for his picture.

"Don't you smile, man!" Brown yelled as teammates sat for their shot. "Remember, this is war."

"They fucked up the whole week," said Charlie Jones, NBC's longtime Fiesta Bowl play-by-play voice. "They alienated everybody there."

"I just thought their shenanigans were stupid," said Bob Costas, who hosted the pregame and halftime shows. "They bought into that good guys–bad guys theme and I think it just sucked some of the energy out of them."

With the festivities devolving into a hostile circus, it was easy to forget that there was a game to play—a game that would determine the national championship. Each program already had a title to its credit during the decade. Penn State's had come in 1982, when the Nittany Lions had rebounded from an early three-touchdown loss to Alabama to deliver Paterno his first national championship. And Miami, of course, had won its title in 1983 under Schnellenberger, ratcheting up expectations for the miracle worker's successor.

One year before, the Hurricanes had come out on fire against Tennessee in the Sugar Bowl, dominating the first few minutes of the game before imploding in a 35–7 blowout defeat that cost them at least a share of the national championship. With seventy million viewers tuned in, the largest television audience in college football history, the Hurricanes again started the game in dominant fashion. On the first snap, Sileo and Daniel Stubbs busted through the Penn State offensive line and buried Shaffer fifteen yards behind the line of scrimmage.

"'Rome!" Sileo shouted to Brown as he returned to the defensive huddle. "We're gonna fucking kill these guys."

Two plays later, Brown and Dan Hawkins, the other two members of Miami's defensive front, sacked Shaffer, forcing Penn State to punt on fourth-and-twenty-seven.

At one point in the first half, the Hurricanes had outgained the Nittany Lions 204 yards to 20. Penn State did manage a 75-yard touchdown drive in the second quarter, but running back Highsmith kept ripping off huge chunks of yardage for the 'Canes. Even though the game went into halftime tied 7–7, it seemed like only a matter of time before Miami got its act sufficiently together to dominate Paterno's overmatched Nittany Lions.

One problem: Testaverde, who had won the Heisman Trophy in a landslide, was not himself. Since the regular season had ended, the quarterback had lost a lot of practice time. First, he had injured himself in a motorcycle accident, missing the final regular-season game against East Carolina. Then Testaverde had gone on the postseason award circuit, picking up one knickknack after another while his teammates prepared back in Coral Gables. "He was busted up," says offensive lineman Matt Patchan. "He didn't practice at all leading into that game. Really, there was no need for Vinny to play. We had Geoff Torretta as his backup, and he would have started for a majority of college football teams." While Testaverde struggled to get into the flow of the contest, Penn State confused him even further, dropping linebackers into coverage on almost every play. Testaverde would throw five interceptions in the game, some of them tossed to linebackers with no Miami receiver anywhere near the play. The golden-armed QB was completely baffled.

With less than a minute to play, the 'Canes trailed 14–10, but advanced the ball to the Penn State five-yard line as Testaverde suddenly came to life. On first-and-goal, however, he was sacked back at the thirteen. With a time-out remaining, the Miami coaches urged a running play against the tiring Penn State defense, but they let the Heisman winner overrule them. "We had been giving it to Alonzo Highsmith, and he had been getting seven, eight yards a crack," says Matt Patchan. "He could have easily gotten it in. Something happened, and we inexplicably decided to throw the ball. It was just a mess." On third down, with no choice but to pass, Testaverde threw an incompletion, bringing up fourth down.

Testaverde surveyed the Penn State defense and noticed that linebacker Pete Giftopoulos was lined up right in the path of his top target on the play's intended pattern. Testaverde audibled. But within moments Giftopoulos moved from his original spot, settling in right where the new pattern was headed. Instead of audibling again, Testaverde took his chances with the play as called.

It probably wouldn't have mattered either way. Like a poker player, the Penn State linebacker had figured out how to read Testaverde, noticing that the Miami quarterback's eyes settled right over the portion of the field where he intended to throw. The Heisman winner threw this pass right into the linebacker's waiting hands, sealing the loss for the Hurricanes and the national championship for the heavy-underdog Nittany Lions. It was the quarterback's fifth interception of the Fiesta Bowl, the most watched college football game in television history.

The outside world rejoiced, the *Phoenix Gazette* trumpeting CLASS BEATS CRASS in the next morning's edition. Just over a year before, Johnson and his Hurricanes had fumed after their thumping of Notre Dame, feeling that the CBS announcers had tagged them with a villain label that they had not deserved. Now they had no one to blame but themselves. And in their moment of defeat, not many people were left to defend them.

If 1986 was a transition year at Notre Dame, it was a colossal disappointment in Coral Gables, perhaps the only place on the map where a college team could win eleven consecutive games and still chalk up the season as a failure.

For Johnson and the 'Canes, things would get worse before they would get better.

If Miami's reputation as a haven for miscreants wasn't reinforced enough by the team's off-field performance at the Fiesta Bowl, some revelations in court documents a few months later helped lock it into place. Safety Selwyn Brown had been charged with sexual battery, an incident alleged to have occurred in the football dormitory. Charges were later dropped, but the academic records of six Hurricanes were subpoenaed during the Brown investigation, and what they revealed was not flattering. Brown's verbal SAT score had been 270, and that was the highest score among a group that also included Michael Irvin, Donald Ellis, Darrell Fullington, Cleveland Gary, and Alfredo Roberts. Ellis had scored a 200, the minimum possible score on that half of the exam.

To this day, Hurricanes from the era are sensitive to charges that they were a collection of flunky mercenaries representing the university on Saturdays while acting as if the library were under quarantine during the week. Indeed, the program's graduation rate under Johnson was exemplary.

"We didn't get extra help from teachers," says Randal Hill, a wide receiver during the Johnson era. "Teachers were even harder on us. We were not even allowed to wear any type of football or athletic paraphernalia to class because we knew the teachers would be that much harder on us. Johnson and the academic support staff told us that was the rule: no athletic apparel to class. You had to dress respectably."

Regardless, Miami's image continued to take a constant beating, and there was a feeling within the program that things were no worse than at any other school—just more extensively reported. That was certainly the view of Joe Frechette, the highest-ranking police official on the University of Miami force. After a spate of incidents had made the papers, Frechette distributed a memo detailing how incident reports involving Miami athletes were to be handled from that point forward. In particular, Frechette demanded that no copies be made of the original reports. That, he believed, might curtail the leaks to the media that had become prevalent. Since Miami was a private university, Coral Gables department procedure dictated that incidents were not supposed to be entered into the public record unless a misdemeanor or felony charge was made. At that time the campus police, working under the town department's umbrella, would hand the information over to Coral Gables PD proper. Frechette was frustrated that officers on his force were using the media to circumvent department protocol, airing all sorts of dirty laundry that otherwise would have stayed in house.

"It appears to me that what's getting leaked to the newspapers is getting out some way," Frechette told the *Miami Herald*. "I'm trying to pin it down. If you'd do the same with every student in this place, I'd be the happiest fella in the world. If it happens with a football player, it makes the paper."

Frechette's immodest, almost defiant support of the Hurricanes raised skepticism about the purity of his directive, including from within his own department. Frechette was a big Miami fan, standing on the sidelines for games and traveling to road games at the athletic department's expense.

What he could not do, however, was jam the genie back in the bottle. Whether the instances of Hurricanes running afoul of the law truly made Miami distinct from other programs around the country was immaterial: Public perception was what it was.

"We did some nutty things," Sileo says. "Our guys were crazy. What can I tell you? We were really crazy guys."

What didn't help was that in Miami in the late 1980s, football was the only game in town. The Florida Marlins of Major League Baseball and the Florida Panthers of the National Hockey League were still a few years from coming into existence. The National Basketball Association was working to establish a franchise in the market, but the Miami Heat would not begin play until 1988, and it would take a few years after that before they actually became competitive. That meant a lot of the media attention, particularly between the afternoon *Miami News* and the morning *Miami Herald*, focused on the Hurricanes and their exploits both on and off the field.

"There aren't many newspaper wars anymore because there aren't many newspapers," says Rich Dalrymple, Miami's sports information director in the Johnson years. "But the war was fueled by any little thing that either of them could find on the University of Miami program. It was very high-profile, and eighteen- to twenty-two-year-old kids are gonna do silly things from time to time. Everything became front-page news. You had these off-field incidents, you had a great team, you had dynamic players and they played in such an enthusiastic, in-your-face style and played so many games on national television that it was just a perfect scenario to attract both good publicity and bad publicity."

In the midst of all that bad publicity, Johnson's team would have to bounce back from the stinging disappointment of two consecutive blown bowl games. To back up the level of bravado the Hurricanes were now displaying, only national championships would do. For the 1987 season to make up for what had happened in Tempe, they would have to harness an almost unparalleled degree of redemptive motivation. For at least eleven Miami players, the path to redemption began before the clock hit zeroes at Sun Devil Stadium.

When Penn State's offense went onto the field to take a final snap and a knee to wind the clock down, the Miami coaching staff began to send out the second unit defense, feeling as if the first team had battled enough all night long to keep the 'Canes in the contest and deserved to relax. The starters balked, however, demanding to finish what they had started—not to mention taking their bitter medicine. "They were going to pull us," Sileo says. "I said, 'Fuck that, we're going out there.' Those guys from Penn State started talking shit at us, saying, 'Look at 'em, look at 'em. We beat 'em. We upset 'em.' I just sat there and said, 'You have every right to talk shit.' I remember us looking at each other and saying, 'We deserve that,' and we took it." Penn State quarterback John Shaffer kneeled with the ball and the revelry broke out all around the Hurricanes, who walked off the field in defeat despite giving up just 162 yards of offense. Only Toledo had gained less on Miami that season.

As difficult as it was to stand through those five excruciating seconds, by taking the field for one last snap, the Miami defense ensured that, even in defeat, the defiant Hurricane spirit shined through. Later, when the team plane arrived in Miami, the players who made the trip back to Florida were greeted by about 150 loyal followers who braved rainy conditions to show their unflagging support. Some of them came dressed in camouflage.

"We had so many rock stars that were part of that team," says offensive lineman Scott Provin. "But we were a true team. It was a collaborative effort to get there. It was a difficult game, and I don't think any of us have put it out of our memory. It's just disappointing that so many of my teammates that year weren't able to walk away with a ring after having one of the greatest teams in college football history."

There was little question that the Hurricanes had outplayed the Nittany Lions. But the national title trophy would be going home with Penn State, which was all that really mattered. Under Johnson, Miami consistently led the country in bravado. But the 'Canes had played three major bowl games under him, and lost all three of them.

"We won our share of big games," says Dave Wannstedt, Johnson's defensive coordinator, "but there's obviously a big difference in winning a big game in the regular season and winning the national championship."

The Fiesta Bowl closed the book on Testaverde's career, and despite his horrid performance in the game, he would go on to become the first selection in the NFL Draft, by the Tampa Bay Buccaneers, and play twenty seasons in the league. The Miami program had produced three first-round quarterbacks in succession: Jim Kelly, Bernie Kosar, and Testaverde. So while the entire team felt pressure heading into 1987, perhaps no one carried a bigger burden than the lightly recruited quarterback who stood next in line.

CHAPTER 6

Building a Program

Unlike Miami, South Bend experienced few instances of overt clashes between the races. But tension on the Notre Dame campus in the mid-1980s was certainly palpable. At the time of Holtz's hiring, there were less than two hundred black students enrolled at the university, and nearly two-thirds of them were varsity athletes. That made life difficult, at times, on black Notre Dame students who were not involved in athletics.

One student reported being asked if all blacks were Muslims. Others sensed immediate discomfort in the dorm when they moved in. When the two black student organizations at Notre Dame sponsored social events on campus, throwing open the doors for all students, they were frustrated to discover that only a handful of their white classmates would show up. Perhaps worst of all, some black students at Notre Dame felt isolated in the classroom. "In many cases," black student Lisa Boykin told the campus magazine, the *Scholastic,* "a teacher's impressions of your performance are affected simply by the color of your skin."

The Notre Dame administration was not oblivious to the university's homogeneity and was well aware of the limiting effect it had on the educational experience. Notre Dame's longtime president, Father Theodore Hesburgh, had served as a major player on President Richard Nixon's Civil Rights Commission. Yet, in 1966, Notre Dame's entering freshman class contained just twelve black students. Before the 1970 Cotton Bowl against Texas, Hesburgh announced that a high percentage of the proceeds from the game would be used to fund scholarships for minority students. That fall, fifty-eight black freshmen enrolled at Notre Dame, more than doubling the previous year's total.

But, scholarships or no scholarships, that momentum was difficult to sustain. The next year the total plummeted by nearly two-thirds.

You didn't have to be an insider to sense Notre Dame's elitist, country club vibe. In the 1980s, players from the Irish's most heated rival certainly noticed it as well.

"Notre Dame was the anti-U," Miami lineman Leon Searcy says. "They exemplified everything that we weren't. We looked at Notre Dame as clean-cut, crew-cut, [fancy] sweater wearing, briefcase carrying, representing a society as a whole that we didn't understand and just didn't like. Notre Dame is what we weren't, and we didn't like it. That's why we had so much animosity toward them, because we figured that they had the better dorms or ate the better meals. We were the anti-everything they stood for."

When Holtz took over the program after the 1985 season, the first action he took was to completely alter the culture within the existing roster, exemplified by months of grueling early-morning workouts. But he also realized that to compete with the Miamis of the world in the upcoming years, and to do so as soon as possible, he would have to begin recruiting the same kind of athletes that those schools were able to put on the field. By 1985, speed had surpassed power as the key ingredient for winning football. "They were just gigantic players," says former Miami offensive lineman Matt Patchan, recalling the 58–7 demolition of the Irish in Faust's last game. "Everyone was big and strong and tall. But looking back, it was a glimpse at how college football was morphing. We had guys that were not as big, but we had explosive players."

To recruit that kind of speed and try to beat the Hurricanes at their own game, Holtz would have to open up new recruiting veins and battle stereotypes about his new school that even its own students admitted were grounded in reality.

———

Vinny Cerrato, Holtz's recruiting coordinator, would help the program cast a wider recruiting net. Tony Rice, the option quarterback from Woodruff, South Carolina, was an early coup for the new staff. For starters, Rice was a black southerner, a demographic that typically had little interest in traveling into cold weather to attend a Catholic university with a predominantly white student body. He was also an academic risk, something the university powers that be did not take lightly. Young and energetic, Cerrato was able to break down racial and cultural barriers that previously stood in Notre Dame's way. He had to get creative, however, to slip potential academic risks—black, white, whatever color of the rainbow you resembled—past Notre Dame's savvy admissions office.

"They would always want the transcripts on the Monday prior to the week the kid would visit," Cerrato says. "If a kid was marginal gradewise but I knew he would do a great job in the interview, I wouldn't turn the transcript in until Friday. The kid would already be on campus. I knew otherwise the kid may get rejected. They might tell me, 'You can't even let him visit.' I knew that this was the only chance I had of getting those kids in."

The tactic didn't endear Cerrato to athletic department academic liaisons like George Kelly and Joe Yonto, but it did give plenty of academic risks the opportunity to impress the admissions office in a face-to-face interview.

"I had to play the game," Cerrato says. "I had to know how the game was played."

That was vintage Cerrato, proud master of the loophole. Such shenanigans helped ensure that the Irish would be able to recruit in margins they hadn't explored under prior regimes. They also ensured that a certain amount of friction, initially sparked when Holtz pushed Tony Rice on the university's admissions office, would always exist between the school and the young, energetic Holtz staffer who would lead Notre Dame's recruiting renaissance.

"Gerry Faust was the best recruiter Notre Dame ever had for bringing in Notre Dame–type people—choirboys," said Mike DiCicco, the director of academic advising under both Faust and Holtz. "[Under Holtz and Cerrato], you had to take a closer look to make sure they belonged here. I sensed that there were some rough kids that came in. I found that I had to push kids to get to class a little bit more. Actually, more than a little bit."

Cerrato was just twenty-four years old when he arrived at Notre Dame along with Holtz. Born in Queens, New York, and raised in Minnesota, he had attended Iowa State University. He was recruited as a quarterback but moved to wide receiver, starting as a junior and a senior. He was a productive college player but not National Football League material. "I wouldn't have drafted me, either," Cerrato said. "My evaluation? Good speed, but not very good running skills." Well before the advent of subscription-based recruiting websites and NFL Draft guides the thickness of phone books, Cerrato made himself a master of such hairline delineations. The difference between "good speed" and "good running skills" could very well be the difference between whether a recruit became an All-American at Notre Dame or spent four years soaking up valuable scholarship money while offering little return on the investment.

Wasted scholarships, to Cerrato, were the worst problem a program could have. Never having been part of a football world full of bloated scholarship rolls, he never had to adjust his scouting eye to keep up with the new times. Understanding the margin for error better than a lot of the old-timers he was battling, he consciously kept the Notre Dame roster lean. Cerrato, for example, rarely recruited the kind of plodding offensive linemen so popular for generations. He felt they would become little more than slow-footed benchwarmers if they didn't progress. He recruited extra defensive linemen instead, figuring that the extra spring in each one's step would increase their versatility and thereby decrease the likelihood of them becoming next-level busts.

That Cerrato became a groundbreaking recruiter was due to a confluence of circumstances. It certainly hadn't been his goal starting out. During his second year at Minnesota, Holtz needed a new recruiting coordinator on his staff. He offered all seven of his graduate assistants the opportunity to interview for the job. Six of them met with him. Cerrato, his heart set on becoming an offensive position coach, decided to pass.

But Holtz wasn't letting him off that easy. As a graduate assistant, two of Cerrato's main duties had been connecting players with summer jobs in their home areas and driving Holtz to the airport for speaking engagements. During one such trip Holtz again asked Cerrato if he was interested in the recruiting vacancy. No, Cerrato said, because he wanted to coach offense. Holtz offered a deal: If Cerrato would take recruiting now, Holtz would promote him to a position whenever one opened.

He never had to. "It was so fun because it was something different every day," Cerrato says. "And you could be so creative." When Holtz took the Notre Dame job, Cerrato was among the members of his old Gophers staff that he brought with him. At some of his previous stops, especially Arkansas, Holtz had been criticized for a perceived indifference to recruiting. At Notre Dame, Cerrato noticed Holtz, though energized, dangerously slipping into his old way of thinking.

"I remember when we first got there, Coach Holtz said, 'We'll outcoach all these people,'" Cerrato says. "Then we went down to Birmingham and got beat by Alabama. He comes running on the bus, sits next to me, and says, 'We have to get players like everybody else.'"

Easier said than done. Certainly, Notre Dame's name recognition opened a lot of doors. And the program's graduation rate, the university's Catholic values, and its international academic reputation all sounded like sweet music to the ears of caring parents or, in a case like Rice's, grandparents. But the academic standards also shrunk the recruiting pool. Even though those standards were relaxed a degree upon Holtz's arrival, the staff still had to battle, cajole, and even sneak such players through the admissions web. The bottom line was that, taking over after some of the worst seasons in Irish history, the coaches had to innovate if they wanted to survive.

Holtz and Cerrato came up with a solution. Instead of nine assistant coaches, the maximum allowed by NCAA rules and the standard at big-time football schools, Holtz would employ eight. Cerrato, while occupying the ninth spot and officially being a member of the Irish coaching staff, wouldn't work with the current roster. Instead, he would spend the week on the road, watching recruits. He quickly developed an eye for talent—an eye so sharp, he could detect talent indirectly. Cerrato, for example, never saw Tony Rice throw a pass. Never saw him break a tackle. But he watched him play basketball, and was confident that the athleticism would translate. As many prospects as he tried to see, he sometimes had to make snap judgments like that. He also had to be pretty much dead-on with his evaluations, and most of the time he was. Working against the perception that Notre Dame was a dead program, a relic, Holtz and Cerrato salvaged the 1986 class, Holtz's first, by utilizing some of the prospect lists they had maintained at Minnesota.

Allen Wallace, publisher of *SuperPrep* magazine and one of the founding fathers of the recruiting cottage industry, calls Cerrato "the first superstar college recruiter." At the same time, he found his youthful arrogance off-putting, a reaction, says Wallace, that was shared by plenty of Cerrato's brethren in the coaching world.

"I wasn't crazy about him," Wallace says. "I met him one time and was very disappointed, actually. He was extremely defensive. Vinny was paranoid and he'd let you know it. You got the impression that he just wanted things to work out for him. In any good business relationship, people want things to work out for each other. Vinny was just looking out for himself."

Regardless of how Cerrato came off to other adults in the college football loop, he had teenagers eating from his hand. Besides his national travels, Cerrato also worked the Chicago Catholic League pipeline, which had been paying dividends at Notre Dame for generations. John Foley, a Prop 48 academic risk like Rice, was the nation's top defensive player and came from Chicago's St. Rita High School. From St. Laurence High School in Burbank, the Irish landed cornerback Stan Smagala, offensive lineman Tim Grunhard, and offensive lineman Jeff Pearson. Smagala had been a holdover Faust recruit, and Holtz encouraged him to instead select one of the Mid-American Conference schools recruiting him, Western Michigan or Akron. That Smagala stubbornly elbowed his way into one of the twenty-two scholarships dispensed by Notre Dame early in 1986 epitomized Holtz's first class of recruits.

"We were kind of a ragtag group," says Grunhard, who would go on to play eleven NFL seasons. "And [Holtz] let us know it too. In our first meeting as freshmen, he told us, 'Most of you wouldn't have been here if we hadn't gotten a late start on recruiting.' So we always had kind of a little chip on our shoulder. We always wanted to prove that we belonged."

"Coach Holtz told us that, talentwise, this was one of the worst recruiting classes he ever had," says tight end Rod West, another member of the class of '86, "and was one of the worst in Notre Dame history."

Recruiting analyst Joe Terranova rated the first Holtz class "between fifteenth and twentieth" in his national rankings, a nice year at most places but considered abysmal at Notre Dame. After that, however, Cerrato really got to work. Because the local talent couldn't match the level that Miami achieved with its South Florida focus, Notre Dame couldn't replicate that portion of the Coral Gables blueprint for success, but the Irish coaches had no problem copycatting another element of Miami's player procurement philosophy.

"We wanted to recruit speed at every position," Cerrato says. "So we would take as many option quarterbacks, running backs, and wide receivers as we could get because they could play so many positions. We wanted to recruit tight ends to play offensive tackle. We wanted to recruit fullbacks and linebackers to play defensive line."

One of those linebackers was Chris Zorich. Like Rice, Zorich hardly fit the Notre Dame student-athlete profile. Although he was from Chicago, he wasn't a Catholic schoolboy who had grown up dreaming of donning the famous gold helmet. Long ago, under legendary coaches like Knute Rockne and especially Frank Leahy, Notre Dame had all but owned the largely Irish, mostly Catholic South Side, basically sticking whoever they wanted on the South Shore train that zipped from the city to South Bend. But changing demographics—the "white flight" that had occurred in so many major American cities after the U.S. Supreme Court's epic *Brown v. Board of Education* decision in 1954—had pushed much of the old guard out to the surrounding suburbs. And as that happened, Notre Dame had lost its grip on inner-city Chicago, particularly the mostly black, economically depressed Chicago public schools.

"Chris Zorich came from the slum of slums in Chicago," says Chicago-based recruiting analyst Tom Lemming. "Before that, Notre Dame used to snub their nose at the impoverished while they went on to Miami to come back to kick Notre Dame's butt. Notre Dame started recruiting the same kind of players, but with better grades. They weren't geniuses, but they had better grades than the Miami players."

Zorich attended Chicago Vocational School, where he was preparing for a future career as an auto mechanic or a skilled union laborer. The son of a white single mother and a black father he never knew, Zorich's school and his neighborhood on the city's far, far South Side were both treacherous places requiring nimble navigation. "You learn three lessons living here," Zorich once said. "Watch your back; don't trust anybody; and when you hear a gunshot, hide behind a car. I'm frightened to death of this neighborhood." At age fourteen, while stopping in a store with a friend on the way home from school, Zorich was caught in a holdup and had a gun pointed directly at him. "I thought I was going to die," he said. "I almost wet my pants. I was terrified."

"There weren't that many options," Zorich says. "The role models were the mechanics who had the car shop down the street and the woman who ran the corner store. Not saying those weren't good role models, but that's all I was exposed to. My sphere of existence was very small."

Zorich's protective mother, Zora, didn't let her son go out for football his freshman year at Vocational, the same school that had produced Chicago Bears legend Dick Butkus decades before. He began attending practices as a sophomore, forging his mother's name on a permission slip. By the time she discovered where he was every day after school, she didn't have the heart to make him quit. The two had been through a lot together. Suffering from diabetes, Zora Zorich was unable to work, and she and Chris survived on $250 a month in government aid. As a little boy, Chris would rummage through the dumpster of a local grocery store for food that had been tossed out, sometimes spoiled hamburger meat. Zora would surgically excise the discolored portions and serve the rest.

By the time he was a junior, Zorich had developed into one of the best players in the city, and his head coach told him for the first time that a scholarship to play football in college was within his grasp. But when Notre Dame coaches made their initial recruiting overtures, Zorich wasn't familiar with the school, just ninety minutes down the way on the interstate toll road.

"I'd love to," Zorich said. "But my mom doesn't like to fly."

The Irish assistant wasn't following.

"There's no way that my mom would fly to France to watch me play," Zorich explained. "You guys have that hunchback guy in the church, right?"

Eventually, Zorich got his geography figured out. But there was a problem: Zorich's cumulative SAT score was just 740. That was better than Rice's, and he was an academic qualifier according to the NCAA's standards and would not have to sit out a season as a Prop 48 casualty. However, the score was still about 500 points beneath Notre Dame's average entering freshman score. The average Notre Dame entering freshman scored in about the eightieth percentile on the SAT. Zorich was somewhere in the tenth percentile of test takers. "Watch him closely," admissions director DiCicco wrote in Zorich's file upon admitting him into the university.

Zorich signed as one of several linebackers in the 1987 Notre Dame signing class. It was Holtz and Cerrato's second, and it was pure gold.

———

While Zorich, who would eventually be moved to nose tackle and develop into a consensus All-American, and offensive linemen like Mike Heldt and Winston Sandri provided the grit and guts of the group, there was also plenty of speed and flash. Wide receiver Todd Lyght was pegged as Tim Brown's successor, and his signing was indicative of Cerrato's magic touch. With mere days to go before signing day in early February, Lyght had all but decided on Michigan State. Cerrato rushed to his Flint, Michigan, home in a last-ditch attempt to change the speedster's mind.

"I went in and said, 'Todd, we're gonna have a serious conversation,'" Cerrato says. "I said, 'We're gonna sit down and we're gonna talk about all the reasons why you should come to Notre Dame.'"

Cerrato drew a line down the middle of a sheet of paper and began naming reasons.

"Academics," he said. "Is that a reason why you should come to Notre Dame?"

"Absolutely," Lyght replied.

Cerrato wrote the word *academics* in one column of his sheet.

"So I go through like twenty things," Cerrato says, "and he said, 'Yeah, yeah, yeah.' I said, 'Todd, you take the pen and write down all the reasons you shouldn't come to Notre Dame.' He sits there for a minute and says, 'I can't think of any.' I jumped up, shook his hand, and said, 'Congratulations, it's great to have you.'"

Among the other players in the class of 1987 were running backs Ricky Watters and Tony Brooks, who selected Notre Dame even though the backfield was filling up and the carries promised to be sparse. (Watters, who would go on to rush for more than ten thousand yards and nearly eighty touchdowns in the NFL, spent most of his years in South Bend playing wide receiver.)

The critics at previous stops who charged that Holtz was a lazy recruiter were not completely off base. When Faust was running the program, he traveled tirelessly, making all three home visits to each prospective recruit that were allotted by the NCAA at the time. Holtz limited himself to one, but tried to make it count. "Holtz himself didn't like to recruit that much," Lemming says. "But in the house, once he got to the house, there was no one better than Holtz."

For someone who fancied himself a raging disciplinarian in the locker room and on the practice field, Holtz's recruiting schtick could be downright corny. A visit from Holtz was sure to include plenty of well-rehearsed quips and one-liners, not to mention a magic trick or two.

"He was losing me with the magic tricks," says Rod West, a tight end from New Orleans. "I didn't want my head coach moonlighting as an amateur magician. But he saw he was losing me and that's when he came to me and said, 'Okay, I'm going to give it to you straight, Rod. You can come to Notre Dame and be a part of the turnaround, or you can go somewhere else and watch it happen.' He changed course. That's when he got my attention."

Eventually—with a push from Penn State coach Joe Paterno, according to Cerrato—the NCAA outlawed the Irish staff structure, with one assistant spending so much of his time on the road visiting recruits and so little of it coaching the current team. But before that, Cerrato, Holtz, and the rest of the Notre Dame staff—not a poor recruiter among them—assembled four consecutive consensus No. 1-ranked recruiting classes. Adding all of that young talent to a hungry veteran nucleus that burned to make sure 58–7 in the Orange Bowl would not be its lasting legacy, Holtz had the personnel to compete with anyone. Now all he had to do was coach them up to their potential. As opposed to his reputation as an indifferent recruiter, his ability to do that had never been in question.

CHAPTER 7

Quarterback U

Entering his senior season at St. Paul, Minnesota's, Cretin-Derham Hall High School, Steve Walsh was a good high school quarterback. And most people understood that Walsh was a good high school quarterback. And most people, particularly those close to the game of football, understood what *good*, as opposed to *great*, high school quarterbacks did when their high school playing days expired.

They went to small colleges and continued to play for sheer love of the game. In fact, if they were really good, and worked extra hard, they might just get a chance to play at St. John's University for legendary coach John Gagliardi, who had already won three small-school national championships.

As his senior season approached, that sounded quite all right with Walsh. And if St. John's didn't work out, there were other options. St. Thomas. Carleton College. It was nice to have choices. "I just wanted to play," he says.

Not that the multisport athlete had completely given up on the idea of attending college on the strength of his right arm. He had simply accepted that it probably wasn't going to be for one of the big boys of the college football block. While Walsh was at Cretin-Derham Hall, Lou Holtz was coaching the in-state Big Ten school, the University of Minnesota. But running his option attack, Holtz had zero interest in Walsh. And when Minnesota didn't show any interest, that was a signal to other Big Ten and major conference programs that it probably wasn't worth a trip to Minnesota to see Walsh throw.

Although Walsh did love to play football, he truly saw football as a chance to secure an education. He was from a blue-collar Catholic family in the Twin City suburbs. His father owned a plumbing shop, and his mother worked for his father. Two of Walsh's older brothers had gone to two-year junior colleges and picked up associate degrees, but nobody in the Walsh lineage had graduated from a four-year school. Even as a teenager, Walsh realized how expensive it would have been to attend a private NCAA Division III school like St. John's—what a burden on the family and its business that might have become. "My dad wouldn't have been able to pay for it," Walsh says. "His plumbing business was small: He probably just had a couple of guys working for him here and there, and that's it. He would have probably been able to grind his way through, but I didn't want him to have to do that."

Luckily for Walsh, as his senior year approached, interest perked up slightly as the blue-chip quarterbacks in the recruiting pool began to fall off the board. In the Big Ten, only Northwestern offered him an opportunity at a roster spot, although coach Dennis Green wanted Walsh to walk on and prove himself while splurging for the most expensive tuition in the conference. Iowa State offered a lifeline, dangling the possibility of a scholarship. It was a low-end major-conference school, but a scholarship was a scholarship.

Before Walsh attempted to secure four years in Ames, Iowa, however, his high school offensive coordinator, Tom Cross, wanted to try one more thing. Cross had gone to high school with a former college quarterback named Marc Trestman, who in some ways had been Steve Walsh before Steve Walsh. Unlike Walsh, Trestman had earned a scholarship to the University of Minnesota. But he couldn't get on the field, and eventually transferred to Moorhead State, before matriculating back to Minnesota to finish his degree. Trestman's path into coaching had been just as circuitous. After attempting a back-door route into the NFL as a defensive back, he moved to Miami in the late 1970s not to get into coaching but to pursue a law degree at the University of Miami, which he completed in 1981. While in law school, Trestman volunteered to help out with Coach Howard Schnellenberger's Hurricanes staff. Before he had even turned thirty years old, he was promoted to quarterbacks coach. And so Walsh's coach Cross decided to work his connection, even if it might be a long shot.

"He called Marc and said, 'No one's really looking at this kid, and this kid can play,'" Walsh says. "So Marc came up to a game to see me, and they sent him away with some film. After watching the film, they were, like, 'Okay, what do we need to do to get him here?' Two months later, I'm on an official visit on a boat. It didn't take much after that to get me to commit.

"Now that I'm coaching high school football myself, I know that there aren't that many kids that are misses, but there are still some diamonds in the rough. If Miami had come up and thought I was too skinny or too short, I probably would have ended up playing Division II or Division III."

When Walsh arrived in Coral Gables in the fall of 1985, the program was still working to cement its place in college football's hierarchy after Johnson's tumultuous first season. But it was already well on its way to becoming a quarterback factory.

———

Like the rest of the process of building Miami into a power program, the beginning of the school's modern quarterbacking legacy—George Mira finished fifth in the Heisman Trophy balloting back in 1962—occurred rather unconventionally. The project began in the tiny town of East Brady, Pennsylvania, a tiny Irish Catholic community about an hour from Pittsburgh.

As early as fifth grade, Jim Kelly would sign drawings he did for classmates with an ornate signature, then explain that they had better hold on to them: "Someday that autograph's going to be worth a lot of money. Someday I'm going to be a pro quarterback—just like Terry Bradshaw."

Kelly's dream drew eye rolls at the time, and even as he developed into a star high school athlete, it didn't seem any closer to becoming a reality. There was no question he had a knack for the game. One of six boys in the Kelly household, Kelly was five inches taller than most of his classmates by the time he reached junior high school. His father, who, as an orphan, had never participated in organized sports while growing up, pushed his talented son hard. As a high school quarterback, Kelly threw for nearly four thousand yards and more than forty touchdowns. Recruiters began descending on East Brady, but Kelly only had eyes for one school: Penn State.

There was one catch: Nittany Lions coach Joe Paterno wanted to pack thirty or forty pounds on his lanky frame and turn Kelly into a linebacker like his older brother, Pat, who had played for the Baltimore Colts and the Detroit Lions. That plan didn't interest Kelly, so in jumped then Miami coach Lou Saban. Leaving the comfort of Coral Gables, Saban attempted to fly into Pittsburgh during a blizzard and instead spent six hours at an airport in Toronto when his flight was rerouted by the weather. When Saban finally arrived in East Brady, the snow made it impossible to read numbers on the houses in Kelly's neighborhood, so he knocked door-to-door until he finally located the right abode. Saban spent his time there drawing up pro-style passing plays and showing them to Kelly, which won the quarterback over. Imagine his surprise, then, when he arrived a year later and discovered that the Hurricanes were running the veer offense instead, a version of the option.

Saban left a year later and Schnellenberger arrived—along, finally, with the pro-style offense Kelly had been promised by the previous regime. Schnellenberger also brought with him former NFL quarterback Earl Morrall to tutor the Hurricanes QBs, and Kelly's development began to progress in leaps and bounds. Although Kelly graduated from Miami before the team success really began in earnest, he did develop into a first-round selection of the Buffalo Bills in the 1983 NFL Draft and went on to an eleven-year Hall of Fame NFL career.

Kelly had helped put Miami on the map, particularly as a destination for quarterbacks, but the two men to follow him would really cement the Hurricanes' reputation as the new "Quarterback U." In 1982, Miami signed two quarterbacks in its recruiting class, Bernie Kosar from Ohio and Vinny Testaverde from New York State by way of a prep school in Virginia. They were two very different players. Kosar's mechanics, to put it kindly, were less than stellar. "He [had] the most awkward throwing style I'd ever seen in my life," Kelly said. "Bernie did everything against the book." Meanwhile, Testaverde was constructed like an NFL prototype. Regardless, their fierce competition for the starting spot advanced nine practices into the fall of 1983 before Schnellenberger and the staff finally decided on Kosar. "We made the decision to go with Bernie, thinking he just might have been a little bit ahead in the offense at that time," Trestman, Schnellenberger's quarterbacks coach, says. "Both guys had really run the first team very, very effectively, but

Bernie had the ability even with the second and third team to move them. It was just a slight edge. You could have flipped a coin." The choice of Kosar over Testaverde turned out to be an inspired one. Kosar led the Hurricanes to the national championship. Testaverde, meanwhile, considered a transfer.

"We talked," Trestman says. "I just really pleaded with him that it wasn't his time right now at Miami to play, it was Bernie's. But there was no doubt that he was going to be a great and accomplished quarterback at the college level."

Testaverde's patience paid off. Kosar graduated in just three years from Miami and challenged the NFL to become eligible for the draft. Instead of backing up Kosar for all four years, Testaverde was handed the job with two years of eligibility remaining. He threw twenty-one touchdowns as a junior, then followed that up with a twenty-five-touchdown season in 1986, winning the Heisman Trophy by a landslide. The loss to Penn State in the Fiesta Bowl might have devastated Miami players and fans, but it had done nothing to dissuade the NFL. The Tampa Bay Buccaneers made Testaverde their no-brainer selection as the No. 1 overall pick in the draft. Meanwhile, Kelly had thrown for more than 5,000 yards and forty touchdowns in a season with the USFL's Houston Gamblers before finally agreeing to terms with the Bills. In Cleveland, twenty-three-year-old Bernie Kosar had thrown for more than 3,800 yards for the 1986 Browns.

So nothing to live up to for Walsh, the skinny recruiting afterthought from the north country. Nothing at all.

"Now I'm the next guy," Walsh says, "and it was, like, 'Hey, what are they going to do with this kid?' The machine was certainly starting to go. The main thing I was doing was replacing a Heisman Trophy winner. But the thing was that Vinny had lost his last game, and that was very disappointing to a lot of people, including Vinny. What I held on to was that I could get back into a position to win a national championship, and that was a way I could silence all the critics."

In his favor, Walsh had not spent the previous two years on the beach. Realizing he lacked Testaverde's natural ability, he nonetheless tried to mentally experience the 1986 season right along with his predecessor. If Testaverde was taking instruction from offensive coordinator Gary Stevens in a meeting, Walsh was thinking through the lessons right along with him. If Testaverde was reading a defense during the season, Walsh was putting himself in his shoes.

That the nation wasn't convinced was apparent when the preseason rankings came out in 1987. Despite the wire-to-wire dominance of the 1986 team, save for a few costly errors in the Fiesta Bowl, the Hurricanes were ranked just tenth to begin the season. At most programs, that was nothing to be ashamed of. At Miami, a No. 10 ranking was an insult.

The 'Canes would take it out on their first two opponents.

On September 5, in-state rival Florida visited the Hurricanes. Even in the best of times, the season opener against the Gators had proven to be a major stumbling block for Miami. The 1983 national championship season began with a 28–3 humbling at Florida's hands. In Johnson's second season, 1985, the 'Canes had to string together ten straight victories to get back into the national title hunt after falling at home to the Gators in their opener.

This time would be different.

With the nation's expectations lowered, the Hurricanes steamrolled the Gators 31–4. Walsh, just a couple years removed from picking through Division III opportunities, threw for 234 yards and a touchdown.

The next week brought an even larger challenge. The 'Canes would have to travel to Little Rock, Arkansas, to play Arkansas, now ranked tenth. The meeting was personal for Johnson, who felt he had been jerked around by his former college coach Frank Broyles, now the Razorbacks' athletic director, when he was granted a sham interview for the Arkansas opening in the late 1970s. By halftime, the Hurricanes led 38–0. The final score was 51–7, with Walsh completing twenty of twenty-eight passes. With the victory, the Hurricanes rose to No. 3 in the Associated Press rankings.

Once again, it appeared that a national title run was shaping up in Coral Gables, and once again on the strength of a blossoming All-American behind center. But then again, that had been the case before. And the 'Canes knew better than anybody that nothing was guaranteed.

CHAPTER 8

"You're the Prop 48"

Tony Rice didn't necessarily think it was going to be easy. What competitor would?

For four years at South Carolina's Woodruff High School, Rice had been the biggest show in town. The starting quarterback from his freshman year on, Rice lost just two games in high school. His sophomore and junior seasons, he helped bring the Class AA state championship home to football-crazy Woodruff in back-to-back autumns. When football ended each year, he transitioned to basketball, earning four varsity letters in that sport as well. By his senior year, Rice was a second-team all-state basketball player.

And then came Notre Dame.

Because of his low cumulative SAT score, Rice would have sat out his freshman year of football at any Division I-A school. Games, of course, but even practices. It was going to be tough, but what choice did Rice have? He would face it like a man.

However, never did he realize how difficult that task would be until Michigan week his freshman year.

The first game of Lou Holtz's tenure generated a level of excitement on campus that most of the current students in South Bend had heard about only in stories told by older relatives. Like most of his fellow Notre Dame students, on the Friday night before the opener Rice walked over to the Athletic and Convocation Center, home of Irish basketball games during the winter and the madness known as Friday-night-football pep rallies in the fall.

Another student, noticing Rice's athletic build and, almost certainly, his dark skin, eyeballed the freshman.

"You look like a football player," he said. "What's your name?"

Rice told him.

A wave of recognition swept across the student's face. "Oh," he said, "you're the Proposition 48."

Rice turned around and walked out of the building.

Irish offensive lineman Andy Heck recalls, "There was definitely a group of students and faculty that had their mind made up about him before they ever met him and were vocal in the papers and even on campus, like, 'What are we doing? We're about something different here.' You know, kind of guilty before proven innocent. But he quickly won those people over and never showed that it got him down. I don't know exactly how he was able to handle that so well."

Sitting out for academic reasons was a shock to the system for a kid who had been handed the keys to an offense in high school that rivaled the most complex college offenses in terms of the mental agility required of and the responsibilities entrusted to the quarterback. "Tony was a smart guy," says Michael Sloan, a split end at Woodruff with Rice and a friend since second grade. "He didn't test well, but he was real smart. He knew the game inside and out."

Things got a little better after that early run-in at the pep rally. Rice endured his year without football, playing in Notre Dame's popular intramural "Bookstore Basketball" tournament to stoke his competitive fires. It wasn't the same, of course, but at least it was something to help bridge the gap. He earned most-valuable-player honors in the tournament's all-star game.

Most important, Rice lived up to his end of the bargain academically. He had survived the brutal first year at Notre Dame, proving the doubters wrong and vindicating his head coach by earning his eligibility. But hiding from the difficulties of his situation as a black, Baptist, academic nonqualifier from the Deep South at an elite, mostly white, almost exclusively Catholic university wasn't always possible. It took its toll. Prior to Rice, there had been just one black quarterback at Notre Dame, and Cliff Brown had started only a few games for the Irish in 1971. "For so long," Brown said then, "the black athlete was thought of as, 'Give him the football and let him run—he can't think.' I think a lot of black athletes probably haven't come to Notre Dame because people have told them they wouldn't have a chance. My being first-string should convince them that a black man can play at the helm anywhere if he's good enough." Unfortunately for Brown and for any aspiring young African American quarterbacks looking for a role model at the position, Brown was eventually supplanted by eventual All-American Joe Theismann. So, nearly two decades later, Rice was answering the same lingering questions.

"If two more people would have said, 'You can't play here, you can't play because you're black,' I might have had to quit," Rice said. "You can only take so much."

There were certainly moments when Rice very nearly did walk away.

"I almost flunked out and I almost walked out," he said. "I got so homesick that I called Momma and cried to come home. I mean, I really cried—real tears. I begged her. She gave me the lecture of my life and I listened, thank God. It took a while, but she finally convinced me that I wasn't a quitter and that I could learn to study and make grades as good as the next guy."

Rice's experience wasn't uncommon among his black teammates. Chris Zorich recalls an almost verbatim heart-to-heart with his own mother.

Finally, however, as spring practice began, Rice could practice with his team. That was the good news. The bad news for Rice was that the way things stood, that was about all he was going to be doing. The Irish already had a quarterback, Terry Andrysiak, who had been waiting even longer than Rice to finally get his chance.

Andrysiak's father, Donald, was a 1958 Notre Dame graduate, and when Terry was growing up, his family had been heavily involved in its Catholic parish near Detroit. But despite those markers, Notre Dame wasn't pushed in the Andrysiak household the way it was in other families headed by Domers. The family were University of Michigan season ticket holders, a near treasonous offense for a Notre Dame alum. Terry's sister even graduated from Michigan.

Football wasn't pushed, either. After averaging twenty-two points a game as a freshman high school basketball player, Andrysiak considered giving up football altogether, an idea his father agreed with, although he was talked out of that by the St. Frances Cabrini High School football coach. One of those athletes who could excel at just about any sport he tried, Andrysiak would unwind from football practice every day in high school by shooting nine holes of golf. By the time he arrived at Notre Dame, selecting the Irish after also considering Michigan, Boston College, and Michigan State, Andrysiak could regularly shoot in the high seventies.

Andrysiak was somewhat of a mystery for the Irish heading into the 1987 season, because he had never held the long-term starting job, a much different challenge from spot duty as a backup. But at the same time he wasn't a complete unknown. He had appeared in nineteen games, twice filling in as an emergency starter for an injured Steve Beuerlein. Andrysiak had made the most of his limited opportunities, completing 57 percent of his passes for 775 yards, four touchdowns, and just two interceptions. Against Navy as a sophomore, he had completed eleven of seventeen passes off the bench to engineer a come-from-behind victory. Some of that success, while still mired behind Beuerlein on the depth chart, caused a young Andrysiak to reconsider his commitment to the university and its football program. "I didn't see myself playing or making headway," he said, "and I didn't know what Notre Dame was all about."

Predictably, some Notre Dame fans pined for Andrysiak to start every time Beuerlein struggled. "Steve went through hell," Andrysiak said. And perhaps there was a small part of Holtz, maybe even a big part, which also wondered how the offense would look with Andrysiak running the huddle from the opening snap. He was, after all, much more mobile than Beuerlein. A sprinter on the track team in high school, Andrysiak's strength was his mobility. But his arm strength was a serious concern, especially since so much of Notre Dame's offensive success would depend on the quarterback being able to get the ball into the hands of Heisman Trophy candidate Tim Brown, the preseason cover boy on almost every national college football magazine.

Because of Andrysiak's deficiencies as a college passer, Holtz understood that he had a narrow margin for error and rode him mercilessly in practices leading up to the start of the season. He made sure that Andrysiak was well aware that if he faltered, there were two very viable options waiting in the wings, Rice as well as six-foot-five freshman blue-chipper Kent Graham. Although Holtz had always been a master manipulator who used psychology to bring the best out of his players, his treatment of Andrysiak, which at times bordered on antipathy, wasn't for show. Holtz called the QB's progress in 1986, when he was an understudy to Beuerlein, "minimal." The two struggled to form any kind of working chemistry, and Andrysiak, an admittedly bad practice player, didn't feel that real progress came until Holtz toned down the yelling, nitpicking, and derision. "I think he started to teach me a little more instead of pulling me off so much to tell me he might have to get another quarterback," Andrysiak said.

Notre Dame's 1987 opener would be a personal challenge for Andrysiak as well as an epic challenge for the Irish as a team. The game was at Ann Arbor, site of a pair of losses under Faust. The 1981 loss was Faust's first as Notre Dame's head coach and knocked the Irish out of the top ranking in both polls. They had not returned to No. 1 since.

More than those previous two games at Michigan Stadium, however, the specter of the 1986 opener in South Bend still hovered over the season-opening showdown. That was Holtz's first game, the game that ended with John Carney's missed field goal for the win, followed by an appreciative roar from the Notre Dame crowd. That was enough for the Notre Dame fans a year ago, but in Holtz's second season—especially after the thriller against USC to end the 1986 campaign—the expiration date on moral victories had passed.

For Andrysiak, his first game as the Notre Dame starting quarterback would take place in a stadium where he had spent many a Saturday afternoon, having grown up just twenty minutes from Ann Arbor. Back then, he was just one of more than one hundred thousand spectators crammed into the "Big House." Now he would be one of the game's focal points. For Notre Dame fans, the contest offered a chance to see the quarterback they had clamored for over the past few seasons. For Michigan fans, it was a chance to see a homegrown blue-chipper who had spurned the Wolverines out of high school fall flat on his face while quarterbacking a heated rival.

Andrysiak, of course, wasn't facing Michigan on his own; it just felt like that—both the blessing and the curse of playing quarterback at

Notre Dame. On offense, the sixteenth-ranked Fighting Irish were fueled by Brown, who had returned two kickoffs for touchdowns the season before while catching forty-five passes for 910 yards (an average of more than twenty yards a reception). With tailbacks Mark Green and Anthony Johnson back, as well as talented freshman Ricky Watters, the emphasis of the Irish offense would shift from the aerial assault to the ground game.

The defense was a bigger question mark. Six of the seven top tacklers from the 1986 season had moved on. Up front, nose tackle Mike Griffin was still somewhat undersized but a nice veteran presence to anchor the unit. Inside linebackers Wes Pritchett and Ned Bolcar were veterans who had bided their time under Faust and then Holtz, while outside linebackers Cedric Figaro and Darrell "Flash" Gordon had started the year before. Cornerback Marv Spence had started most of 1986 but was surrounded by youth and inexperience.

In Michigan, the Irish would be facing a team that had won seventeen of eighteen season openers under coach Bo Schembechler. They would be trying to slow down a team, ranked ninth in the country, that had never lost a home opener under the man known around the state simply as "Bo."

And they would make it look like child's play.

Any doubts about Andrysiak were largely settled after an efficient eleven-for-fifteen passing day that included an eleven-yard touchdown pass to Brown in the opening quarter. A year after John Carney's difficulties had helped doom the Irish at Notre Dame Stadium, new placekicker Ted Gradel drilled field goals of forty-four and thirty-eight yards.

But the real star was the inexperienced Irish defense. Having long awaited their opportunity, the newcomers made the most of the chance. The first three Notre Dame scores were set up by turnovers, all of them by players (Figaro, Jeff Kunz, and Cornelius "Corny" Southall) who were either new to starting or, in Kunz's case, had done so on an extremely limited basis the previous year. Before the day was over, the Irish had forced seven turnovers and won 26–7 to avenge the season-opening defeat the year before.

"It was the first game of the year and we wanted to start off on a good note," Southall says. "We needed to do well. For a lot of juniors, including myself, that was our coming-out year, our turn to take the torch that was passed along to us and to show what we could do."

With Michigan out of the way, the Irish began picking up steam. Michigan State, a team that had added to the Irish heartbreak the season before, was no match for a Notre Dame team that had gone from being unsure of itself to brimming with swagger. The Irish scored the game's first 31 points in their triumphant return to Notre Dame Stadium.

The night game in South Bend had one of the more bizarre beginnings one will ever see to a football game. Notre Dame kicked off and Blake Ezor, Michigan State's deep man on kickoffs, fielded the ball at the two-yard line. Instead of trying to run the ball upfield, however, Ezor was confused about where he stood. He took a couple of steps back and dropped to one knee. In the end zone. Safety, Notre Dame. The game clock still showed 15:00 and yet the Irish led 2–0.

But that was just the warm-up act. The game was supposed to be an early-season Heisman Trophy showdown between Spartans running back Lorenzo White and Notre Dame's Brown, and it was a lopsided battle royal if there ever was one. Late in the first quarter, Brown returned a Michigan State punt seventy-one yards for a touchdown to put his team up 12–0. Then, with less than twenty seconds to play in the quarter, the Spartans were forced to punt away their next possession as well.

Looking for the kill, the Notre Dame coaching staff called for a punt block, and ten Irish players crammed the line of scrimmage with no blocking scheme set up. Brown returned the kick sixty-six yards for the score. Meanwhile, the inspired Notre Dame defense held White to just fifty-one yards on nineteen carries.

Game.

Set.

Heisman.

Buried in all the excitement was the college debut of one Tony Rice. The sophomore's debut was nothing remarkable, particularly in light of what Brown had done. He completed one pass in two attempts and managed to break off a twenty-three-yard run. However, it was significant in that Rice's long journey—from the public housing projects of

Woodruff, South Carolina, through the frustration of the SAT examination room, through his year in exile at Notre Dame—had finally led to a college football field in an actual game.

———

It doesn't take long for a strain of national championship fever to spread through South Bend. In September and October of 1987, it took exactly three games. Victories over Michigan, Michigan State, and Purdue catapulted the Irish from sixteenth in the Associated Press poll, where they had begun the season, to fourth as they prepared to travel to Pittsburgh for an October 10 matchup.

Pitt, little more than a decade removed from a national championship, had stumbled horribly in the weeks leading up to the game. Two wins to begin the season had raised hopes, but then came the ultimate indignity, a 24–21 home loss to Temple, which the season before had gone winless in eleven games. Pitt hadn't yet recovered, grinding out an ugly 6–3 victory over West Virginia the week after and then falling 13–10 to Boston College.

In particular, the Pitt offense was in shambles, and second-year coach Mike Gottfried was pinning a lot of the blame on his quarterback, Sal Genilla. After Genilla had thrown four interceptions against Boston College, Gottfried had allowed a pair of freshmen to take snaps with the first-team offense during Notre Dame week. Combined with the recent dominance of the Notre Dame defense under the direction of former Pitt head coach Serafino "Foge" Fazio, it seemed like a safe time for the national media to anoint the Irish a contender for the national championship.

"A!" former Irish coaching luminary turned CBS analyst Ara Parseghian told *South Bend Tribune* columnist Bill Moor when asked to grade the current Notre Dame team.

"What better year for a football miracle at Notre Dame," a fawning article in *Sports* magazine dreamt, "than this, the school's 100th anniversary?"

Meanwhile, one person tried to pour cold water over the excitement. Lou Holtz had not voted his own team in the top fifteen that week.

Bah humbug. While Pitt's quarterback Genilla was bearing the brunt of the criticism, from both inside and outside the program, for his offense's collapse, Notre Dame's Andrysiak had developed into an expert game manager. With the defense, Brown, and a committee of explosive running backs carrying most of the water, the pressure was largely off, an unusual but blissful state for a Notre Dame quarterback. After his long wait, Andrysiak's season could not have gone any better. And neither could Notre Dame's.

By the time the two teams took the field in Pittsburgh, three ranked teams had already been upset earlier in the day. All the Irish had to do was dispose of this struggling Pitt team, and when the world woke up on Sunday morning, they would be all that remained of the herd of college football's unbeatens.

By halftime, it was 27–0 Pitt.

At the start of the game, Genilla had stormed out of his coach's doghouse, passing for a touchdown and running for another. Craig "Ironhead" Heyward, an offensive guard masquerading as a tailback, bulldozed his way into the end zone twice. Notre Dame's longest play of the game, a thirty-eight-yard completion from Andrysiak to Brown, had culminated in a fumble deep in Pitt territory. It had been that kind of half for the fourth-ranked team in the country. As halftime approached, things couldn't get worse for the Irish.

Except then they did.

Late in the first half, with things going badly for Notre Dame and getting worse by the second, senior offensive guard Tom Freeman was flagged for a holding penalty. The coaching staff immediately pulled him out of the game to teach him a lesson, sending in sophomore Tim Grunhard.

Grunhard would eventually develop into a fantastic offensive lineman at Notre Dame, and would go on to start more than 160 games with the Kansas City Chiefs in the NFL, including 120 in a row. But in midseason 1986, he was a raw sophomore who had absolutely no chemistry with the starting offensive line and only a rudimentary knowledge of the communication that was employed at the line of scrimmage.

On one of Grunhard's first plays, starting tackle Byron Spruell barked out the assignments for the offensive line and Grunhard got into position, satisfied that he understood the call. But when Spruell, lined up next to Grunhard, fanned out from the play, Grunhard mistakenly plowed inside and ahead. That left a clear path between a Pitt rusher and the now vulnerable Notre Dame quarterback Andrysiak.

"The next thing I know, Terry got hurt," Grunhard says. "Of course, the seniors and fifth-year guys and Terry let me know: 'Hey, you got me hurt.' And then the guy from my class came in and never came back out. So Tony Rice can thank me. Tony owes me for that one."

Onlookers who hadn't realized the severity of Andrysiak's injury, a broken collarbone, were surprised to see Rice trot onto the field to begin the second half. They were even more surprised when he didn't begin the half behind center but instead walked up behind one of his offensive guards. A crackling bundle of nerves, Rice had initially lined up behind the wrong offensive lineman. But with that out of the way, something remarkable happened: Notre Dame, playing on the road and demoralized after a half that saw its opponent storm to a four-touchdown lead and then saw its senior starting quarterback knocked silly, came storming back.

Rice started the comeback himself, rushing for a sixteen-yard touch-down late in the second quarter, then finding wide receiver Pat Terrell in the end zone for the two-point conversion. A blocked punt set up a touchdown early in the fourth quarter. By the time running back Mark Green ran one in from seventeen yards and Brown ran in for the con-version, 1:29 remained in the game and the large Pitt lead was down to 30–22.

When Notre Dame recovered the ensuing onside kick, it looked as if another miracle, similar to the previous season's comeback at the LA Coliseum, was in the works at the school that specialized in them. But then Rice's inexperience emerged. With the clock ticking down and no receivers visibly open as he rolled right, Rice scampered out of bounds to stop the clock before it hit zeroes. One problem: It had been fourth down. Possession transferred, and Notre Dame didn't even get to take a final shot at the end zone to complete the comeback and salvage a tie.

Rice's boneheaded decision to voluntarily surrender his final bullet was indicative of his first-year growing pains.

"Tim Brown was calling audibles for Tony in some of those games," recalls wide receiver Steve Alaniz. "I remember playing Boston College and being on the field with Timmy, and Timmy's yelling, 'Switch the play!'"

Ultimately, however, it was better that he made those mistakes in 1987, with the Irish out of the national title picture, than the following season, when they could start fresh.

"Tony, not having played in '86, and Tony, being inexperienced in '87, you could see was making mistakes," says Tim Prister, the longtime Notre Dame beat writer. "Now Andrysiak did a nice job. But you knew that the more Holtz could get Rice on the field in '87, the more quickly that this thing could get turned around."

———

Notre Dame traveled to Miami in late November boasting an 8–2 record, the Heisman Trophy front-runner in Brown, and an insatiable desire for revenge. A lot had happened in the two years since the 58–7 bloodbath at the Orange Bowl in Faust's last game. The Irish under Holtz didn't in any way resemble the group that went through the motions that night. But for those players who had participated two seasons before, the impending trip to South Florida opened a wound that was fresher and rawer than many of them probably realized.

The Irish, however, were not the only team with plenty of motivation. A year after the devastating Fiesta Bowl loss, the Hurricanes had survived one real scare—a one-point victory against Florida State—but otherwise had rolled through their schedule untouched and ranked No. 1. Not that complacency was an issue in a program with so much to prove after three straight disappointing season endings, but a November visit from Tim Brown was more than enough to light the late-season fire anew. There was a phrase in the Miami locker room about the opposing team's star player: The 'Canes were determined not to let him "show out," or use the 'Canes as a stepping-stone to national prominence.

"Any time you're playing a potential Heisman Trophy winner, it's an opportunity to go out and make a name for yourself," says Dave Wannstedt, Jimmy Johnson's defensive coordinator. "At Miami, even though we were undefeated and we had great teams and great players, probably the underlying storyline is that we always felt like we had to go out and prove ourselves.

"I think if a lot of other programs would have won as many games as we did, they would have crowned them the team of the century and it would have been America's love story," Wannstedt adds. "We were always kind of the bad boys and the team that had to go prove ourselves because maybe we weren't for real and maybe we weren't as good as the scores were indicating."

Miami wouldn't keep Brown from winning the Heisman Trophy. Although it wasn't the runaway victory that Testaverde had captured the year before, Brown still easily outpaced second-place vote-getter Don McPherson of Syracuse when the vote was announced a week later, drawing nearly twice as many first-place votes as the quarterback.

What the Hurricanes did accomplish, however, was to create probably the most frustrating afternoon of the future nine-time NFL Pro Bowl player's college career. Some of it was self-wrought. Even though Rice had his issues as a passer at that early stage of his career, he hit Brown in stride along the left sideline in the first half. Brown, with a step on two 'Cane defensive backs, let the ball fall right through his outstretched hands. One Irish series in the third quarter was particularly frustrating. While trying to get off the field after a two-yard run out of the backfield, Brown was pelted with items tossed from the wound-up Miami student section. During the resulting official's time-out, Jimmy Johnson was animated in pleading with the students to cut it out. They did, but the chastising also incited the Orange Bowl faithful to grow even louder. A few plays later, with the Irish near midfield on the same drive and very much still within striking distance of the Hurricanes on the scoreboard, Brown flat-out dropped a well-thrown ball from Rice. On the next down he dropped another one, this time after Miami linebacker Rod Carter leveled him just as the football arrived.

Brown gained just ninety-five total yards, his lowest total since the season opener. Afterward, he was incensed at the Hurricanes' posturing.

"Miami had no class during the game," Brown said. "Afterward, no class again. That's the way they play the game. They do a lot of talking."

Worse than other teams? Brown was asked.

"Yeah, a million times worse," he said. "Things you can't put in your newspaper."

"I remember guys jawing at us from the opening kickoff about what they were going to do to us," says Irish defensive lineman Andre Jones.

"I remember having a strong dislike for them, more so than [for] any other team we played against. Their coaches let them play with no boundaries."

The game wasn't a complete waste for Notre Dame. In its season to that point, Miami had turned the football over just nine times. In the first quarter alone against the Irish, the Hurricanes twice gave away possession, including a Melvin Bratton fumble inside the Notre Dame one-yard line. Because Notre Dame's offense was largely inept, with Rice still struggling to pass at a level befitting a starting college quarterback, the Irish were unable to take advantage of those Miami miscues. But hope was not completely lost. The teams would meet again in a year, and Notre Dame's defense understood that it had the capability of goading the Miami machine into mistakes. But that was all in the future. At the Orange Bowl that afternoon, any signs of progress by the Irish since the last time the two programs had met were subtle, and you had to really be looking for them to find them. "It had to be bad if the punter was named Chevrolet MVP," says Vince Phelan, Notre Dame's punter in 1987 and, as it turned out, the recipient of that honor near the end of the CBS broadcast.

"They were a better football team," says Rod West. "That's all it was. They had more people who knew how to play together and knew how to win."

But did Miami know how to win the big one? That question still lingered, particularly over Johnson. Unapologetically, the Hurricanes were a team that approached their tasks at a high emotional pitch, an approach that certainly wasn't condemned by their head coach. Against the Irish, Miami had won the coin toss and, as instructed by the coaching staff, elected to defer, putting the nation's stoutest defense on the field to begin the game. The decision made complete sense, but wide receiver Michael Irvin flipped out. In front of seventy-five thousand fans at the Orange Bowl and a television audience of millions, the future NFL Hall of Famer threw a temper tantrum that would have been shameful if performed by an infant, let alone a soon-to-be college graduate. Later, after catching a benign eight-yard out, Irvin waved his arms until he finally received the roar he was looking for from the Miami crowd. The game was still scoreless at the time. "We're sitting on the sidelines, saying, 'Did he just score? What the hell is he doing? They're on the forty-seven yard line,'" says Notre Dame's Jones.

"You know what the difference between insanity and passion is?" says former 'Canes defensive lineman Dan Sileo. "It's very small. And sometimes, when you get too close to the edge, you can become insane with your passion."

————

The performance against Notre Dame, not to mention the entire 1987 season, showcased a Miami program that had truly come of age. The nation got to see a head coach with the intelligence and personality to be a major success in the game put it all together for the first time. Johnson's early teams were flush with swagger but exposed as flawed when it really counted, in the Sugar Bowl against Tennessee and, even more notoriously, in the painful loss to Penn State in Tempe just a year before. Proud, perhaps overly so, of his psychology degree from Arkansas, Johnson had pumped his early Hurricanes teams full of bluster, setting them up for one inglorious fall after another when they couldn't live up to their image. By 1987, however, he had absolutely perfected the fine art of button pushing. He began issuing challenges during the recruiting process and continued relentlessly twelve months a year.

"He asked me if I had the strength to find out how good I really am," lineman Marty Golloher recalls about a trip to Johnson's office during his official recruiting visit. "He said, 'Do you want to find out how good you really are, or can be, at this game? Do you want to be an old guy with regrets? Or do you want to be sitting in the rocking chair, knowing exactly what you were capable of?'"

In their 1985 game against the Irish, the 'Canes had kicked a team that was as down as it was possible to be and, in the process, falsely passed themselves off as a program ready to dominate the sport. In the case of their dominating 24–0 victory over the Irish at the tail end of the 1987 season, however, the Hurricanes were every bit as good as the results had indicated. A few weeks after shutting down Notre Dame and Brown, the Hurricanes welcomed Oklahoma into the Orange Bowl with the national championship on the line.

"Going into that season," Steve Walsh says, "I had made a vow to myself that if we got back into the position like we were in the year before in the Fiesta Bowl, I wasn't gonna lose that game."

Oklahoma's Sooners had the nation's most dominant defense, holding six opponents to single digits and allowing a high of just thirteen points in a single game. During the week leading up to the New Year's Day battle, however, Hurricanes offensive coordinator Gary Stevens constantly ragged on the offenses the Sooners had faced in the Big Eight conference, mostly option teams that resembled the Hurricanes only in that they dressed eleven men.

"He was just ripping our competition," Walsh says. "'These guys haven't played anybody. Don't get worried. Don't get fooled by this film.'"

The teams played to a 7–7 halftime tie. But early in the third quarter Hurricanes placekicker Greg Cox nailed an attempt from fifty-six yards. The 'Canes would never trail again, going ahead 20–7 before Oklahoma tacked on a late touchdown to make the final score 20–14. Miami's players carried Johnson off the field, and he kicked his arms and legs through the air with the enthusiasm of a small child.

After those near misses in his first two seasons, finally winning the national title provided some redemption for Johnson. But more and more, it seemed like the odds of him staying at Miami much longer were growing slim. It is not uncommon in big-time college football for a coach and a university president to clash over some issues, considering their very different aims. An academic reach here, a slipup at the microphone and some accompanying bad publicity there, and the relationship can disintegrate in a hurry. But usually, as long as the wins continue to stack up, they find a way to coexist. In this case, however, the gulf between Johnson and Miami president Edward T. "Tad" Foote was becoming increasingly difficult to bridge. Foote thought the football team's demonstrativeness reflected poorly on the university, the academic profile of which he hoped to raise. Johnson felt that Foote was every bit the grandstander that his most exuberant young players were. Johnson was perturbed when, at a postseason team banquet, Foote announced gleefully to the crowd that Johnson was going to sign an extension soon, in order to silence rumors that had been swirling about Johnson and Southern Cal. Johnson felt as if his president had made the announcement just to make himself look like the hero of the hour. A few weeks later, Johnson felt that his suspicions were confirmed when Foote summoned him into his office to order him into a press conference to apologize for his players' actions in Tempe at the Fiesta Bowl.

"What does this do to my contract status?" Johnson asked as athletic administrators Paul Dee and Sam Jankovich stood uncomfortably by.

"That's not something we're going to talk about," Foote replied.

Johnson slammed the door and stormed out of the room, planning in that moment to resign at the press conference Foote had called. Instead, he merely seethed while offering a semi-apology that pinned the issue largely on the public's misguided perception of what had gone on in Tempe.

A year later, in the immediate wake of the national championship, Johnson couldn't believe what he was reading when he opened *The New York Times* to read Foote heaping praise upon the program, calling the title a "glorious condensation of life" and "a merging of the emotions that exist in all of us."

"When we won the national championship, our trip to the White House was delayed because it didn't meet Tad Foote's schedule," says wide receiver Randal Hill. "Ten players on the national championship team were not allowed to go to the White House because Tad Foote took ten of his family members. Unacceptable. Totally unacceptable. But it's the truth."

A few weeks later, Johnson finally received his extension. However, with the leverage of a national title on his side, he negotiated out the $100,000 buyout clause that had previously been in his deal. He was free to leave anytime he wanted, no strings attached. But Foote wanted some consideration from Johnson as well. According to Johnson, Foote sent an addendum asking that the coach never publicly state that Foote had backed out of an oral agreement the winter before to extend Johnson's deal.

"You take this paper here and you tell Foote to stick it up his ass," Johnson told Paul Dee.

For the first time under Jimmy Johnson, the 'Canes would enter a season hoping to defend a national championship. Never had their us-against-the-world tune been sung at a higher pitch, particularly now that the team felt it could add its own university to its list of enemies.

PART TWO

Catholics versus Convicts

CHAPTER 9

Tunnel Vision

In late August of 1988, Doug Browne was an anonymous Notre Dame freshman from Reno, Nevada, still trying to acclimate himself to life on the South Bend campus. Like the rest of his first-year classmates, Browne had arrived in Indiana a few days early in order to go through orientation. Also beating the rush of students back to Notre Dame were the members of the *Observer* student newspaper staff, and as Browne strolled across campus late one evening, he grabbed his first copy of the publication from a stack in Notre Dame's south dining hall.

Browne had just attended a campus-sponsored "ice cream social" and had at one point during the evening also managed to down a few beers. Afterward, he and one of his two roommates headed up to their dorm room, where Browne flipped through the newspaper. An item in the classified section caught his eye.

"Beat the rush," it encouraged readers, followed by the phone number and address of the University of Miami football office. It was around seven p.m., with dusk just starting to fall over South Bend. And probably, Browne thought, Coral Gables as well. Browne decided to dial the number.

The phone rang a few times. Finally, a man answered.

"University of Miami football office," he said. "Jimmy Johnson speaking. Who is this?"

Expecting, at best, for the call to be answered by a UM secretary, Browne recovered from the shock of his good fortune quickly enough to move the conversation forward.

"I'm a freshman at Notre Dame," he told the Hurricanes coach, "and I'm beating the rush."

"What rush?" Johnson said.

"I'm beating the rush," Browne said. "I hate you now."

"He asked a couple other things," Browne recalls, "and then he started to scream and yell. He was, like, 'Who the hell is this? Why are you calling me?' He was all pissed off. Then I think he hung up on me."

And that was that, Browne figured. A laugh between roommates. He tried to tell others on campus.

"They thought I was full of shit," Browne says.

But then the weekend rolled around.

Johnson spoke to a group of Miami boosters at a breakfast event on Friday morning. At the moment Notre Dame was about the last thing on anybody's mind. As the Hurricanes geared up for another possible national title run, the Irish were hardly the most daunting obstacle on the schedule, particularly with the way Miami had handled them in recent years. And besides, the weekend ahead brought an opening game showdown with No. 1–ranked and favored Florida State. But in South Bend, Johnson said, they already had their minds on the Hurricanes. He told the story of a Notre Dame freshman who had called him that week, sounding "like a little girl." Johnson then verified the story Browne had been circulating around the Notre Dame campus verbatim.

On Saturday morning, Browne returned to his dorm room after running some errands to find articles about Johnson's breakfast speech clipped from major national newspapers and taped to his door. But that was hardly the end of it. As the October 15 game date drew closer, and Miami and Notre Dame climbed the national rankings, Browne went from anonymous freshman to quasicelebrity. David Letterman had a top-ten list on his show one night: Reasons Notre Dame Fans Hate Miami Coach Jimmy Johnson. Number one: "He was rude to our freshman caller."

Not everyone found the incident so amusing. Browne received anonymous phone calls in his Keenan Hall dorm room telling him he had helped contribute to heated feelings between the two schools and football programs that were apt to become dangerous when Saturday rolled around. After Browne granted a couple of lighthearted interviews, his Reserve Officers' Training Corps officer called him into his office and warned him to "lay low." Luckily for Browne, fate bailed him out of major temptation on game day. CBS play-by-play announcer Brent Musburger had called him, requesting an interview at Notre

Dame Stadium for the pregame show. But Browne wasn't going to be anywhere near the stadium for the Miami game. He had already scheduled a deer hunt back home in Nevada, so he was long gone.

————

On August 12, 1988, Lou Holtz gathered his full squad for the first team meeting of the year. Before he began getting into the nitty-gritty of expectations for the 1988 season, he felt compelled to address something that had been making its way into the news that summer on a much-too-regular basis: accusations of impropriety during his two years at the University of Minnesota, and perhaps even NCAA violations.

"There are a lot of things we need to cover tonight, even though you may not want to hear some of them," Holtz began. "The first thing is the situation at the University of Minnesota. You probably read and heard a lot of accusations. I could talk about this situation for about an hour, but I don't think that would serve a useful purpose. I've been a head football coach for eighteen years and been involved in the game of football as a coach for twenty-eight. In twenty-eight years, I've never done anything illegal to gain an advantage. I have never cheated."

That Holtz had to address the situation at all with his team was illustrative of something that most close observers of the sport already knew: When you hire Lou Holtz, you also hire his baggage.

In his first season at Arkansas, Holtz had suspended three starters: thousand-yard rusher Ben Cowins, leading receiver Donny Bobo, and fullback Michael Forrest, before the Orange Bowl after allegations of a rape in the athletic dorm surfaced. The situation quickly became a racial flashpoint in the program—and the state. The United States Supreme Court had only months before, in *Coker v. Georgia*, banned the use of the death penalty in rape cases. But attorneys for the three players still worried about what kind of harsh penalty a southern judge might mete out, having for too many years watched how charges in similar situations—the players were black, the alleged victim was white—played out.

When no charges were filed, the players hired two of Arkansas's top civil rights lawyers to battle their suspension. Meanwhile, several black

Razorbacks threatened to boycott the Orange Bowl in protest. When court proceedings looked like a possibility, Holtz was represented by the office of young Arkansas attorney general Bill Clinton, who could see the toll that the situation was taking on the first-year head coach. "I really believed there for a while that he was going to resign," said Clinton. "He felt like he was under so much pressure, everyone was calling him a racist. I thought he was going to quit." One reason Holtz was upset about the situation was that he felt the university was putting far too much of the decision making during a very combustible chain of events on the football coach without coming to his aid or stepping in. "Not once did I receive a phone call from anyone associated with the University of Arkansas either supporting me or questioning what had happened," Holtz said.

He did, however, pique the interest of some important people in South Bend.

"That's when I first noticed him," Edmund Joyce, the school's vice president, would later say. "I was impressed by the way he stood up for what he thought was right and then kept his team united and went out and won the game. After that, I sort of kept an eye on him."

That situation was eventually smoothed over—it didn't hurt that the Razorbacks, even without the three starters, demolished heavily favored Alabama 31–6—but the rest of Holtz's tenure in Fayetteville was far from smooth. *Arkansas Gazette* columnist Orville Henry felt that Holtz was distracted from recruiting by his interests outside of football—namely, public speaking appearances and commercial endorsements. When Oklahoma coach Barry Switzer started having success poaching top players from Arkansas, unrest among the program's fans began to grow.

Years before he assembled the recruiting machine at Notre Dame, the word on Holtz was that he could not recruit black players. And if that indeed was the case, he did himself no favors in 1983 when he began to flaunt his friendship with United States senator Jesse Helms, with whom Holtz had struck up a friendship during his time in Raleigh. While Helms was trying to stop a bill to make Martin Luther King Jr.'s birthday a national holiday, Holtz was speaking at a $1,000-a-plate Helms dinner. When he filmed two campaign commercials for

Helms, Arkansas athletic director Frank Broyles had had enough. He fired Holtz.

As salacious as some of the ups and downs of Holtz's tenure at Arkansas had been, however, they were really of no concern to Notre Dame. The budding situation at Minnesota, where Holtz had landed just days after leaving Arkansas, very much was.

The situation at Minnesota was, to put it mildly, a mess, and that well predated Holtz's arrival. The current firestorm had begun when $186,000 went missing from university funds, an amount eventually traced to rogue administrator Luther Darville. Minnesota believed that a lot of the missing money had been dispersed to athletes, including many football players. Darville, for his part, wasn't interested in sticking around to find out where the university's internal investigation led. Facing a felony indictment because of the missing money, he fled to the Bahamas.

Meanwhile, several players were alleging that former Gophers coach Joe Salem, Holtz's predecessor, had paid players from 1979 through 1983—which wouldn't have affected Holtz, except for rumblings that the pay-for-play practices didn't cease when the regime changed. Worst of all for Holtz was an allegation by former Minnesota academic advisor LeRoy Gardner that Holtz had given him $250 specifically earmarked for Gophers linebacker Jerry Keeble. That had allegedly taken place in 1984, which would spare Notre Dame from any NCAA repercussions even if it was judged to be true. So would an allegation by former Minnesota running back Raphael "Pudgy" Abercrombie that Holtz assistant Jim Strong had taken him on $100-plus shopping mall spending sprees, an allegation to which Strong offered an odd but emphatic defense when speaking to the *Minneapolis Star-Tribune*: "I do not spend that kind of money on my daughter, who I love and who lives in my own home."

But whether or not Notre Dame was within the NCAA's jurisdiction on the Minnesota matters—Strong was a member of Holtz's Irish staff—the school's reputation was on shaky ground. And if the Minnesota culture of lawlessness had extended on Holtz's watch past September 1, 1985, the NCAA was within its bounds to punish Holtz and, by extension, Notre Dame.

As the 1988 season got under way, however, any problems Holtz did or didn't have with the NCAA were pushed to the back burner. The Irish had more pressing problems. Notre Dame, alma mater of Joe Montana, Joe Theismann, and Heisman Trophy winners Angelo Bertelli, John Lujack, Paul Hornung, and John Huarte, had quarterback problems. Major quarterback problems.

When Holtz had battled for Rice's admission to Notre Dame in 1986 despite his low standardized test scores, he had vouched for Rice in two areas, promising that Rice would be up to the academic workload at the university, and swearing that Rice would be a terrific quarterback. Through the early portion of the 1988 schedule, the junior QB had flirted with failure in both areas.

After working around the clock in 1986–87 to make his grades and earn his eligibility for the following season, Rice let his performance in the classroom slip in 1987 as his playing time increased. Instead of going back to South Carolina in the summer, he would stay back in South Bend, where he had to take three courses—and earn at least a B in each of them—to retain his eligibility for the following fall.

On July 22, a *Chicago Tribune* gossip item speculated that Rice could be ineligible for the fall. Then, in early August, things really hit the fan. The CBS television affiliate in South Bend, WSBT, reported that Rice had failed to lift his grade point average over 2.0 and would thus be ineligible to compete in the fall. The report by sports director Mitch Henck touched off several days of hysteria as other media members scrambled to either verify or refute the story. Notre Dame officials explained that grades had not been turned in yet while at the same time pushing Henck for his source on the piece, which he refused to give up. In actuality, Rice had earned two A's and a B in his three summer school courses, lifting his overall grade point average to 2.1. It was just enough to keep him on the field. WSBT retracted the story on all four of its Monday local news broadcasts, and Henck, the man who had initiated the report, resigned.

The report had turned out to be erroneous, but it was a harsh reminder of the chance Notre Dame had taken when it allowed Rice through its doors. Instead of being angry about the botched news story, Rice was frustrated with himself for allowing the situation to develop in the first place.

"I don't think I was applying myself," he said. "If you don't make it, it's because you don't want to. There are so many people here who helped me. I'm competing in both the classroom and on the football field. I've grown up a lot. I'm not the playful little Tony all the time anymore."

But that wasn't his only struggle. If Rice didn't improve as a quarterback, and do it quickly, he could ace nuclear physics and it wouldn't make much difference to Holtz.

Rice's experience in the second half of 1987 had been valuable, but it was also telling that the coaching staff decided to go with Andrysiak, a senior using up what remained of his eligibility, in the Cotton Bowl against Texas A&M rather than the supposed quarterback of the future. One reason was that Rice's future as Notre Dame's starter was hardly assured. His time on the field in 1987 was not the coronation of the next Irish great but rather an extended tryout. And Rice was bad as often as he was good. Lining up behind the guard in his first snap against Pitt was funny; rushing for just fourteen yards on ten carries against Miami was not. Neither were his final passing numbers for the season: a 42.7 pass completion rate, four interceptions, and just one touchdown. During one practice, Holtz actually tackled Rice after the quarterback botched a read. "He just lost his fucking mind," said defensive tackle Dan Quinn. Most of the other takes on the incident were milder than Quinn's, and Rice himself laughed off the bizarre takedown, but there was no question that Holtz was not pleased with the quarterback for whom he had gone to the mat at the university admissions office.

Holtz declared open competition in spring practice, and one of Rice's competitors was Kent Graham, a six-foot-five-inch sophomore-to-be with a golden arm. Graham, a Chicago product, had been named the national high school quarterback of the year as a senior. Slow-footed, he wasn't the perfect fit for Holtz's offense by any means. But if Rice couldn't pass well enough to make himself even a mild threat, his option skills would largely be useless anyway. A lame-armed Rice was still good enough at running the football to beat the lesser teams on Notre Dame's schedule—he had thrown just five passes against old Irish nemesis Air Force in 1987—but Notre Dame stood little chance against its elite opponents if Rice didn't improve drastically as a passer.

In a spring scrimmage, Rice completed just six of twenty passes. Even worse, he lost sixteen yards on nine rushes. Holtz's impatience grew. "There were times when he showed a great release and great timing," he said. "They stand out in my mind because they are the exceptions." Only Graham's more putrid performance kept Rice in the huddle as the 1988 season began. (Graham would transfer to Ohio State after the '88 season before going on to a long, successful NFL career.)

With so much to prove, Rice got off to a terrible start to the '88 season. He completed just three of twelve passes in a season-opening 19–17 victory and was bailed out only when Michigan placekicker Mike Gillette missed a forty-nine yarder as time expired. The next week he was just two for nine in a 20–3 victory over Michigan State. In Rice's defense, it wasn't all his fault.

"On most days the receivers were bad," wrote Bill Bilinski, the Notre Dame beat writer at the *South Bend Tribune*. "On others they were terrible."

Holtz was barraged with fan letters begging him to make a change. But he felt that his options were severely limited. Graham had been given his chance to earn the job, and he had thrown more poorly than Rice. Senior Steve Belles was another option, but he had almost no game experience. Desperate for better play from his sophomore, Holtz provided Rice with a dartboard, which the QB hung on his dorm room door. Rice's arm strength was never at issue, but his touch was decidedly off. "Tony was trying to throw the football like a ninety-nine mph fastball," said Holtz. The darts experiment drew a lot of attention, which Rice said was "overblown," although he did agree to pose next to a dartboard for a spread in the *Sporting News*. But whether it was the dart throwing or just the benefit of experience, there is no question that Rice's passing improved right around that time. He was outstanding in the third game of the season, a victory over Purdue, and completed eleven of fourteen passes against Stanford. During one stretch, Rice completed ten consecutive attempts over two games, tying a school record.

The week before the Miami game, Notre Dame found itself locked in a 17–17 tie against Pittsburgh in the third quarter.

"Boy," Rice said to Holtz on the sideline, "this is fun, isn't it, Coach? This is a heck of a game."

Notre Dame went on to win 30–20. The Irish, left out of many pre-season top twenty polls, were unbeaten and ranked fourth in the country. Finally, Miami was next. Against a defense that had already pitched a pair of shutouts in the season's opening month, Notre Dame would sink or swim with Tony Rice under center.

———

While most had considered the Irish a year away from a title run, the Hurricanes seemed to be a year removed from their peak. They simply had too much to replace for them to dominate the way the 'Canes had in running the table in 1987. Daniel Stubbs, an All-American defensive end who had led the defense with nine and a half sacks, was gone. So was fellow All-American and third overall NFL Draft selection Bennie Blades, a safety who had made 124 tackles and five interceptions for the national champions. Walsh was back to engineer the passing game, but receivers Michael Irvin, Brian Blades, and Brett Perriman, along with tight end Alfredo Roberts, had all been drafted. So had the team's top two rushers, Warren Williams and Melvin Bratton. Bennie Blades and Irvin were both first-round picks, chosen among the first eleven selections in the draft, and Irvin would go on to become a Hall of Famer and a cornerstone with three Dallas Cowboys Super Bowl championship teams in the 1990s. Overall, eleven Hurricanes were chosen in that draft's twelve rounds, including six in the opening three rounds.

Not that the Hurricanes were in dire straits. The heir apparent at tailback, Leonard Conley, had averaged more than six yards a carry the season before in limited duty. The defense had lost its top three tacklers from 1987 but was about to plug in defensive linemen Russell Maryland and junior college transfer Cortez Kennedy. Kennedy would develop into the third overall selection in the 1990 NFL Draft, with Maryland going first overall a year later.

But in late summer of 1988, those two, along with the rest of Miami's thirteen new starters on offense and defense, were virtual unknowns. Giving Johnson and the program the benefit of the doubt, voters in the Associated Press poll still voted the Hurricanes fifth to begin the season, while the coaches voted them sixth. If that rankled anybody—and Miami's players were always sifting through the evidence for signs of disrespect—the 'Canes would quickly prove their worth. Coming into the Orange Bowl to begin the season in a prime-time CBS matchup were the Florida State Seminoles, the No. 1–ranked squad in both major polls. The Hurricanes had defeated their in-state rivals the year before in a 26–25 thriller, but the Seminoles believed this was their year, and they weren't afraid to flaunt that fact.

Two days before the game, the Hurricanes convened for a team meeting. As players settled into their seats, Johnson pulled out a video cassette tape and popped it into a player. Three years before, the NFL's Chicago Bears had created a sweeping sensation by releasing *The Super Bowl Shuffle*, a boastful and entertaining rap video. Then the team had backed it up, rampaging its way through the playoffs and capping the year with a dominant performance in Super Bowl XX. In 1988, the players of Florida State thought that their time had come. With head coach Bobby Bowden supposedly out of town for a few days during the summer, the players recorded *The Seminole Rap*, a four-minute ode to themselves.

The first player to rap in the video was Seminoles running back Sammie Smith, who said his first lines—"My name is Sammie and I love to run, just give me the ball and I'll get the job done"—over a highlight film of him scampering freely through the Hurricanes defense the year before. Rhythmically challenged quarterbacks Peter Tom Willis and Chip Ferguson followed, both in sunglasses à la Chicago Bears quarterback Jim McMahon. "Bring on Miami," tight end Dave Roberts boasted. All-American cornerback Deion Sanders, who seemed to take his thirty seconds of film time about as seriously as anyone, rapped over a highlight of him viciously taking down a Hurricanes wide receiver in slow motion.

There were plenty of references to a potential national championship run, and the chorus refrain left no room for humility: "We are the Seminoles of Florida State. We know we're good, some say we're great."

"If we would have done all that before the season, the country would have been on us like we just killed the president," steamed Miami cornerback Donald Ellis.

With two days to absorb what they had just watched, the Hurricanes were ready on Saturday night. Florida State gained just forty-two yards rushing on the young Miami defense, with recording star Smith grinding out all of six yards on ten carries. Willis and Ferguson combined to throw five interceptions. It was a dominant performance from start to finish, with the Hurricanes blasting the nation's top-ranked team 31–0. Before the game, Miami had let the Seminoles do the talking—and set it to music. Now it was the 'Canes turn to squawk.

"Our third-stringers could have put up a better game," said defensive end Willis Peguese. "I felt Florida State quit after the first series. They didn't give us any threat. No challenge."

"When we were up 17–0, three of their defensive linemen whipped off their helmets and threw them to the ground," said offensive lineman Mike Sullivan. "Their backups were playing harder."

It wasn't that the Hurricanes hadn't incorporated personality and individualism as a part of their program through the years: They certainly had. No one could say that Jerome Brown and Michael Irvin, for example, had not displayed their unique personalities—flamboyantly so at times. And perhaps the only reason the Miami players weren't the ones starring in their own rap video was because they simply didn't think of it first.

Or perhaps it was because they were too busy sweating bullets on the practice field all summer. Not that the Seminoles or other good programs didn't have a strong institutional work ethic, but Miami took it to another level.

"It was a fight for your life every day in practice," says former 'Canes tight end Rob Chudzinski.

"During the week, we fought like brothers," says Marty Golloher. "I don't know if you've ever seen two brothers get into a fight and a third person steps in, but it was a lot like that. Practice was ferocious. If you ran across the field and hit somebody, you better come close to taking their life. Every shot counted and everybody was watching everything that you did."

Most important, Johnson ran a true merit system, with no room for favoritism. You worked hard, you produced, you played.

"They knew in order for them to be successful that they needed everyone around them to be successful; they knew it was a team sport," says Mike Azer, Miami's long snapper. "They weren't golfers, they weren't tennis players, they weren't swimmers. They were football players and they were part of a team. When you walked into the locker room, there was no hierarchy."

———

Miami soared to No. 1 in both polls after the victory, but the Hurricanes would find themselves humbled in a hurry. Feeling pretty good about themselves on Monday afternoon, with an open weekend on the schedule, Johnson put the players through their "twelve-minute run" drill at the end of practice. The drill combined steady jogging with occasional forty-yard sprints and devoted the final minute to an all-out dash to the finish line. But this time, eleven minutes in, Johnson was unhappy with the intensity the Miami players were displaying. He ordered them to start over.

Even so, the Hurricanes came out flat two weeks later in their next game, at Michigan. Four years before, the Wolverines had been the last team to beat the Hurricanes in a true road game. And with about seven minutes remaining, it looked as if Coach Bo Schembechler's team was going to do it again. Michigan led 30–14, dominating the game's time of possession and forcing the Hurricanes, who had turned the ball over just once against Florida State, into four turnovers.

Utilizing their hurry-up offense, Miami scored twice on Walsh passes, including a forty-eight-yard strike to Cleveland Gary with just under three minutes left. Trailing 30–28 with its national title hopes in jeopardy, the Hurricanes attempted an onside kick. Safety Bobby Harden fell on the football, and the Hurricanes were alive. A couple minutes later, with forty-three seconds on the clock, kicker Carlos Huerta put a twenty-nine-yard kick through the uprights to make the 'Canes shocking 31–30 winners.

In previous seasons, Miami had started a tradition of holding four fingers up on the sideline as the fourth quarter of games began, a signal to the world that the 'Canes owned the fourth quarter. Through a combination of superior conditioning and unparalleled tenacity under fire, they had backed it up yet again.

"I mean, hey, did the twelve-minute run do that?" says Miami tight end Randy Bethel, recalling Johnson's tactics less than two weeks earlier. "I don't know, but it got us back focused. If we were not focused the way we were focused at the time, would we have had the composure to come back from that? Probably not."

The next two weeks weren't nearly as difficult as the Michigan battle had been. Jolted back to life by the Michigan scare, the Hurricanes outscored Wisconsin and Missouri 78–3 in two victories at the Orange Bowl. The regular-season winning streak was now thirty-six games long, and Miami had a week to rest before it took its top ranking into Notre Dame Stadium against an Irish team that clearly wasn't the same punching bag the Hurricanes had knocked around the previous few seasons.

———

They began popping up around campus early in the week. By Friday they were ubiquitous. By broadcast time on CBS on Saturday, the entire nation knew about the T-shirts. Produced by some creative Notre Dame students as a surefire moneymaker, they read CATHOLICS VS. CONVICTS, and they were an instant sensation.

"That whole CATHOLICS VS. CONVICTS thing," says former 'Canes defensive end Greg Mark, "that's money. That's TV ratings. Let's face it, if you looked at the police logs across the board, they were probably about even. But that was the perception that sold tickets and made it a spectacle and made it more than just another college game on Saturday."

"The fans wanted good guys versus bad guys," says Rob Chudzinski, Miami's tight end in 1988. "The Notre Dame players at that time weren't exactly choirboys, either. But they got the good-guy tag and we got the bad-boy tag."

Holtz was asked about the T-shirts. He swore he hadn't seen them.

"Our secretaries don't wear them," he said. "My coaches don't wear them. The players don't wear them. And my wife doesn't wear one. And those are the only people I'm around this time of year."

One person who had seen them was Notre Dame vice president Reverend William Beauchamp. While Notre Dame's supporters thought the shirts were a hoot, buying them up as quickly as they could be printed, the VP was troubled by the ugliness the series was beginning to bring out in the fans.

"To me, that was very problematic," says Beauchamp. "It was not the way we welcome people to our campus."

During the week, what was meant to be a humor column in the Notre Dame student newspaper, the *Observer*, took things a little too far. The piece was written as a parody from the point of view of Johnson, trotting out every stereotype about the Hurricanes that the writer could fit into the space allotted.

"You intellectual snobs like to poke at . . . our academic program," the author wrote. "Now, we may not have any Rhodes Scholars, but I'll have you know that we have the nation's leading programs in intramural bowling, gator wrestling, drug running, and sports car appreciation."

Although he preferred to stay above the fray, Holtz was finally forced to respond. The last Notre Dame coach to write to the *Observer* had been men's basketball coach Digger Phelps, who had done so to thank the students for their support in an upset victory over No. 1-ranked North Carolina. Holtz, on the other hand, wrote his letter as a gentle rebuke—and a preemptive move against the possibility of more ugliness on Saturday when the Hurricanes arrived.

"When I first came to Notre Dame," wrote Holtz, "I was impressed with four things about this student body—its competitiveness, its intelligence, its intense desire to succeed and its closeness and caring for other people. I would hope our students display those same traits when it comes to football rivalries.

"We look forward to welcoming Miami's team and fans for our next home game. Let's make sure that the Hurricanes leave our campus impressed with the classiness of our program and fans."

In the other team's camp, meanwhile, Miami cornerback Donald Ellis wasn't nearly as diplomatic.

"People say Notre Dame and it's like that's supposed to mean something," he said. "I don't see Notre Dame as greater than Toledo or Wisconsin or anyone else. I don't see them any different than Central Florida."

Asked about the previous season's taunting and numerous late hits at the Orange Bowl, Holtz saw an opening to opine about Miami's program, although he did it with a light touch. Officials, Holtz explained, were taking a closer look at those kinds of extracurriculars in 1988.

Why?

"The reason it was brought around, as I understand, was two games that specifically almost turned into ugly riots," he said. "One of them was the Miami–South Carolina game and the other was Miami–Oklahoma. I think that's the way some people play the game, but they're not going to be able to play that way this year."

In this game, the fireworks would begin well before kickoff.

It had been easy for the two teams to mask their contempt for the other, to swear mutual respect when the players had been bunkered in their separate campuses during the week of buildup. But the charade fell apart as they moved into close quarters, the snug tunnel behind the north end zone of Notre Dame Stadium. As Notre Dame Stadium filled up with fans, Miami's players, headed back to the visitors' quarters in South Bend, took a shortcut through a Notre Dame punt drill. "Total disrespect," says Andre Jones.

"I think there was a sense out there that you could intimidate Notre Dame," says Barry Alvarez, Holtz's defensive coordinator. "That was the wrong crew to try and intimidate."

The Irish took exception and tempers quickly flared. Barking players from both teams moved toward the exit tunnel.

Notre Dame linebacker Ned Bolcar, one of the men who had endured the 58–7 thrashing three years before, began jawing with Miami's Leon Searcy, who, along with his Miami teammates, liked to put on a show to intimidate opponents but never really expected to have to engage anybody for real.

"Ninety percent of the guys on our team couldn't fight worth a lick," Searcy says. "But we had to give that impression, that intimidation. We had to give that impression that we were the so-called bad boys, *Miami Vice* thug-life-living guys.

"A lot of the guys that you saw out front with their chest all out, half those guys weren't gonna play, first of all, and half of them couldn't fight. So there were some guys on that team that grew up on the streets and in the deep heart of the ghetto of Miami. But the majority of those guys—and I look back and I laugh about it now, watching some of the games—I see the guys who were out front bouncing around, man, half those guys were from the suburbs."

Another team might have backed away, sparing the Hurricanes the challenge of actually backing up their tough talk and posturing. But the Irish, with memories of those recent beatings very much in their minds, had no intention of blinking first.

"I turned around and said, 'Get the fuck off the field,'" Bolcar says. "[Searcy] turned around and said something derogatory to me, and then I said something back, and then maybe one of us said something like 'Your mom . . .' and then I punched him right in the fucking throat. The next thing I know, at that point the whole field just erupted into a fight."

The fracas quickly moved from the end zone to the tunnel leading to the locker rooms. Some Miami players had already entered the tunnel and were waiting in line to head to the locker room, their backs turned toward the field and the quickly escalating conflict. Linebacker Jason Hicks and Walsh stood near the back, oblivious, but they would be drawn into things quickly enough.

"They smack Steve Walsh in the back of the head," Hicks says. "We had our backs turned, so they smacked Steve. Steve's off balance, so what am I to do? So I yell, *'Yo!'* and so ensued the brawl in the tunnel. I wasn't about to allow them to disrespect the 'U,' which they did. So they started it. They started it."

The teams performed hand-to-hand combat in cramped quarters while police and stadium security rushed over to pull players apart.

"It erupted into a two-hundred-person brawl," recalls Notre Dame linebacker Wes Pritchett. "It was full-on. I think that set the tone: We were telling them, 'You're not going to intimidate us. You're not going to push us around.'"

In the Notre Dame locker room after the dustup, the adrenaline was still flowing. Irish defensive end Frank Stams, who had stayed to the side during the fight, located fellow defensive starter Pritchett, who had yet to come down from all of the excitement.

"I got him! I got him!" Pritchett exclaimed, fire in his eyes.

"Who did you get?" Stams asked.

A lineup of Miami stalwarts raced through Stams's mind: gargantuan All-American candidates like tight end Rob Chudzinski or maybe defensive tackle Russell Maryland.

"I got the kicker!" Pritchett said.

"The kicker?" Stams asked. "What did you do?"

"I stepped on his foot!"

Stams broke up laughing. And all around him, a fired-up Notre Dame team could not be calmed down.

"Everybody was going nuts," Pritchett says. "Guys were throwing helmets. Somebody broke the chalkboard."

Because there wasn't enough room in the Notre Dame Stadium home locker room, some of the freshmen and walk-ons usually watched games in street clothes from the seats with the fans. But because Holtz wanted everyone in his program to experience what promised to be one of the special days in Notre Dame football history, he had his entire roster suit up. They dressed across the street in the basketball locker rooms at the Athletic and Convocation Center. The group walked to the stadium, through the cheers of the fans congregating outside the gates, then into Notre Dame Stadium, down the stairs, and into the empty Notre Dame locker room. The quiet was soon broken by the whooping and hollering of nearly a hundred raging bulls dressed in blue and gold.

"The guys started running up the stairs," says Lindsay Knapp, a freshman who didn't play in the game, "and, I mean, you'd never seen people like that. I mean, they were just going crazy. They had blood on their hands. We're just kind of sitting there saying, 'What the hell is going on?' We had no idea what had happened."

"I'm seeing this," says Justin Hall, another freshman who was held out of the game due to an injury, "and I'm, like, 'Jesus, what the hell am I doing here? This is unbelievable.'"

As much as emotion had fueled Miami's performances the last few seasons, particularly in the Hurricanes' biggest games, the scene in the visiting locker room was quite different from the chaos that reigned in the Irish quarters. Far from being fired up to go play, the defending national champions were annoyed with the unnecessary distraction before the biggest game of the season.

"Usually that kind of stuff—the sideline stuff and the stuff before games—if you really look back, somehow it's always found to be a walk-on or a kid who's played three plays in a game at most," says offensive lineman Mike Sullivan. "The guys who are really getting ready to play, you generally don't want to expend that much energy. In warm-ups, you're just trying to get off the field.

"It was exactly that: It was a kid, a freshman, that had cut through their line, and the kid probably had more than enough room to run around the edge, but it was probably his first trip away," he continues. "The unfortunate part about being at Miami, as time went on, were the kids who went to Miami expecting to carry the mantle of swagger that didn't understand the guys who came before them were football guys first and showmen later."

Instead of intimidating Notre Dame, the Miami freshman had ignited a pack of blue and gold dynamite. Holtz finally coerced his team to calm down and then ripped into them for letting the Hurricanes draw them into the pregame fight. That wasn't the Notre Dame way, he said. Holtz continued to talk for about ten minutes, skillfully bringing a room about to boil over down to a low simmer. Finally, as kickoff approached, he began to draw perhaps the most important lecture he would ever deliver to a conclusion.

"You have an afternoon to play, a lifetime to remember," Holtz said. "But I want you to do one thing: You save Jimmy Johnson's ass for me!"

"I was thinking to myself, *That was great. But Jimmy Johnson could probably kick your ass,*" says Hall.

No matter. In character, Holtz was a master at manipulating his players' emotional highs and lows for his benefit. Stepping out of character, as he had at the end of the speech, he was able to unleash a blind fury that few teams would have stood a chance against that afternoon.

"He never swore," Chris Zorich says. (In fact, each year in practice, Holtz set a limit of ten curse words within his earshot by his team, himself included.) "So when he says, 'Save Jimmy Johnson's ass for me,' we about broke the door down. We would have went through four brick walls for that man."

"I couldn't stop crying," Jones says. "I must have cried for thirty minutes."

The Irish, finally calm to that point, charged back up toward the tunnel that was the scene of the crime a few minutes before. Three years earlier, the Hurricanes had humiliated Notre Dame on national television. Now it was payback time.

CHAPTER 10

Fumble!

During the week leading up to Miami's visit, Holtz phoned Michigan coach Bo Schembechler. The Wolverines had been the one common opponent for the Irish and the Hurricanes early in 1988, and had put a serious scare into both teams.

"I asked him, 'Can we beat Miami?'" says Holtz. "Not 'What do we have to do to beat 'em?' but 'Can we beat 'em?' That's all. And he thought and he said, 'Yeah, playing you both, yeah. You're gonna have to play well. They're awfully, awfully good. But you are too.' So after you talk to somebody who played both and he says, 'Yeah, you're capable,' then the biggest problem becomes getting your players to believe they could win."

Whatever Holtz did, it worked. The Irish showed a ferocity from the opening sequences of the game that they had not been able to unleash against the Hurricanes for some time. Miami received the opening kickoff. Then, on the Hurricanes' fifth offensive snap, Notre Dame's Stams, a converted fullback who had endured the humiliation in '85, battled through Miami's offensive line to grab Walsh's arm near the elbow just as Walsh was on the verge of beginning his throwing motion. The officials ruled it a fumble, with the Irish recovering. Although Rice and the Notre Dame offense were not able to convert the opportunity into any points, the Irish had landed the game's first jarring blow on Stams's sack and forced fumble. A few plays later Stams again blew through the Miami offensive front. Again he separated the Miami quarterback from the football just as Walsh was stepping into his throwing motion. The replay seemed to show that, even more than the previous mauling by Stams, Walsh's arm was still moving backward when the ball slipped from his hand. Watching the play in real time, however, the officials believed they had witnessed an incompletion. The Hurricanes were forced to punt.

"I remember meeting with [CBS announcer] Brent Musburger during the week," Stams says. "I remember him asking, 'What's your plan to sack Steve Walsh?' I don't think he'd been sacked all year. I said, 'My plan to sack him? I just want to get back there and touch him and see if he's real. He's a figment of our imagination. I don't think he can be sacked. But if I get to the ball as fast as I can and pressure him, good things can happen.'"

One reason that Stams was able to roam free into the Hurricanes' backfield was because the Irish had a budding All-American occupying Miami blockers on the interior of the line. Zorich had been recruited as a linebacker. He had not played in a game as a freshman, during the 1987 season, but he had turned Holtz's head on the practice field. The Irish were preparing for Michigan State early that season, and the Spartans ran an unusual defensive scheme that overloaded the defensive line while sacrificing linebackers. Since the Irish didn't have enough linemen to mimic the Spartans personnel in practice, Holtz had the undersized Zorich fill in for the week.

"At that time," Zorich says, "we had this All-American center named Chuck Lanza, and we just battled all week in practice. We just fought and fought and fought, and at the end of that week Holtz called the team up and said, 'Hey, I just wanted to let you guys know I think we found a new nose guard. Chris, how do you feel about moving to nose guard?'

"What do you say? No? I said, 'Yes, sir,' and then I stayed on the scout squad all year and then over the summer and into the spring. I lifted, got faster, and then I started as a sophomore."

Despite his background as a child of the streets, Zorich was a pussycat away from the football field. His favorite television show, even in college, was *Mister Rogers' Neighborhood*. To relax, he enjoyed feeding the ducks at the lake on the Notre Dame campus. After football ended for him, he dreamed of opening a flower shop someday. "Go pick your little flowers," roommate Tim Ryan barked at Zorich at practice one day after winning a one-on-one battle.

Zorich missed Chicago, especially his mother, whom he called twice a day to remind her to lock the doors to her apartment, which had been broken into five times in ten years. He loved the safety of South Bend and the Notre Dame campus, but, like Rice, struggled to feel comfortable in surroundings so different from those he had come from. He had difficulty sleeping in his dorm room because, compared to home, the campus was simply too quiet. The media attention Zorich received at Notre Dame brought to light another issue: a vocal stutter that sometimes turned interviews into exercises in supreme patience on the part of both Zorich and his interviewer. "He just had to pause a lot to say what he wanted to say," says Charlie Adams, a sportscaster in South Bend. "It wasn't like he had a huge stuttering problem; Bill Walton may have had a bigger problem with it, but Chris certainly had to battle it. As an interviewer, you just learned to be patient and nod."

Whatever his idiosyncrasies and obstacles away from the field, on the field Zorich was a maniac. "My dream [is] to knock the quarterback's head off, then watch it go rolling down the field," he explained to a reporter. Zorich's high school coach, John Potocki, once gave his former player a plaque that read: *Though I walk through the valley of the shadow of death, I shall fear no evil. 'Cause I'm the meanest son of a bitch in the valley.*

"We had a scrimmage before the '88 season," said Holtz, "and I remember after every play he was looking for somebody to fight. Well, finally he found the one guy who would fight him, and that was me. I was so upset that I grabbed him by the face mask. We had quite a few words—all one-sided, of course."

Since that confrontation, Zorich had learned to bottle his intensity and play with a controlled rage, dominating Michigan's offensive line in the season opener and forcing every opponent after that to game plan around him. Miami was no different than the rest of them. And even though the Hurricanes' line had been a brick wall for Walsh all season, with Zorich dominating the line of scrimmage, they stood almost no chance.

———

The Irish also started off well on the other side of the ball. For the past few years Miami's defense had stymied Notre Dame's offense. In fact, the Irish had not scored a meaningful offensive touchdown since early in Gerry Faust's tenure. That changed, however, as Notre Dame marched seventy-five yards for the game's first score. The final thrust into the end zone displayed much of what had been missing for the

Irish the previous few meetings: athleticism, competitive savvy, and the occasional display of flawless execution. That said, the execution on the play that set up the score was anything but flawless. On second-and-twelve from the Miami fifteen-yard line, Rice faked a handoff to tailback Mark Green, then found himself in no-man's-land. Rice pirouetted all the way around as the rest of his team surged right to block the play that was actually called, as opposed to the play that the junior quarterback was now improvising. Instead of panicking, however, after realizing his mistake had caused a busted play, Rice just ran to daylight. He was finally forced out of bounds nine yards later. Rice ran the next play correctly, as did the rest of the Irish offense. As the Notre Dame right tackle and tight end sealed two Miami defensive linemen, Rice kept the football and patiently waited for his lead blocking back, Tony Brooks, to engage a lurking Hurricane linebacker. As soon as Brooks impeded his man, Rice was able to practically walk into the end zone. Less than four minutes remained in the first quarter, and the Irish led 7–0 as pandemonium swept through Notre Dame Stadium.

As the first half progressed, the Irish continued to put pressure on the 'Canes in nearly every facet of the game. While Rice had beaten the Hurricanes with his feet on Notre Dame's first score, he was surprisingly deadly with his arm on their second, a response to Miami's first touchdown, which put Notre Dame on top 14–7. The big play of the second-quarter drive showcased Rice's strengths as a passer. Inaccuracy had plagued Rice since his arrival to college football, but the rocket launcher that had made recruiters swoon back in his South Carolina high school days was still operational. Backed up to his own sixteen-yard line and facing third-and-long, Rice leaned back and let one fly. When it finally came down, freshman Raghib "Rocket" Ismail was waiting for it, a step behind Hurricanes safety Bubba McDowell. Off balance after catching Rice's heave in stride, Ismail tripped at the twenty-five, but the gain of fifty-seven yards set up Notre Dame's second touchdown, an easy fullback pass from Rice to Braxston Banks.

———

Raghib Ismail came from Wilkes-Barre, Pennsylvania. That state had always been fertile Notre Dame recruiting territory, but mostly for quarterbacks, linebackers, and the tough guys in the trenches. College coaches often had to scour warm-weather states for speed, but Ismail clocked a legitimate 4.4-second forty-yard dash, and he seemed to play even faster than that.

"The guy that's probably happiest today is our track coach," Holtz said on national signing day.

Like Tony Rice and Chris Zorich before him, Ismail was no prototypical Notre Dame recruit. Although he had come of age in Pennsylvania, Ismail, his two younger brothers, and his parents had lived in Newark, New Jersey, for the first few years of his life. His parents went by the names of Ibrahim and Fatma Ismail, and penciled in the Sudan as birthplace on the birth certificates of all three of their children. Raghib and his brothers grew up believing they were the sons of African immigrants, a ruse that Ibrahim would carry to his grave and Fatma would not unveil to her sons until Raghib was at Notre Dame.

In the 1970s, with the United States only a few years removed from the civil rights movement, the Ismail brothers attended the Islamic Clara Muhammad School in Newark. It is a relic of the time period that a black man would choose to navigate the world as a Muslim rather than as an African American ancestor of slaves in America, but that is exactly what Ibrahim Ismail had done. Born in the Deep South, Ibrahim spent a lot of his upbringing in the New York–New Jersey area, a history he hid even from his wife, a teenage convert to Islam herself. Mentally and emotionally freed from the low expectations of his country during the Jim Crow era, he devoted himself to his faith and his studies with the zeal of a serious scholar and instilled that same drive in his three sons. "My father gave me a thirst for knowledge," Raghib said. "He said it was the key to everything."

Unlike his sons—Qudry would go on to play at Syracuse University and in the National Football League—Ibrahim Ismail was no athlete. He had been the victim of a serious fall when he was just five years old, and the resulting injuries left one leg five inches shorter than the other. As middle age approached, he was beset by serious kidney problems. He died in 1980, when Raghib was just ten years old, taking the secret of his origins with him. After her husband's death, for the first time in her adult life, Fatma Ismail worked outside the home. But multiple jobs were not enough to pay the tuition at the boys' private Islamic school, and they were exposed for the first time to what it truly meant to be black in America while attending inner-city Newark's public schools. They were taunted for their intelligence and academic work ethic, and a concerned teacher urged Fatma to remove her sons from the toxic atmosphere. She did, migrating to Wilkes-Barre, Pennsylvania, to live with her mother-in-law. There was one condition: that the boys attend a Protestant church, not a mosque. But for a young man who would be Notre Dame–bound in a few years, the exposure to different faiths was good training for the deep spiritual introspection that awaited him in college. "I don't know what Almighty God really prefers to be called, and neither do you," Rocket told *Sports Illustrated*. "I am just a young man. Some things are not for me to know yet."

On another positive note, their exotic names and the novelty of their supposed immigrant roots gave her sons some currency in the mostly white school district, Fatma said. "If my boys had been named Jones, they could only have gone as far as people let them," she explained. "Ismail? You can go as far as you want."

That may have been true in the classroom, but Holtz was skeptical as he traveled to Pennsylvania to watch the highly touted prospect perform.

"I'd never heard of a good football player named Raghib," Holtz said. "At his size, how good could he be? I wasn't high on him. Then I went to his hometown. I loved his personality. I could sense this was someone people genuinely loved. There was something special about him. Intensity. Awareness. Unselfishness."

Oh, and speed.

"Every time that guy touched the ball, it was, like, 'Hey, what's he going to do with it?'" says Justin Hall, a member of the 1988 recruiting class with Ismail. "Rocket was actually the first guy I met walking into the dorm as a freshman, and I didn't know anything about him. I didn't follow recruiting that much when I was getting recruited. But I knew even watching him in practice before that season that the guy was something special."

Ismail's presence in the Notre Dame offense in 1988 was a godsend: Tim Brown, the 1987 Heisman Trophy winner, was now beginning what would turn out to be a Hall of Fame career with the Los Angeles Raiders in the National Football League. However, Ismail wasn't as polished a receiver as Brown, and even though Rocket had been an every-down running back in high school, the Irish backfield was already overloaded, with Ricky Watters, Braxton Banks, Tony Brooks, and Anthony Johnson—not to mention Rice—all sharing carries. What's more, Ismail was small, a wispy five feet ten inches and 170 pounds. Using him out of the backfield, at least as a featured, between-the-tackles back, would expose Notre Dame's most dangerous new asset directly to the potential of physical harm on every down.

It took all of one practice for Holtz to move Ismail from running back to wide receiver. Like anyone learning a new position, it had taken him a few weeks to get down the basics, but Ismail had been chipping away at senior starter Steve Alaniz's playing time throughout the early part of the season. Alaniz had not been pleased to see his position handed to a freshman—it was inevitable that Ismail would be the starter soon, or at least handle the bulk of the snaps—but, watching the newcomer dart by McDowell and under Rice's heave, even he understood that Ismail was something special.

When Lou Holtz took over the Notre Dame program, he had recognized immediately that it was sorely lacking in game-breaking speed, the kind of speed that made programs like Miami so dangerous. The Rocket was Holtz's most obvious attempt to fix that problem.

———

While the Rice-to-Ismail toss had been the biggest offensive play of the first half, Stams and Pat Terrell had combined for the biggest defensive play of the opening two quarters. Stams had harassed Walsh all afternoon, forcing the Miami quarterback's first-quarter fumble and battering him on the other near fumble that had been ruled an incompletion. In the middle of the second quarter, Walsh completed a pair of intermediate passes, to tight end Rob Chudzinski and fullback Cleveland Gary, to move the Hurricanes into Notre Dame territory. After taking some of Notre Dame's best shots early on, Walsh was starting to look a little too comfortable scanning the field for targets from the pocket. Barry Alvarez, Notre Dame's defensive coordinator, decided to bring the blitz. The Hurricanes were ready, however, picking up the charging

Notre Dame pass rushers. Leonard Conley, a Miami running back, meanwhile slipped out of the backfield and into the flat, turning around to await a Walsh toss with lots of room to run. Another completion could have demoralized the Notre Dame defense, which would have sent its best shot at Walsh and still found itself burned for a long gain. Stams, however, had read the play perfectly. Staying home in his rush lane, he didn't hesitate as Conley passed by him. Instead, he kept coming at Walsh, raising his arms, timing it perfectly.

Deflected, the ball altered direction, and Terrell was in position to react. He grabbed it out of the air at the Notre Dame forty-yard line, then raced untouched for sixty yards for the touchdown to put the Irish ahead 21–7.

A few weeks before, down big in the fourth quarter, the Hurricanes had come charging back in Ann Arbor. So they were no strangers to this uncomfortable position. With about two minutes to play in the first half, Miami faced a fourth-and-four at the Notre Dame twenty-four. Rather than send in placekicker Huerta, however, Johnson decided to go for it. Stams, the one-man wrecking crew for the Notre Dame defense to that point, had been momentarily sidelined after getting poked in the eye. With that danger neutralized, Walsh again looked to his running back Conley in the flat to pick up the needed yards. Conley picked up the four that Miami needed and then some, beating Irish defensive back Todd Lyght in a footrace to the right corner of the end zone to make the score 21–14. It was precisely the kind of conversion that would test the resolve Holtz was working so hard to instill in his team.

Holtz had wanted to use the Hurricanes' go-for-broke swagger, embodied by Johnson's decision to pass up the field goal attempt on fourth-and-four, down two touchdowns, against them. In the previous year's game, Notre Dame had held stiff near midfield during the second quarter, forcing Miami to punt and seemingly stalling the Hurricanes building momentum. But, rather than kick the ball away, punter Jeff Feagles pretended the long snapper shot the ball over his head. While Notre Dame reacted to the well-executed fake out, Conley received the snap and shot out of the backfield. By the time anyone on the Irish defense noticed, the 'Canes had a first down deep in Notre Dame territory and would kick a field goal.

It had been a discouraging turn of events for Notre Dame on the way to a 24–0 defeat, and Holtz was determined not to allow something similar to eat at his team's confidence again. "Every time [Johnson] did something like that," Notre Dame defensive back George Streeter says, "Lou Holtz had us conditioned that it was an act of desperation. Whether it was successful or not, in our mind that meant, *We've got 'em. They can't run their regular offense. They can't run their regular defense. They can't do what they've normally done because we've got the upper hand.* Our confidence grew every time he attempted one of those things."

It was a neat bit of reverse psychology by Holtz, but strong as Notre Dame's resolve was, as the first half wound to a close it couldn't hide the fact that the Irish appeared winded. Fueled by the adrenaline of meeting the 'Canes head-on in the tunnel before the game, Notre Dame had dominated the first quarter and a half. But the defending national champions were steadying themselves, a scary thought for the fifty-nine thousand Irish fans who had been given an official warning just a few minutes earlier after tossing oranges on the field after Terrell's touchdown return. After the Miami defense held the Irish offense to just one set of downs after the Conley touchdown, Walsh again picked apart the Notre Dame secondary. The last two plays of Miami's last-minute drive looked easy: a twenty-three yard pass to Andre Brown, followed by a fifteen-yard touchdown to Gary with just twenty-one seconds to play in the first half. Notre Dame had played the best half game of football against the Hurricanes that the Irish had managed in years, surging ahead by two touchdowns with a frenzied crowd behind it. Yet, heading back through that tunnel, they now found themselves in a 21–21 tie against the No. 1 team in America.

———

In some ways, Pat Eilers was the typical Notre Dame football player, and in other ways he wasn't. A star in the classroom, Eilers was a double major, in biology and mechanical engineering. He was also a double Notre Dame legacy, not at all uncommon at a school that values its family lineages. Eilers's father, Vincent, had graduated from the university in 1956, and Pat's sister Anne was a 1985 graduate. Eilers's switch

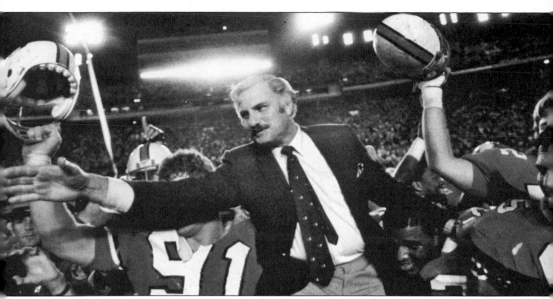

ABOVE: In the last game he ever coached at Miami, Howard Schnellenberger capped the ultimate rebuilding task with a national title-clinching victory over Nebraska in the Orange Bowl. *Miami Herald Staff Photo*

BELOW LEFT: The sight of Lou Holtz leading the Irish onto the field was a familiar one from 1986 through 1996. Holtz had to reenergize the program after Gerry Faust's difficult tenure, which preceeded his. *University of Notre Dame*

BELOW RIGHT: Recruited as the perfect match for Coach Lou Holtz's option offense, Notre Dame quarterback Tony Rice worked hard to become a throwing threat to keep opposing defenses honest. *University of Notre Dame*

ABOVE LEFT: Miami quarterback Vinny Testaverde, right, and defensive tackle Jerome Brown, left, arrive for the 1987 Fiesta Bowl against Penn State wearing combat fatigues. The style choice became a major controversy for the Hurricanes. *Brian Smith/Miami Herald*

ABOVE RIGHT: Miami coach Jimmy Johnson's first two seasons in Coral Gables were difficult. However, the lowest point was probably the stunning Fiesta Bowl loss to Penn State to end the 1986 season. *Bill Frakes/Miami Herald*

BELOW: As he followed in the footsteps of Heisman Trophy winner Vinny Testaverde and NFL stars Jim Kelly and Bernie Kosar, Steve Walsh found himself in the glaring spotlight as he took over as Miami's starting quarterback to begin the 1987 season. *Joe Rimkus, Jr./Miami Herald*

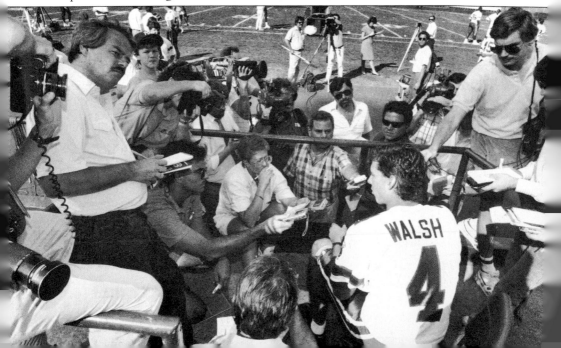

ABOVE: Jimmy Johnson was able to put his difficult first three years at Miami behind him with an Orange Bowl victory over Oklahoma to cap the Hurricanes' perfect 1987 season. *Bill Frakes/Miami Herald*

BELOW LEFT: Miami quarterback Steve Walsh embraces teammate Sandy Jack after the Hurricanes' Orange Bowl victory over Oklahoma to conclude their perfect 1987 season. The victory helped exorcise Miami's Fiesta Bowl loss to Penn State the year before. *Brian Smith/Miami Herald*

BELOW RIGHT: Notre Dame quarterback Tony Rice had to sit out his first season in South Bend as an academic casualty. He lost just one game in his two full seasons as starting quarterback for the Irish. *University of Notre Dame*

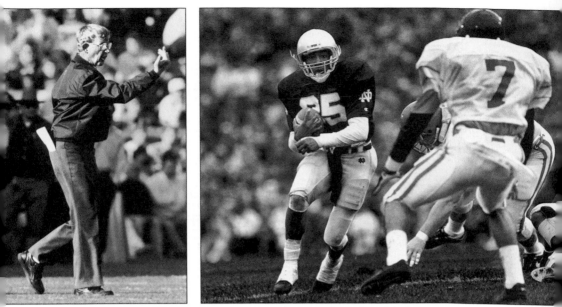

ABOVE LEFT: Notre Dame coach Lou Holtz rose from humble beginnings, hitchhiking from his home to the Kent State campus every day while a student. He walked onto the football team, despite being severely undersized, as a means to jump-start a coaching career. *University of Notre Dame*

ABOVE RIGHT: After spending his high school career as an every-down running back, Raghib "Rocket" Ismail was converted to wide receiver shortly after arriving at Notre Dame. *University of Notre Dame*

BELOW: Notre Dame wide receiver Raghib "Rocket" Ismail stretches to haul in a pass against Purdue. The speedster would develop into the most explosive player in college football. *University of Notre Dame*

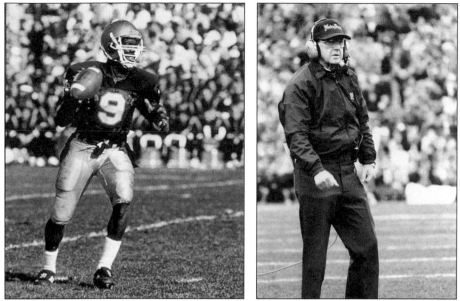

ABOVE LEFT: Notre Dame's top recruiter Vinny Cerrato urged head coach Lou Holtz to pursue Rice despite the fact that Cerrato had seen Rice play only basketball at South Carolina's Woodruff High School. *University of Notre Dame*

ABOVE RIGHT: Lou Holtz called the offensive plays throughout his tenure at Notre Dame, but also began running the defense after new coordinator Gary Darnell's defense struggled to begin the 1990 season. *University of Notre Dame*

BELOW : Notre Dame's defense stacks up Miami running back Stephen McGuire in the 1988 game between the two teams. The Irish defense surrendered a lot of yards in the 31–30 victory but forced seven turnovers. *University of Notre Dame*

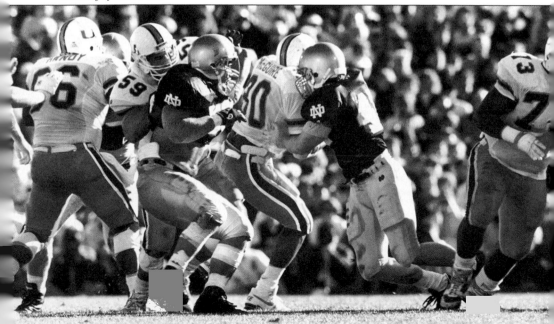

ABOVE: Notre Dame placekicker Reggie Ho puts one through the uprights in the 1988 game against Miami. The 31–30 victory over the Hurricanes is still considered perhaps the most memorable game in the storied history of the Notre Dame program. *University of Notre Dame*

RIGHT: Miami running back Leonard Conley battles for yards in the 1988 game against Notre Dame. Conley would be the intended target of Steve Walsh's two-point conversion pass at the end of the game.
University of Notre Dame

BELOW: Notre Dame defense back Pat Terrell leaps to break up Miami's two-point conversion at the end of the 1988 contest. The break-up preserved Notre Dame's epic 31–30 victory and helped boost the Fighting Irish to the national championship. *University of Notre Dame*

ABOVE: With Miami's All-American defensive linemen creating havoc up front, middle linebacker Bernard "Tiger" Clark had the game of his life in the Hurricanes' 27–10 victory over Notre Dame in 1989. *Walter Michot/Miami Herald*

BELOW LEFT: Notre Dame coach Lou Holtz talks strategy with tight end Derek Brown, a major national recruit the Irish were able to lure out of the Miami area. The Hurricanes program had been built on not allowing top recruits to leave south Florida. *University of Notre Dame*

BELOW RIGHT: First-year Hurricanes coach Dennis Erickson celebrates his team's 27–10 victory over Notre Dame in 1989. Erickson had replaced Jimmy Johnson prior to the season. *Bill Frakes/Miami Herald*

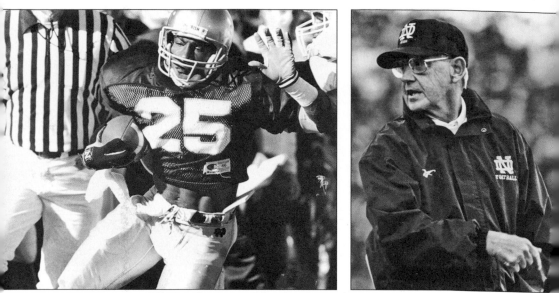

ABOVE LEFT: Raghib "Rocket" Ismail battles for yards against Miami in the 1990 Notre Dame victory in the final game between the two teams. Ismail established a season high for total yards in the game, which included a kickoff return for a touchdown. *University of Notre Dame*

ABOVE RIGHT: Notre Dame coach Lou Holtz took over immediately after one of the biggest embarrassments in the storied program's history, a 58–7 loss to Miami to conclude the 1985 season. *University of Notre Dame*

BELOW: Notre Dame's Raghib "Rocket" Ismail returns a kick against Colorado in the Orange Bowl after the 1989 season. Ismail was one of the most prolific kick returners in college football history. *University of Notre Dame*

from safety to flanker before his senior season was very typical of Holtz's coaching philosophy: He was constantly managing his roster like a jigsaw puzzle, working overtime to arrange his athletes in ways that maximized their talents, even if that meant retraining them or giving them responsibilities they had never before undertaken.

On the other hand, Eilers was much different than the collection of blue-chippers and former high school All-Americans that surrounded him on the Notre Dame sideline. Eilers had been a standout athlete at the Saint Thomas Academy in Mendota Heights, Minnesota, playing running back and defensive back and captaining the baseball team. Away from school, he was a good enough downhill skier to compete in the Junior Olympics.

But Eilers's father was an orthopedic surgeon in the Twin Cities, and after a lifetime of mending broken bones, tendons, and ligaments, he had warned his son about the dangers of playing football, and the need to build a life's plan distinct from the game in case things didn't work out. His father's warnings came to fruition during Eilers's final high school season, when he broke his collarbone. Almost immediately, major football schools that had been recruiting him backed away.

"People are interested, then you break your collarbone and they're no longer interested," Eilers remembers thinking. "That tainted the appeal a little bit."

So, in the fall of 1985, Eilers, who dreamed of following his father into the operating room, enrolled at Yale University to play football and accumulate his premed credentials. Ivy League football, however, was played at quite a different level from the football played by Notre Dame and Miami. For one thing, there are no athletic scholarships awarded, and the Ivies, to this day, do not participate in the postseason Football Championship Subdivision playoff, even though the league's top teams would surely make some noise in the postseason. Also, in Eilers's day, freshmen were not eligible for varsity play in the conference. That rule relegated Eilers to the grandstand at the Yale Bowl on Saturdays during his freshman year, and while sitting up there during the Yale-Harvard game he was struck with a revelation: *They don't take football seriously enough here.* Eilers shared that thought with his father, who was sitting with him, and they both agreed that Pat would stay enrolled at Yale through the academic year, then revisit a transfer possibility if he still felt the same way at the end of the spring.

In May, Eilers drove from New Haven to his home in Minnesota, stopping in South Bend on the way for his sister's graduation. While passing through, he met with new Irish coach Holtz, who offered him the opportunity to walk on to the Notre Dame football team the following fall. Eilers went back to New Haven to tell his position coach what he was going to do.

"Pat," the coach told him, "you'll go there and never play."

Eilers wasn't discouraged but rather more motivated than ever. He spent his first season at Notre Dame as a scout team running back, running the opponents' plays to ready the first-team defense for its next game. Dedicated to earning a scholarship, Eilers would run the plays to completion, sprinting forty yards down the field and making first-team defenders continue their pursuit. It wasn't a great way to make friends, but the coaching staff noticed. His second season at Notre Dame, Eilers was switched to defensive back. When he gave George Streeter a run for his money for the starting spot, Holtz followed through on his pledge and put Eilers on scholarship.

Early in fall camp, he was leveled on a play by offensive lineman Andy Heck. Holtz was not pleased.

"You should have stayed at Yale!" he shouted, grabbing Eilers by the face mask.

The play was called again, and this time Eilers ran it to perfection. Holtz patted him on the helmet and told him he thought he was going to be all right at Notre Dame.

And he was. Eilers was moved to flanker during the off-season preceding 1988. During the first half against the Hurricanes, Holtz liberally shuffled in talented running backs, including Mark Green, Tony Brooks, and Braxston Banks. Ricky Watters, a future NFL Pro Bowler, lined up as a flanker. So loaded was the Irish backfield that there wasn't room for Pat, the overachieving former Yalie trying to scratch his big-time football itch.

Eilers's moment to shine, however, would come soon enough. The teams traded turnovers early in the third quarter, Rice throwing a wounded-duck pass that was intercepted by Miami's Bubba McDowell, and the Hurricanes' Leonard Conley coughing up the ball on the very next snap. Walsh also threw his third interception of the game in the third, this one to Notre Dame defensive tackle Jeff Alm.

The game, tied at 21–21, would turn Notre Dame's way midway through the third quarter, when one of Holtz's pregame prophecies came to fruition. The Hurricanes had driven the ball nearly to midfield, a rare possession when they had not yet succumbed to Notre Dame's front-four pressure by coughing up the football. Johnson sent in punter Tim Kalal. A year before, at a similar key moment, punter Jeff Feagles and up man Conley had run a fake to perfection. This time, Kalal was standing back in punt position while Matt Britton stood in Conley's old spot. The snap went directly to Britton, and he was stuffed almost immediately behind the line of scrimmage and the Irish took over on downs.

In a game with one big play after another, this one had real consequences. Having just a few minutes earlier thrown his worst pass of the day, the interception to McDowell, Tony Rice on the next play threaded an NFL-caliber toss along the left sideline, hitting Watters in stride inside the Miami five-yard line.

Holtz sent in his three-back wishbone offensive formation. In that alignment, the receiver playing the split end position stayed wide, just to leave open the possibility of a pass and keep the defense honest. But the flanker moved into the backfield. Watters, Notre Dame's most talented player at the position, was winded after the long grab the play before. So Holtz sent in his backup, Eilers. Eilers took the handoff and started running to his right, trying to find enough daylight to get to the goal line. Already stumbling around the three-yard line, he placed a hand on the ground to steady himself, then bumped into the backside of behemoth offensive lineman Dean Brown to knock himself further off balance. By the time gravity finally yanked Eilers to the turf, he had barely pushed the ball over the goal line. In just a couple of short years, Eilers had gone from the grandstand at Yale to the end zone at Notre Dame Stadium. And just three years after falling 58–7 at the Orange Bowl, the Irish led the Hurricanes, winners of thirty-six consecutive regular-season games, 28–21. A few minutes later, kicker Reggie Ho booted a twenty-seven-yard field goal.

Heading into the final quarter of the regular-season game of the decade, a stirring meeting between college football's traditional powerhouse and the team of the 1980s, Notre Dame led 31–21. But Miami had come from behind before in 1988, and the 'Canes were more than capable of doing it again.

———

If anything marred what otherwise was shaping up to be a college football game for the ages, it was the officiating crew's inability to correctly rule on fumbles. Twice in the first half, Walsh had coughed up the football on hard hits by Stams. The crew had made the wrong call on each of those plays. On a play late in the first half, they made another mistake. As the 'Canes drove deep into Notre Dame territory, trailing 21–14, Walsh connected with tight end Chudzinski in open field. Chudzinski secured the ball, then turned to head upfield. He took two steps and then *bam*: Notre Dame's Pat Terrell crashed into him, sending the football to the ground. The Irish recovered almost immediately, but the sequence was ruled an incomplete pass, and Miami had new life. The Hurricanes concluded the march with Walsh's touchdown pass to Cleveland Gary, the fullback's seventh catch of a dazzling first half.

The Hurricanes cut the Irish lead to 31–24 very early in the fourth quarter on a short Carlos Huerta field goal. A few minutes later Miami was driving again deep into Notre Dame territory, and this time Jimmy Johnson was determined not to settle for a field goal. So when fourth-and-seven from the eleven-yard line rolled around with the Hurricanes still trailing by a touchdown midway through the final quarter, the Miami offense stayed on the field.

By that point Walsh had already thrown three interceptions. On the other hand, he was nearing four hundred yards in passing, having broken the single-game Notre Dame opponent record early in the fourth quarter. Now, though, he faced his most critical down of the game and the most critical play for the Hurricanes since the comeback in Ann Arbor. Walsh dropped back to around the sixteen-yard line and began scanning the field for receivers. He had good protection, but the pocket started collapsing around him a few seconds after the snap. An Irish rusher, bearing down on the Miami quarterback, was rerouted by a Hurricane offensive lineman a few yards behind Walsh, giving the passer a few more precious moments to find an open man. Just as that backside pressure collapsed in on Walsh, he let go of the football. Backing off the line of scrimmage a few yards, Zorich leaped in the air and reached out, trying to get his hand once more on Walsh's tight spiral or even match his line mate Jeff Alm with an interception. But this one eluded his fingers by a few inches.

The target of the pass, yet again, was Gary, and Walsh delivered the ball right into his numbers at around the Notre Dame two-yard line, a few feet right of the left hash marks. The Miami fullback had run an underneath route, escaping the notice of the Irish secondary until it was too late. A line of Notre Dame defenders bore down on him, trying to keep him out of the end zone for what would likely be the tying score. Safety George Streeter was closest, and as the force of the pass caused Gary to stumble, Streeter dove in an attempt to halt him short of the goal line.

He had been conditioned during the week on how to handle just such a moment.

"Lou Holtz used to tell our running backs to have three points of pressure on the ball," Streeter says. "Cleveland Gary didn't. He often had just two. I wouldn't say he was careless, because it worked in the past, but there was an opportunity that he might cough it up if you hit him in the right spot. If you ever see a photo of Cleveland Gary making cuts, you see that his elbow's high, the ball is tucked in his hand and his elbow, and it's away from his body a lot of times. It was just one of those situations like that."

Losing his balance and twisting forward, Gary lunged to break the plane. Whatever happened, it seemed that the situation was going to be extremely favorable to Miami. If Gary got into the end zone and Hurricanes kicker Carlos Huerta nailed his fourth extra point of the day, the game would be tied 31–31 going into the final few minutes, with the Notre Dame offense coming off of its worst drive of the afternoon. If, however, Gary's dive, or Streeter, stopped him short, Miami's offense would have the ball inside the Notre Dame one-yard line on first-and-goal.

With Gary parallel to the ground, Streeter reached out with his right arm and grabbed at Gary's own right arm as the Miami fullback flew past him. Earlier in the game, Streeter had been involved in a similar play: On Miami's first touchdown, early in the second quarter,

Streeter had seemingly stopped Hurricanes receiver Andre Brown at the one-yard line, Brown's knee striking the ground before his arm extended the ball over the plane. An official on top of that play, however, had immediately raised his arms into the air to signal a touchdown, yet another questionable call on a crucial play. This time the football, cradled precariously between Gary's outstretched right hand and his wrist, began to come loose. As his body made impact with the grass, the ball squirted out of his grip. Its backspin carried it backward out of the end zone, where the closest Notre Dame defender, linebacker Michael Stonebreaker, pounced on it.

Players from both sides immediately surrounded the two officials on top of the play, asking for a definitive ruling. Walsh sprinted into the fray, repeatedly pointing at the ground to frantically plead his team's case.

"One of the referees," Walsh says, "as I was in the huddle trying to state my case, said, 'Don't worry, it's your ball, we're just trying to figure out where it's going to be placed.'"

Walsh backed away a step and waited for an officials' meeting to sort out the mess. Instead, a couple of seconds later, without consultation, the other official near the goal line signaled that the ball belonged to Notre Dame. While the players on Notre Dame's defense pranced back to the sideline, arms raised in celebration, the Irish offense dashed onto the field before anyone decided to change his mind. On the Hurricanes sideline, Johnson signaled repeatedly with his arm while yelling, "First down! First down!"

At that moment nobody in the stadium was prouder of the Irish defense than its coordinator, Barry Alvarez.

"If you watch," Alvarez says, "when that ball hits the ground, we had eleven players point to it immediately. Sometimes, when everyone reacts, the official reacts too."

The game took place years before instant replay was instituted as a check on just that sort of bang-bang play. And that fact, along with the limited camera angles available on the goal line replays, make the broadcast seem like an anachronism. CBS broadcasters Brent Musburger and Pat Haden almost immediately deemed the Gary fumble the correct call. And even if instant replay had been in place in 1988, it is far from certain that the ruling on the field would have been overturned.

Although the ball didn't separate completely from contact with Gary until his arm hit the ground, the CBS overhead replay does appear to show that the ball may have begun to escape Gary's possession before his body slammed into the ground, perhaps rolling up his wrist if ever so slightly. That would have negated Walsh and Johnson's argument that the ground caused the fumble and the ball should have belonged to the Hurricanes at the one.

Seeing everything develop from behind the play, Walsh and Johnson were at poor angles to understand what the real dispute should have been: whether Gary, by stretching his arm to hold the ball out, had broken the plane of the end zone before the ball began to come loose. Without a camera peering right down the goal line from the sideline, the replay angles also make it difficult to determine precisely where the ball was, in relation to the goal line, when it began to come free. Because of the poor camera angles, had the play occurred years later, there is a good chance it would not have been reversible, no matter which way the officials on the field decided to go. But in 1988 the point was moot: The ball belonged to Notre Dame, which clung desperately to a 31–24 advantage.

———

When Holtz gathered his first Notre Dame recruiting class in the fall of 1986 to emphasize to them what a collection of misfits and last resorts they were, the speech didn't really resonate with wide receiver recruit Pat Terrell.

"The whole time I'm sitting there," says Terrell, "I'm thinking, *He must be talking about my teammates, because I know he's not talking about me.*"

Before he had ever called a play in a game at Notre Dame, Holtz's reputation for keeping the ball on the ground was already well established. But any difficulties that might have presented in recruiting wide receivers was neutralized by the presence on the Irish roster of Tim Brown.

When Holtz and his staff fanned out in late 1985 and early 1986 in search of a last-minute class, Brown remained two years away from picking up the Heisman Trophy at New York's Downtown Athletic Club, but he was already making it clear that whoever coached him was going to have to find a way to involve Brown heavily in both offense and special teams. In a part-time role as a freshman in 1984, Brown caught twenty-eight passes. A year later, Faust's final season, he caught twenty-five passes and displayed even more explosiveness, introducing himself to the world with a ninety-three-yard return of the second-half kickoff against Michigan State for a touchdown.

Terrell had noticed, and when Holtz told him that he envisioned him as "the next Tim Brown," Terrell listened.

There was, however, one big hang-up.

Terrell attended Lakewood High School in St. Petersburg, Florida, right in the heart of the Howard Schnellenberger–established "State of Miami." The Hurricanes may have changed coaches, but Jimmy Johnson hadn't gotten to where he was because he was a stupid man. As the Hurricanes experienced more and more success, the Miami brand name allowed the coaches to widen their net and recruit nationally. Even so, the core of the Miami program would still consist of South Florida kids. They were tough, fast, and, for the most part, wanted nothing more in life than to play their home college football games at the Orange Bowl.

As Terrell's senior season at Lakewood High progressed and his successes mounted, so, too, did the pressure to head to Coral Gables after graduation. It seemed like the perfect fit. It was home, after all, and unlike a lot of the stodgy midwestern and eastern football programs, the Hurricanes liked to put the ball in the air and into the hands of their playmakers.

As the competition for his services heated up, Terrell's father sat him down for a man-to-man conversation.

"What schools are you looking at?" Terrell's father asked.

Terrell named a couple of Florida schools.

"How much are those schools worth a year?"

After performing some quick calculations in his head, Terrell answered: "Four thousand dollars."

His father stuck his hand out.

"Congratulations," he told his son. "Because of your hard work academically and athletically, you've earned $16,000 worth of education."

He wasn't done.

"What other schools are you looking at?" he asked.

Notre Dame, Pat told him. Price tag: approximately $25,000 a year.

The elder Terrell pulled out a piece of scratch paper and a pen and did some fast calculations.

"All right," he said. "You can get a $100,000 education or a $16,000 education. Your decision."

Then he walked out of the room.

"I kind of knew where he was leaning," Terrell says. "But really, I just knew that Notre Dame was going to make a move athletically in the right direction. I thought Lou Holtz was the right person for the job. And I truly thought that Notre Dame and its athletes were all headed the same direction that I knew I wanted to go. Miami is a wonderful academic institution. They do a great job. It's a tough school to get into. I just felt that Notre Dame was the right place for me academically, spiritually, and careerwise. It seemed like it had the best of all worlds wrapped into one."

Being labeled "the next Tim Brown" didn't hurt. And for a while it looked as though that might happen. Thanks to the team's need, Terrell was switched to the defensive secondary as a freshman. But the subsequent spring game, back at receiver, he caught five passes for eighty-seven yards. When injuries chipped away at Notre Dame's depth at receiver in the middle of the 1987 campaign, Pat started five straight games, lining up in the same wide receiver corps as Brown himself.

But Terrell's skill set—blazing speed but hands of stone—made him a prime candidate for a switch to defensive safety, and as the 1988 season dawned, that's where he found himself. Terrell started his first game against Pitt the week before the Miami showdown. As the game against the Hurricanes kicked off, Terrell felt he had a lot to prove. To the folks back home, he had to show that he had indeed made the right decision coming out of high school—a judgment that, at least for the moment, would be based on the score when the two programs got together. To Lou Holtz and the Irish coaching staff, he had to prove that he could be a major contributor to the program's success, even if the flaws in his game would prevent him from ever becoming the next Tim Brown, as had been hoped.

In the developing struggle against the Hurricanes, Terrell's opportunity would come. But not before a few more twists and turns on the way to a classic college football ending. Late in the fourth quarter, the

Irish seemed to have the game won when Stams, continuing to harness every bit of emotion he had been left with after the 58–7 drubbing three years before, forced his second fumble of the game. Zorich immediately pounced on the ball, and Notre Dame took over inside its own thirty, a couple of first downs from milking the clock to the end.

But on third down and seventeen, Holtz inexplicably lost his steely conservative patience, while Rice reverted back to the mistake-prone first-year starter from a season before. Instead of satisfying himself with running the clock and punting the ball away, Holtz called a deep pass play. The injury-ravaged offensive line gave way to the Miami pressure almost immediately, and Rice fumbled as he was clobbered. Instead of taking over with a long field to traverse after a Notre Dame punt, the Hurricanes offense had the ball at the Notre Dame fifteen, a catastrophic turn of events after the way the Irish had played all afternoon. As they had on Gary's fumble a few minutes before, the Hurricanes soon faced a fourth-and-seven from the eleven. This time Walsh threw the pass into the end zone, where it was hauled in by a diving Andre Brown, who kept his hands underneath the ball and secured it long enough as he rolled over to earn the touchdown signal even as the football squirted free and out of bounds a moment later. With forty-five seconds to play, Miami had made the score 31–30. Now Johnson faced his biggest decision of the season.

Coming from a soccer background, Miami placekicker Huerta lagged behind his teammates when it came to the intricacies of football strategy. So he considered himself fortunate to learn the game at the side of a coach he considered a football genius. To keep himself mentally involved in the contests between his brief spurts of activity, Huerta paid close attention to Johnson's decision making. Huerta might not have known a zone blitz from a Cover 2, but when it came to game management, he started to understand how remarkable Johnson's intuition for making the right decisions was.

"I never saw him make a bad call," says Huerta. "It would amaze me. I would sit there and critique to see if he would screw up in the turmoil that many of those games turned into: It was either right or left, or punt or not, or call a time-out or not, or go for two or not. He always made the right call."

So after the touchdown Huerta wasn't surprised when Johnson

raised one finger in the air to send him on the field for an extra-point
try that would make the score 31–31, as it likely would remain when the
clock hit zeroes. This wasn't the sexy call in the situation, but it was the
sensible one. The Hurricanes were already ranked No. 1 and were
the defending national champions, playing on the road against a Notre
Dame team that clearly deserved its top-five ranking. Salvaging a tie in
such a hostile environment, after coming from double digits behind
twice—on a day the Irish had put everything they had on the line—
would likely keep the 'Canes firmly in the driver's seat in their push to
become the sport's first repeat national champions since Oklahoma in
1974 and '75. A loss, on the other hand, would wrest that control from
Miami's hands. And with the way the Irish had played, it seemed more
than feasible that they would run the tables the rest of the way.

Huerta began to trot onto the field to boot the chip shot that would
keep his team's national title hopes intact. But then, a few steps into his
jog to the huddle, he heard maniacal shouting behind him: Huerta was
being called back by both Johnson and 'Canes offensive coordinator
Gary Stevens.

"I got this sinking feeling down my spine," says Huerta. "It was one
of those things. I just got a feeling. Not that it was the wrong call. It
might have been the right one. It was the indecisiveness that I worried
about."

As the Hurricanes broke from the huddle after a time-out to ease
the chaos, Terrell had just one thought: *No trick play. For the love of God,
no trick play.* In the shadow of Touchdown Jesus, the nickname for the
towering mural that overlooks Notre Dame Stadium, Terrell bargained
with the Almighty: He was more than willing to let the play come his
way, to his man, just so long as the Hurricanes played it straight. Starting only his second game as a defensive back, Terrell had no burning desire to be a hero. He just didn't want to be the goat.

After a day in which Walsh had thrown for 424 yards and four
touchdowns, there was little chance that the Hurricanes would attempt
to run the ball in for the two-pointer to win. Instead, Walsh rolled out
while scanning the field for his receivers and running backs. For a
split second he began to pull the trigger, but pulled back when a Notre
Dame pass rusher broke free, in order to avoid a batted ball at the line
of scrimmage. That crisis averted, Walsh lofted a pass toward the back

right corner of the end zone, the same location and trajectory as the touchdown throw to Brown the play before.

Leonard Conley, the intended receiver, never really had a chance. Like a veteran defensive back, Terrell jumped the route and batted the ball down with both hands. Terrell would go on to become a second-round selection in the NFL Draft and play nearly a decade in the league. Any time his name was mentioned on a network broadcast, it was almost certain to be followed by a note that he was the man who broke up Steve Walsh's pass in the corner of the end zone to end Miami's thirty-six-game regular-season winning streak.

"I think I appreciate that play so much more than I did immediately after it happened," Terrell says. "I always used to think, *Well, man, I had a big-time interception return for a touchdown in that game, too, and nobody ever talks about that.* But now that I've been retired and I have children of my own, I appreciate that play so much more than I did while I was still an active player."

The remaining forty-five seconds were saturated with the sound of the Notre Dame Stadium crowd savoring the program's first upset of a No. 1–ranked team since Gerry Faust's second team had upset Pittsburgh on the road late in the season. However, it was the first time the Irish had toppled No. 1 at home in fifty-two years. Even the great Ara Parseghian had three times in his Irish career, which included two national championships and several other near misses, welcomed No. 1 to South Bend three times and lost each one.

The Irish crowd shook the old stadium's foundation as the defense trotted off the field after Terrell's pass breakup. The commotion rose again when the Irish recovered Miami's onside kick attempt. The Notre Dame fans roared and didn't stop when Rice fell on the football a final time with about twenty seconds to play, cradling it like a newborn.

By the time the CBS camera crew reached Holtz on the field, the celebration around him was fully under way. "Shut up!" he barked at some revelers, before turning his attention back to interviewer John Dockery. Holtz declined to talk about the details of the contest, instead steering all questions back to his crediting of the "Notre Dame Spirit."

It was hokey, of course, and classic Holtz to credit the victory to something as celestial as the "Notre Dame Spirit." But on that afternoon, at that moment, it struck the perfect chord.

No such thing as the "Notre Dame Spirit"?

Tell that to Pat Eilers, who had left Yale for South Bend on a wing and a prayer and scored the winning touchdown.

Tell it to Tony Rice, once nearly turned away at the university's gate but now assured his place in Irish lore for eternity.

Tell it to Chris Zorich, who not long before was sure that Notre Dame was in Paris.

And tell it to Tim Grunhard. Once part of the "ragtag" first recruiting class Holtz and Cerrato had cobbled together in the winter of 1986–87, Grunhard had severely injured his ankle the week before against Pitt. The plan had been to hold him out of the Miami contest, and indeed he did not start. And yet, in the game footage, there is No. 75, raising his arms to the heavens after an Irish touchdown.

"There was no way that I should have played in that game," Grunhard says. "I couldn't walk until about Wednesday. But it would have broken my heart if I couldn't have played or participated in that game. It was huge for me. It proved that if I put my mind to do something, that I could get it done. I willed myself out there. I learned a lesson in that game. That game was a turning point for me and I think it was a turning point for a lot of different people, not just on the football field, but in life."

CHAPTER 11

Almost Heaven, West Virginia

After the Miami victory, the rest of Notre Dame's season seemed imbued with an air of inevitability.

"After that game," says tight end Rod West, "we expected to beat the shit out of whoever we played, period, end of discussion. It became business at that point."

"Coach Holtz doesn't want to hear this," says Todd Lyght, "but half the time all we had to do was show up and we'd win a game. That's how good we were."

Inside the Notre Dame locker room, Holtz and his coaches managed to keep alive the no-one-believes-in-you, us-against-the-world rhetoric that had originally launched the team's rise from the lower reaches of the top twenty to the top of the polls. But from the outside looking in, the perception of Notre Dame was changing rapidly. No longer were the Irish a collection of overachieving also-rans straining to slow the Hurricanes. Rather, this was the Notre Dame of old, blessed with advantages that other programs could only dream of, granted the benefit of the doubt at every turn.

"Notre Dame is as good as the media makes it," Navy fullback Deric Sims groused after his team's 22–7 loss, "which means you build them up to be Superman and put an 'S' on their shirt. They are not as strong as the media builds them up to be."

There was one last major obstacle on the Irish regular-season schedule, and it was a potential doozy. In late November, Notre Dame traveled to Los Angeles to face Southern California. It was true that Miami was Notre Dame's archrival of the moment. It was also true that geographic proximity, along with the fact that the game traditionally kicked off the season for both teams, had turned the annual contest with Michigan into one of each season's most pivotal early-season college football games. But where tradition was concerned, few matchups in the sport could hold a candle to Notre Dame–USC.

Prior to 1980, a good part of the history of college football had been an extended battle of one-upsmanship by these two programs. Tim Brown's Heisman Trophy in 1987 had given the Irish seven of the awards in their illustrious history. But USC was no slouch: The Trojans had won four Heismans, most recently by Marcus Allen in 1981. In the 1970s, certainly a memorable decade for Notre Dame football, the Irish had won a pair of national championships (1973 and 1977) under a pair of coaches (Ara Parseghian and Dan Devine). Not to be outdone, Southern Cal had captured *three* titles during the decade (1972, 1974, and 1978), also under two different head coaches (John Robinson and John McKay).

The series had started in 1926, just a couple of years after Knute Rockne actually turned down overtures from USC to remain in South Bend. From 1928 through 1932, the two programs passed the national title back and forth as if it were a hot potato. In 1964, Parseghian's first year at Notre Dame, the Irish flew to Los Angeles undefeated, ranked No. 1 and a double-digit favorite over the Trojans. The Irish led 17–0 at halftime and seemed to be well on their way to a national championship before USC rallied in the second half for a stirring 20–17 victory. A few years later, the 1977 game between the teams would forever go down in history as the "Green Jersey Game" as the Joe Montana–led Irish scored twenty-eight unanswered points en route to a 49–19 victory and, eventually, the national championship. Then there was, of course, the game two years prior, when Holtz's first Notre Dame squad had staged a second-half rally at the LA Coliseum to finally establish itself as a team to be reckoned with in the future. "All the other rivalries were good too: Michigan, Michigan State," says Kris Haines, Montana's prime wide receiver target. "But nothing compared to USC. That was it. That was the game."

And yet, remarkably, in the long, storied history of the series, never had Notre Dame and USC met as the first- and second-ranked teams in America. That would change on November 26, 1988. The Trojans, led by quarterback Rodney Peete, had rampaged through the Pac-10 conference, with only Washington giving them a real scare. They had clinched their spot in the Rose Bowl, seemingly a birthright when you elected to play at USC; and with the Irish coming to town, the Trojans had designs on an even bigger goal.

All season, nothing could impede Notre Dame's march to a national title. Not the potential distraction of Holtz's Minnesota past hovering over late summer proceedings. Not Rice's passing woes early in the season. Not even the mighty Miami Hurricanes. The Irish had stared down each of those beasts and bested them.

And then, in late November, it seemed that Notre Dame finally met its match: a California shopping mall parking lot.

———

Even if Navy's Deric Sims was reading the situation correctly—that the nation was trying to essentially will Notre Dame to a national title—the sentiment definitely wasn't unanimous. There was one person out there, a Texan transplanted to sunny South Florida, a good ol' boy with perfect hair, who was pulling for Notre Dame's demise every week.

Losing to Notre Dame in October had hardly derailed the Miami Hurricanes Express. But before they moved on to the rest of their schedule, the controversy regarding Gary's fumble near the Notre Dame goal line continued to simmer. The biggest catalyst was an article in the *Miami News* afternoon newspaper the following Monday, purporting to quote an anonymous official working the game.

"There was no fumble," the quote read. "The ruling was the ball went over on downs. We probably made a mistake."

Miami's players and fans were apoplectic when they read that interpretation. If there had not been a fumble, the Hurricanes would have earned a first down and would have had four opportunities to punch the ball in from the one-yard line. It would have been a preposterous ruling, a mistake of epic proportions in an epic rivalry game with national championship implications, and that's exactly what Collegiate Independents Football Officials Association director Art Hyland said when reached for his response to the report.

"Does that sound plausible?" he said. "With seven officials out there—and all seven responsible for down and distance—it's about impossible that somebody wouldn't rescue that error."

Hyland was just getting started.

"I don't believe one word of it," he said. "My officials are not permitted to talk to the media and don't. None of the officials ever made such a comment, or have even talked to a reporter, coach, or any other person about that call or the game."

Hyland indicated that the official who had made the call had reviewed the tape of the play and come away confident that the correct decision had been rendered.

"It's unfortunate," he said, "and, quite frankly, irresponsible, that the alleged quote of the CIFOA official was made public without confirmation."

The Hurricanes, already convinced that they had been robbed, saw the follow-up story, flimsy sourcing notwithstanding, as complete validation for what they were already convinced was the case. Hostile television announcers. Rampant media criticism. T-shirts. Questionable officiating. Rather than viewing everything as a series of coincidental events, it was all part of one very large, orchestrated whole, an amalgam of anti-'Canes sentiment that had finally cost Miami on the field.

"We thought we never got good calls or fair calls at Notre Dame anyway," says Shannon Crowell, who rotated in at running back that game along with Gary and Leonard Conley. "I think when someone refers to you as a whole as a group of convicts, it suggests what the general opinion of your team is when you come into their venue."

Early in the week following the game, while the newspaper account fueled the fires of discontent among the Hurricanes, Johnson popped in a tape of the play for the team to watch one more time.

"They blew it," Johnson announced. "They blew the call."

Then, however, Johnson said he would hear no more talk about the goal-line call from that point forward. "We had to move on from that," Chudzinski says. "That's the last he wanted to talk about it."

After the loss, Miami demolished Cincinnati 57–3. The Hurricanes pounded East Carolina 31–7. They blasted Tulsa 34–3. "It definitely got us more pissed off than it did dejected," says Mike Sullivan. "We went into every year really believing that there was nobody on the schedule that would beat us or *should* beat us."

Then, on November 19, came the most impressive showing of all. LSU was coming off a 10–1–1 season when 1988 began and had showed few signs of a letdown in coach Mike Archer's second season. With the Hurricanes coming into Baton Rouge, the Tigers had already clinched a share of the SEC title. For a Miami team harboring renewed national championship dreams, the trip to play in one of the country's most intimidating venues was the biggest opportunity to showcase themselves since the Notre Dame loss. In a driving rainstorm, the Hurricanes blew out LSU 44–3.

As the Hurricanes had hoped, people noticed, and no one more so than Lou Holtz. Confronting his own momentous road challenge, Holtz picked up the phone in his office early in the week and dialed the same number that Notre Dame freshman Doug Browne had punched in a few months before. The Notre Dame coach hoped that he wouldn't elicit the same reaction the "freshman caller" had, but braced for it nonetheless.

"I thought long and hard before making this call," Holtz began after Johnson answered the phone. "I hope our relationship is such that I can do it. I know you want us not to win, but I need your help."

"Sure, Lou," Johnson replied. "What can I do?"

Holtz told Johnson how much he admired Miami's success on the road. In their last twenty-six regular-season road contests, the Hurricanes had been defeated just twice, including the 31–30 loss to Notre Dame.

Now, with the Irish facing their own stern road test at USC, Holtz wondered if Johnson might be able to share some of the secrets of his success.

"It's sort of fed on itself," Johnson explained. "But basically it's a matter of the players developing so much pride in showing opposing crowds what they can do. We remind them that's why they came to Miami, to play in big games: South Bend, Baton Rouge, Ann Arbor, Norman, wherever."

Johnson's insights were not exactly revelatory: When it comes to motivation, so much of coaching is in the delivery anyway, as opposed to the messages, which are often retread. But that he was willing to talk at all represented a thawing of the ice that had begun to form when Johnson was unhappy with his perceived treatment on the Notre Dame Stadium sideline in 1984—ice that solidified when the Miami coach poured it on at the Orange Bowl in Gerry Faust's final game at Notre

Dame, then became all but unbreakable in the tunnel before the Irish victory in South Bend.

Like a couple of old friends, the two coaches began to chat about that contest, played barely more than a month before.

"So many people say it was a classic," Johnson said. "I hate to hear it because we lost. But it was a hell of a game. Lou, we've taken so much flak for taunting, but we play clean and there wasn't any taunting."

"When the whistle blows," Holtz agreed, "it was as hard a game as I've ever been in. But clean."

Any initial awkwardness now out of the way, Johnson continued with further advice for Holtz's road-bound Fighting Irish.

"You can't believe how actually excited our players were to play in Baton Rouge," Johnson said. "I mean, who's going to be excited about playing in Baton Rouge—against the Southeastern Conference champs? I told them we have a chance to show the nation what we can do in a place like that. You know, Lou, a lot of teams can play at home. A team's own crowd bails it out of a lot of psychological letdowns. But you don't have that on the road, and an average team exaggerates its letdowns. So it takes a team that's strong mentally to overcome it, to turn it back around. The team has to know the only effect a crowd has is psychological. You have to make everyone—the staff, the team—believe you won't be intimidated by the crowd."

"I'm not embarrassed to call somebody," Holtz says of his conversation with Johnson. "They had success on the road, so I called him and asked, 'Why do you win on the road?' Everything is so much mental, so much about how you prepare. You've got to be sound fundamentally. You've got to teach them blocking and tackling. And your theories. But getting them ready mentally is every bit as critical."

The two exchanged some more pleasantries, Johnson good-naturedly wished Holtz's team ill in the showdown in Los Angeles, and they both hung up and got on with the tasks of pursuing a national championship.

———

When Holtz arrived at Notre Dame after the 1985 season, his first step was to institute a code of rigid, almost militaristic discipline to his team's daily routine. Promptness was expected, and no wiggle room was offered. Holtz often referred to "L.L.H. Time"—Louis Leo Holtz Time—constantly reminding his players that stragglers were not accepted and that they should be situated and ready to go well ahead of meeting times.

By 1988, however, a certain laxness had developed among some team members. It was an odd phenomenon, since Holtz had made the pursuit of perfection one of the central themes of fall camp. But it was something that had come over them nonetheless. "We talked to the players and ran them when they were late," said Holtz, "but we weren't getting the desired effect."

For about twenty-four hours in late November, it looked as though the team's loose punctuality would cost the Irish their first national championship in more than a decade.

Holtz had scheduled a six o'clock team dinner on the Friday night before the showdown against USC. Within minutes, the team managers informed Holtz that two players, running backs Ricky Watters and Tony Brooks, were not present. Holtz was frustrated when any players were even a few seconds late, but this duo's absence was particularly galling. Back in South Bend just a couple of days earlier, the same pair had been late to a team meeting. Watters explained that he had been turning in an architecture class assignment, and Holtz let it slide with a stern warning to let nothing of the sort ever happen again. According to Holtz, both Watters and Brooks made the trip to Los Angeles with the understanding that they were one slipup away from being sent right back home.

A few hours before the dinner was to begin on Friday, Californian Brooks excitedly told Watters and a few other Irish players, mostly freshmen, that a local friend of his was willing to let them borrow his car so that the players could follow a group of girls to an LA-area mall. Watters, Brooks, and the rest became separated from the girls almost as soon as they arrived at the mall, so they opted to do a little Christmas shopping instead. All seemed well when they decided to leave, figuring they had plenty of time to get back for the team function. But there was one problem: The exit they were staring at looked nothing like the place they had come in. By the time the disoriented players realized that they had entered on another level, the race against the clock was on. "We thought we still had a chance to make it in time," Watters said, "and pushed the speed limit the whole way back."

Holtz has maintained that the players were forty minutes late for the meeting. Watters disputes this. "We arrived to the luncheon with the doors just closing in front of us," he said. Regardless, an order was an order, even when No. 1 was playing No. 2 on the season's final Saturday. After he was done speaking with the rest of the team, Holtz ordered Watters and Brooks, the two repeat offenders, back to their hotel rooms.

With every intention to send the two players on the first plane home the next morning, Holtz gathered his senior leaders into a conference after dinner, pulling them out of a movie that the team was enjoying. The meeting had about it all the solemnity due a papal selection, with Holtz sitting at the head of the table, puffing on a pipe. Rather than try to talk Holtz into letting Watters and Brooks stay in California and play against the Trojans, the group backed his tentative decision to send them back to South Bend.

"In the leadership group of the seniors, there were no dissenters," says offensive lineman Andy Heck, who actually pushed for the pair to be tossed off the team altogether. "It was unanimous and there was no hesitation: 'This is what we should do, Coach, and we're behind you.'"

Holtz walked back into the room where the rest of the players were watching the movie *The Untouchables*, and announced that he had come to a decision. While most of the players remained silent, one stood up and said that Holtz was making a mistake. Defensive end Frank Stams, one of the players who had been with the program since the 58–7 drubbing against Miami in 1985, grew angry at the guy who made the comment.

"I don't care what all of you guys think," Stams thundered. "If you're not ready to play this game tomorrow, then I want you to just get the hell out of this room. I don't care if I'm the only one on the field."

Until the moment their plane left the runway, Watters and Brooks thought that they were embroiled in an elaborate ruse meant to teach them a lesson.

Prior to the game the next afternoon, Holtz flipped the no-respect card one last time. "We were the No. 1 team in the country going into the game," linebacker Wes Pritchett said, "but all they said in the papers was how USC was a better football team. I think coach Holtz did a great job using that as a motivating factor on us." There was at least some merit to what Holtz was selling. The Trojans, playing at home, were about a field goal favorite. And the losses of Watters and Brooks were not minor. Brooks would end the 1988 season with more than seven hundred rushing yards: His absence was no small loss, even on a team that shuffled talented running backs into the game. Watters would finish the year with a team-leading sixteen receptions. When Holtz sent him home, he also removed a lot of the big-play potential from the Irish offense. Watters had averaged more than twenty-one yards per catch. "Knowing Holtz," says Tim Prister, who covered the game for *Blue & Gold Illustrated*, "it's almost like his eyes lit up when he got the opportunity to make a statement. Not that he was trying to screw Watters and Brooks, but it was an opportunity to provide the ultimate motivation and he went for it."

Even without the two stars, the game was never really that close. Although USC outgained the Irish by about a hundred yards, and held the ball for about ten more minutes than Notre Dame, defensive coordinator Alvarez had gone into the game scheming for big plays, and the strategy paid dividends. Running more blitzes than was customary, the Irish kept quarterback Rodney Peete on the run all afternoon long. Alvarez used five different defensive ends, hoping to keep them fresh in the California heat. It worked. Stan Smagala intercepted a pass near the end of the first half and returned it sixty-four yards for a touchdown to put Notre Dame ahead 20–7. In the battle between No. 1 and No. 2, No. 1 would triumph 27–10.

———

Although Tony Rice had wanted to transcend the role of "black quarterback" from the time he had arrived in South Bend, the matchup for the Irish in the Fiesta Bowl would make that harder than ever to accomplish. No. 3 West Virginia—the Irish had not given in to Johnson's pressure for a No. 1 versus No. 2 rematch against the Hurricanes—were also guided by a black quarterback of considerable talent: Major Harris.

Wrote Ben Smith, columnist for the *Fort Wayne* (Ind.) *Journal-Gazette*:

For all their differences...both arrived at this week's Fiesta Bowl and Gala Three-Ring Media Circus having been hardened in the same crucible. They have trashed the critics who said they didn't throw well enough or were more suited to playing other positions. And, with quiet dignity, they have refuted those severely brain-damaged individuals who suggested they might be too black to lead a team to the pinnacle.

Harris, just a sophomore, had finished fifth in the Heisman Trophy voting behind Oklahoma State running back Barry Sanders. He received more first-place votes than Miami's Walsh, who finished one place ahead of him, in fourth. Dangerous on his feet while more developed as a passer than Rice, Harris had thrown fourteen touchdown passes and run for six. He wasn't West Virginia's only weapon, however: Harris took refuge behind a massive offensive line that had paved the way for more than three thousand rushing yards.

With no history between the two teams, Holtz was not in a position to push the same sorts of emotional buttons that he had been able to manipulate in the moments before the Miami game. His own emotions had been stirred in the morning, when Holtz turned on the television in his hotel room to see that ESPN was showing a documentary about the history of the Notre Dame program. But he resisted any temptation to stir the locker room echoes, instead keeping his pregame speech—to use his own word—"placid."

The strategy worked. Or perhaps Notre Dame was just that much better and more battle-tested than the Mountaineers. With the national championship on the line, Rice had one of his best games as a Fighting Irish quarterback. He threw for 213 yards while running for seventy-five, winning the individual duel with Harris. "Before the game," said Notre Dame running back Mark Green, "they were talking about how their offense was unstoppable. It was kind of the other way around." The Irish won 34–21, and it wasn't even that close. Harris injured his shoulder very early in the game and was ineffective much of the night as he tried to tough it out. Notre Dame led 16–0 before the Mountaineers even registered a first down. By halftime it was 23–6. "As long as I live," Holtz said, "I'll always remember this team."

With victories over Miami, Michigan, USC, and West Virginia, Notre

Dame became the first team since 1945 in college football to beat four teams in the final Top 10 on the way to a national championship. By completing their undefeated season in Tempe at the Fiesta Bowl, the Irish did their part to lay a foundation for an altered future in college football. The Fiesta Bowl, with no conference tie-ins, had for the second time in three seasons played host to the national championship game, the first being Penn State's epic victory over the Hurricanes. Now that Sun Devil Stadium had been the scene of the final step of Notre Dame's climb from the depths of Faust's final game, its status as a major destination on New Year's Day was cemented; it would be made official a few years later, when the new Bowl Championship Series selected the game in its rotation of major sites over the Cotton Bowl, despite the latter's longer, more storied history.

In the bigger picture for Notre Dame, the national championship ensured that the Irish would leave their stamp on yet another decade of college football, one that had been threatening to get away from them just three years before. The Hurricanes still held the mantle of "Team of the '80s," but Holtz's squad would surely enter the next season ranked No. 1, with a clear path ahead of it until the much-anticipated season finale at the Orange Bowl.

In the meantime, things were about to change drastically in Coral Gables.

CHAPTER 12

End of an Era

As stirring as the victory was, as essential to the trajectory of Lou Holtz's program—indeed, the trajectory of all of college football—as "Irish 31, Hurricanes 30" had been, that result alone had not made Notre Dame a team in complete charge of its own destiny.

On the university's campus, atop all-male, eleven-story Grace Hall dormitory, was perched an eight-foot-tall sign that read: *No. 1.* Whenever an Irish athletic team ascended to the top of the national rankings in its sport, the sign was illuminated. On the night of October 15, 1988, the roof of Grace Hall remained shrouded in blackness, as there remained one team ahead of Notre Dame in both major polls: UCLA. And the Bruins seemed like they wanted to stay there.

On the day Notre Dame beat Miami, UCLA defeated Cal in Pac-10 play. The following week the Bruins trounced Arizona 24–3 to keep the Irish at No. 2. Next up for coach Terry Donahue's team was Washington State.

Usually irrelevant in the Pac-10 race for the Rose Bowl and coasting along in late October with four victories against three defeats, the Cougars seemed like no real threat to UCLA's reign at the top of the polls. Behind quarterback Timm Rosenbach, Washington State's offense was dangerous. But its defense was one of the nation's worst. In the second half, UCLA built a 21-point advantage and seemed poised to cruise home against the Cougars, who had lost twenty consecutive games in Los Angeles against UCLA and USC. Then, inexplicably, the momentum began to swing. "When we got down that far," Rosenbach says, "we just kind of saw red and decided to go after it."

Trailing just 30–27 in the fourth quarter, the Cougars ran thirteen consecutive running plays on their go-ahead drive, despite having a

talented quarterback behind center. They went ahead 34–30 on a one-
yard run by sophomore running back Rich Swinton, who was playing
only because the leading rusher in the conference, Steve Broussard, was
injured.

Behind All-American quarterback Troy Aikman, the Bruins drove to
the Washington State six-yard line with forty-four seconds remaining,
and it appeared they would survive the scare. But, unbelievably, Aikman
fired four consecutive incompletions. Game over.

"Call it the luck of Notre Dame's Irish," wrote *LA Times* columnist
Mike Downey, "because guess who's No. 1 now?"

As predicted, when the polls came out a couple days later, Grace
Hall's roof was bathed in light and would remain so for the next few
glorious months. Thanks to the also-rans from Pullman, Notre Dame's
season had changed—permanently, it would turn out.

So, too, had the career of Washington State's young and rising head
coach, Dennis Erickson.

———

Later, when the smoke cleared and the narrative became too oft-told to
allow for variances, Jimmy Johnson would feel that the shared history
between him and Texas oil tycoon Jerry Jones, his "college roommate,"
had been vastly overstated.

As teammates at the University of Arkansas in the late 1960s, the
two offensive linemen had been paired by coach Frank Broyles for
room assignments thanks solely to the alphabetical similarity of their
last names. Johnson and Jones weren't roommates in the traditional
sense, as in sharing the tight space of a dormitory room. Both married
during college and kept off-campus apartments. But Broyles felt that
teams should isolate themselves from the world on the eve of battle,
and so his Razorbacks stayed together at one hotel, with teammates
paired off in rooms. This was true even when Arkansas was playing at
home.

"How well do you get to know a guy on a few Friday nights in the
Holiday Inns of Waco or Fort Worth or Austin?" Johnson would later
write. "Maybe you lie there on your beds talking about the opponents

for a few minutes, or bitch a little about how hard practice has gone all week, but that's about it. Lights out."

Maybe Johnson and Jones weren't as tight-knit as the world would soon come to believe, but neither were they exactly strangers. After college, when Johnson began pursuing a coaching career, Jones went into business—first life insurance, then gas and oil exploration—and steadily amassed a fortune. Jones's business endeavors in the Southwest put him in contact with some of the biggest movers and shakers of the college booster universe, and Jones actually helped broker Johnson's initial contact with the Oklahoma State athletic department in the early 1980s. On occasion, Johnson said, the pair would make flippant conversation about someday teaming up and running an NFL franchise together. But Jones was no wild dreamer. Less than two years out of Arkansas, he had made a serious bid to purchase controlling interest in the San Diego Chargers. At age twenty-four, he backed away on the advice of his father, but a seed had been planted.

In August of 1988, Jones gave Johnson a call to tell him he was thinking about making a bid to buy the Dallas Cowboys.

"I'm only interested in buying them if you're interested in coaching them," Jones said.

"I'm interested," Johnson replied.

On the evening of February 24, 1989, *Dallas Morning News* sportswriter Ivan Maisel, who covered the college beat at the newspaper, had been pressed into Cowboys duty. Rumors were flying that Jones was about to purchase the team and perhaps even dismiss iconic head coach Tom Landry. Gossip that juicy had set off a full-scale sprint for the story among Dallas–Fort Worth news agencies. After staking out a hotel for several hours, Maisel was finally granted permission by his editors to call it an evening. Along with his girlfriend, he headed to a Mexican restaurant called Mia's. Within minutes, in one of the great instances in the history of sports of a reporter falling into a major scoop, in walked Jerry Jones and Jimmy Johnson.

"Mia's turned out to be a nice, small place," Johnson said. "But it was very crowded. And little did we know that it was one of Tom Landry's favorite restaurants. At least Landry wasn't there that night. He was the only element missing from a complete fiasco."

Maisel called on a photographer, who snapped shots of the two new faces of the Dallas Cowboys dining together. The next morning, the *Morning News* carried the photo, along with a news story by Bernie Miklasz that had been aided by Maisel's serendipity. Jones was buying the team from H. R. "Bum" Bright for $130 million. And he wasn't arriving alone.

"By all indications," the story read, "the purchase, which could become official Saturday, would abruptly terminate the twenty-nine-year regime of Tom Landry, the only head coach in the Cowboys' history. Jones, according to several sources close to him, plans to replace Landry with University of Miami coach Jimmy Johnson."

Most football fans know the rest of the story. Johnson's hiring by his "college roommate" was widely lampooned in the Dallas media, largely owing to what people felt was an unceremonious, undignified, and almost completely avoidable end to the coaching career of the legendary Landry. But Johnson didn't fail. A guy whose lack of NFL experience frightened a lot of onlookers, he fleeced one veteran general manager after another in stocking his roster. By the time he left "Big D," Johnson had transformed the Cowboys from NFL laughingstock to back-to-back Super Bowl champions. Today, Miami is seen as little more than a footnote on Johnson's journey to the place where his real legacy would be forged: the NFL.

"If Jimmy had stayed at Miami," says Dave Wannstedt, Johnson's defensive coordinator, "he could have won five national championships and he'd be in the Hall of Fame. He knew that and he chose to keep moving on. That's what drove him, new challenges."

As obvious as the move had been for him, however, and as successful as he would end up being in the NFL, at the time Johnson also realized that he would be leaving a lot behind. Said Rich Dalrymple, Miami's sports information director during the Johnson years: "The day he left Miami for the Dallas Cowboys was the only time I saw him cry."

After the news broke, Johnson hustled back to Miami to meet with his players. He avoided the press for a few days, choosing instead to make his public reemergence at his upcoming introductory press conference in Dallas.

Johnson's final speech to the Hurricanes he was leaving behind was short and emotional.

"You know the job you have to do," he said. "Players win championships, not coaches."

Johnson began to walk out of the room, then turned back briefly.

"And one more thing," he said. "You get after Notre Dame's tail."

———

Johnson's exit left a void in college football. Howard Schnellenberger had built Miami into an unlikely modern power, but it was Johnson who had transformed the Hurricanes from a likable underdog into the most polarizing brand in college football and perhaps all of sports during the 1980s. It was Johnson who had encouraged his players to express their personalities, managing the difficult task of balancing individuality with the team concept. This was new to college football. The previous generation of great coaches, men like Bear Bryant and Woody Hayes, preached an obsessive sublimation of personal expression for the sake of the team. Johnson was one of the first children of the 1960s to rise in the coaching ranks. While General Patton disciple Hayes, for example, abhorred the sixties counterculture movement with every fiber of his being, Johnson grew up alongside it: Janis Joplin had been in his high school history class. And although Johnson was no hippie, some of the lessons of the era had definitely taken. Johnson's predecessors in coaching had watched great athletes like Ted Williams march off to war; Johnson had watched Muhammad Ali refuse to go. Jimmy Johnson had changed college football, and college football, it seemed, would be a less interesting sport without him involved.

And what was true for the sport as a whole certainly seemed to be true of the best rivalry going, the one between the Hurricanes and Notre Dame. By piling on the points against the Irish in Faust's final game, Johnson had awakened something in the Notre Dame players right at a time when somebody who could do something about it was waiting in the wings. It had not happened overnight, but by the time of Notre Dame's 1988 victory, a series that had been one-sided for much of its history now promised a new era of competitive contests and genuine animosity. Holtz had been the drill sergeant who brought the Notre Dame program back up to speed, but Johnson had been the director of the rivalry's great drama: His personality and philosophy had made the series into such compelling theater. And now, just like that, he had left for greener pastures. The 1989 rematch, which would have been the most anticipated game on the coming year's schedule, was still many months away. Could the rivalry survive a coaching change?

―――――

Before he became Miami's athletic director in 1983, Sam Jankovich spent several years in the same job at Washington State. He had, however, missed the arrival in Pullman of head coach Dennis Erickson by a few seasons: Erickson had become the Cougars' head coach before the 1987 season, more than four years after Jankovich's exit.

At the same time, Jankovich still had plenty of ties to his old school. And although he was working clear across the continent by the spring of 1989, he was well aware of the football program's recent renaissance under Erickson. During Jankovich's own tenure at Washington State, the Cougars qualified for a postseason bowl just once, losing to BYU in the Holiday Bowl after the 1981 season. So when Jankovich settled into a seat for the 1988 Aloha Bowl, played on Christmas Day, he was well aware of how far youthful Cougars coach Erickson had brought the program. The 24–22 victory over the University of Houston was the school's first in a bowl game since 1916. What's more, it gave "Wazzu" nine victories in a season for the first time since 1931. The Holiday Bowl was merely a side excursion for Jankovich during a trip to see the Miami basketball team play in Hawaii. But less than two months later, it was clear that the performance of Erickson's team had left an impression. So much so, in fact, that when Johnson officially proffered his resignation as Miami's football coach on the morning of Sunday, February 26, Erickson was one of the first people the Miami athletic director called, at around 3:30 p.m. Miami local time.

"Are you interested?" Jankovich asked Erickson point-blank.

"No," Erickson said. "I just couldn't leave Washington State at this time."

Erickson had become a head coach at just thirty-four years of age, taking over an Idaho program in 1982 that had lost seven of its final eight games the year before. The turnaround under Erickson, a passing game innovator, was immediate. The Vandals, then playing at the

NCAA I-AA level, won nine games in his first season. In his final year, 1985, Erickson's team won the Big Sky Conference and qualified for the second time under him for the I-AA playoffs. After that season he made the leap to Division I-A, taking his innovative spread offense to the University of Wyoming.

In that first year in Laramie, Erickson improved the Cowboys from 3–8 to 6–6. That was good news and bad news for Cowboys fans, who had recently been jilted in short order by up-and-coming coaches like Pat Dye and Fred Akers. And in that tradition, it didn't take long for Erickson's name to begin circulating in the coaching rumor mill for major conference openings. When Wisconsin began the search for a permanent replacement for Dave McClain, who had died of a heart attack before the 1987 season, Erickson was among the people interviewed. When he took his name out of the running, Erickson was greeted with a thunderous standing ovation at halftime of the next Wyoming basketball game.

Less than two weeks later, he was gone.

Eleven days after Wyoming fans rattled the foundation of their campus basketball arena in his honor, Erickson was offered the Washington State job while he was in California at a coaches' convention. He didn't return to Wyoming to break the news or even to pack up his belongings. Instead, he left it to his wife, Marilyn, to handle the logistics of relocating. After his departure became public news, a rock was thrown through the window of his home, and people called in death threats.

"They'll be packing them in with can openers and checking shotguns at the door," Erickson's successor at Wyoming, Paul Roach, later joked about an impending visit to Laramie from Erickson and the Cougars.

Not that Erickson condoned threats of violence, but he certainly understood the fan base's anger.

"I was a young idiot," Erickson would say less than two years later. "I didn't do it right."

And so, in late February 1989, when one of the nation's top two programs came calling, Erickson's initial impulse was to turn the overture down. At least for the moment, he didn't think he could put himself, his family, or Washington State's fans through the same kind of hell that had followed his exit from Wyoming just two winters earlier. As news began to leak of Erickson's increasing interest in Coral Gables, however, angst began to grow in the Pacific Northwest.

"Who is this guy?" wrote *Seattle Times* columnist Steve Kelley. "Is he going to become the Larry Brown of college football? He leaves after one year at Wyoming without saying goodbye to his players. He flies to Miami after declaring, 'I am not interested in that job.' The fact is, Dennis Erickson owes Washington State more than two fleeting seasons."

In the end, after plenty of soul-searching, Erickson didn't agree. He took the job.

"You're talking about one of the greatest programs in college football at that time," Erickson says today. "How many opportunities do you have like that in your career? When it was all said and done, I felt like I had a chance to compete for a national championship, which I wasn't going to be able to do at Washington State at that time. For me, it was an upgrade in what I was doing for a living."

———

Erickson grew up in the state of Washington, the son of longtime high school football coach Robert "Pinky" Erickson. A high school quarterback, Erickson didn't play for his father but for a rival high school.

After playing at Montana State, Erickson began climbing the coaching ranks and was eventually hired as the offensive coordinator at Fresno State under his old college coach, Jim Sweeney. Sweeney was less than impressed by his new assistant.

"Dennis, the reason I hired you was that you were the greatest competitor as a player I've ever known," Sweeney told Erickson. "But as a coach, you're a zero."

"He was permissive," Sweeney would later recall. "He would accept shoddy performances. I said, 'You've got to quit running a popularity contest.'"

Sweeney claimed that Erickson shaped up after that, but old habits die hard, and it didn't take long for that reputation to trail him to Miami.

Washington State's academic performance the previous fall had been, quite simply, shameful. While the all-sports grade point average on the Pullman campus was 2.63, Erickson's Cougars carried a 1.94 in the fall. Five of Erickson's former players were ineligible to participate in spring practice because of low grades the previous semester.

"Some people like to study," offensive lineman Mike Utley explained. "I don't. I never enjoyed school here. I would never have come to college if it wasn't for football. If it wasn't for football, I'd be out working construction right now. Once we saw how good we were, going to class didn't seem so important."

Certainly, nearly every college football team—even studious Notre Dame—has a few Mike Utleys on its roster, players more than willing to use the system to their advantage. But even the diligent students in the Washington State program were giving academics short shrift after experiencing a taste of football success. For example, running back Rich Swinton, the unlikely star of the upset over UCLA, had been a National Merit Scholar in high school who had considered going to Harvard. But because of grade issues he would watch spring practice from the sidelines.

"I don't think it had anything to do with the coaching staff," says Steve Broussard, one of the men ruled ineligible. "Everything was in place, the academic support and so forth. It was more on the individuals taking it upon themselves to get lackadaisical in the classroom."

Regardless, the Washington State situation raised eyebrows in Coral Gables. Whenever Miami was accused of being a haven for miscreants who spent more time in lockup than in English 101, Johnson had a ready retort: his program's graduation rate. Maybe some of the Hurricanes got in a little trouble from time to time. Maybe a few of them were too eager to take advantage of what "Suntan U" had to offer. But boys will be boys, and what Johnson said was true. His program's graduation rate, always hovering around 80 percent, was among the best in the country. Under fire for bringing in borderline students so long as they could run, jump, or tackle, Johnson had even placed a moratorium on accepting Prop 48 players. Within a month of accepting Johnson's old job, Erickson said he would consider reversing that policy. "I like the core curriculum requirement, but I'm not in favor of the test," Erickson said. "My feeling is if you believe a young man has a chance to succeed, you've got to take a look at him." Sound logic or not, it only added to the new coach's image as someone who put *X*s and *O*s way ahead of *A*s and *B*s.

"Yeah, I know that whole rap," says Rosenbach, Erickson's quarterback at Washington State. "The nature of the beast in college football is win games or you get fired. What do you want? Abide by the rules, do the things you're supposed to do on and off the field, get the best players you can, and win games. That's what people want. That's what universities expect of you when they hire you. If they want to win, it goes both ways. They can't all be Rhodes scholars."

The Washington State baggage was fodder for a large segment of the Miami community that had not wanted Erickson hired in the first place.

Gary Stevens had been Johnson's offensive coordinator and was beloved by both his players and the Miami community. The city's police and fire departments had both put out press releases encouraging Jankovich, a one-man search committee, to hire Stevens. Miami students hung banners from their dorm room windows in support of him. One of the results of the us-against-the-world culture that had been encouraged at Miami was the development of a real hostility toward outsiders. And Erickson was decidedly an outsider.

"He wasn't accepted right away," said Russell Maryland. "Our first team meeting, these guys from Washington State show up with these big tweed jackets. They looked like they had just got off a plane from the tundra. After having had Jimmy Johnson for three years, when Coach Erickson and his staff showed up, it was like, 'Who are these guys who are going to try and take over what we've established?'"

Jankovich said he had selected Erickson over Stevens for one simple reason, and that was head coaching experience. Erickson had it. Stevens didn't. However, plenty of people weren't buying the explanation, particularly once it was revealed that Erickson and Jankovich had known each other for two decades.

"Standard cronyism," says Shannon Crowell, a running back at Miami. "It was disheartening, because Gary Stevens was a phenomenal coach."

"All of us were Jimmy Johnson's recruits and we were loyal to Jimmy Johnson," says wide receiver Randal Hill, an eventual first-round NFL Draft pick. "Everybody wanted Gary Stevens as the head coach, and because everyone wanted Gary Stevens to be the head coach, Sam Jankovich went the other way. Just because."

Jankovich was frustrated by the cold reception that his new hire received.

"I'm not the one who left for the Cowboys, Jimmy Johnson did," he said. "I'm not the one who took five assistant coaches, Jimmy Johnson did. I have no animosity toward Jimmy. But here I am, the villain, because I'm just trying to do my job."

Erickson tried to lay off his players and figure out the lay of the land in his first few weeks. Unfortunately for him, it was viewed by some of his new players as that very permissiveness that had previously tainted Erickson's reputation.

"Practice wasn't as demanding, it wasn't as disciplined, it wasn't as structured," Crowell says. "The level of care for the players and their performance wasn't there. Of course, the level of care for the outcome was there, but you get out of something what you put into it, and there just wasn't the same kind of dedication, the same kind of experience— the same kind of intensity—as there was under the Johnson staff."

"Erickson was a good enough guy; he wasn't a bad guy," says Jason Budroni, a Hurricanes offensive lineman in the Erickson years. "All the guys who were there before me, though, they were always talking about Johnson: 'Under Coach Johnson, you wouldn't get away with this' or 'If Coach Johnson were here, you wouldn't be able to do this.' That was always the big thing. Not that they were against Erickson, but I don't think that they respected him the way that they respected Johnson."

Erickson's defense is that he didn't need to push the Hurricanes because, by 1989, hard work and on-field discipline was second nature to the holdovers in the program, who then passed on those qualities to the next generations.

"I learned how hard to practice from those players," he says. "It was important to them, and they really enjoyed playing the game, more so than at any other place.

"They were self-motivated," Erickson explains. "There was great leadership, peer pressure, whatever you want to call it. They all wanted to be the best, and if you weren't giving your best effort, you'd hear about it. I don't know that I ever had to say one thing about practicing hard or playing hard. I don't think I ever had to say that in six years."

When Dennis and Marilyn Erickson moved to Miami, they brought with them sons Bryce, fourteen, and Ryan, ten. The two Erickson boys wanted to know one thing: Would Steve Walsh be back as Miami's quarterback in 1989?

So did the Miami fan base. When Erickson was hired over Stevens, most people assumed that it also meant the end of Walsh's career as a Hurricane. He was on pace to finish his degree in finance in the spring and would be entering his fifth year at Miami. There were plenty of reasons to return, including the possibilities of a Heisman Trophy and a national championship. But after his stellar 1988 season, the QB appeared NFL-ready. If Walsh was going to learn a new offense at this stage of his development, he felt he ought to be drawing a paycheck to do so.

The offense that had been run at Miami under both Schnellenberger and Johnson had been extremely successful. It had, in many ways, altered the way college football was played. Quarterbacks Kelly, Testaverde, and Walsh had helped the game close the door on the stodgy 1970s, when coaches like Ohio State's Woody Hayes would have been hard-pressed to decide between walking over hot coals and putting the football in the air. But the main difference between the way Miami ran its offense and the way offense had been played in the college game before that had been the frequency of pass plays, not necessarily the plays themselves. The Hurricanes' setup was quite conventional, including two backs and a quarterback who dropped back deep to scan the field from a stationary position in the pocket.

What Erickson and offensive coordinator Bob Bratkowski did was completely different. They utilized just one running back in the vast majority of their formations, heresy to college football traditionalists. Quarterbacks were not treated as statues but instead frequently rolled out and asked to quickly hit short targets. The new Miami offense was much more similar to the modern-day spread offense (the foundation of the University of Florida's two national championships in the 2000s) than it was to anything that had been run before in college football. Many of the players were skeptical. "You could talk about it, you could say this is what we've done in the past," says Bratkowski. "None of that stuff really mattered to anybody until we started to get on the field and play the games and show how successful it could be."

At Washington State, Erickson's offense had ranked third in the nation in total offense, and Rosenbach had led the country in passing efficiency.

"It's kind of a nightmare to prepare for," said UCLA defensive coordinator Bob Field, whose team Erickson's had knocked from No. 1.

"It's not an offense you shut down," said Arizona State defensive coordinator Dennis Brown. "You let it run its course and hope for mistakes."

For years Miami had cultivated an image as an outlaw program shaking up college football. There was, then, perhaps no bigger sign that the Hurricanes were now firmly entrenched in the establishment than the fact that their quarterback was considering exiting because the new offense was just too unconventional for his taste.

At first, when Erickson was hired, Walsh seemed to be as good as gone. In early March, however, he surprised many onlookers by announcing that he would begin spring practice with the Hurricanes. He had until April 10 to enter the NFL's supplemental draft, held between the first and second rounds, and appeared ready to use every second of the time he had to make an informed decision.

Walsh practiced with the Hurricanes eight times in the spring, and he didn't look at all like the quarterback who had led the nation with twenty-nine touchdown passes the previous season. In two spring scrimmages he completed just twenty-one out of forty passes for 195 yards and one touchdown. Meanwhile, backup Craig Erickson (no relation to the coach) had thrown for 240 yards and had connected on three touchdown passes, and he had done it all in eleven fewer attempts. Whether it was indeed the case or simply a function of his heart not being in it any longer, just a few months removed from a top-five finish in the Heisman Trophy voting, Walsh looked like the lesser fit in the new Miami offense.

In early April, Walsh, the likely Heisman Trophy front-runner at the most famous quarterback factory in America, opted out of his fifth year of eligibility and instead entered the NFL supplemental draft.

"All of my college goals have been accomplished," he explained.

Walsh's exit only added to the consternation about the outside coaching hire. In early April he wrote a letter to the editor, published in the *Miami Herald*, thanking the South Florida fans and media for their support during his Hurricane career and casting a vote of confidence for Erickson's new system.

"That style of offense had no bearing, whatsoever, on my decision to enter the professional ranks," Walsh wrote. "I want our fans to understand this."

The quarterback wasn't being honest: Erickson's new system *was* the reason he had decided to leave Coral Gables.

"There were a couple times when I said, 'Hey, can we do *this*?'" Walsh says. "Dennis was kind of reluctant to make a lot of changes in his system. I don't blame him, because it was his offense, but I just didn't feel welcomed to really give a lot of my input."

Walsh especially didn't like how streamlined the decision making seemed to be for the quarterback. In Stevens's offense, Walsh had been given three or four progression-read options on every snap. Under Erickson, with the system's trademark quick decision making and release, he would be limited to one or two. He thought it would stifle his growth as a quarterback. The thought was not unfounded. As the spread would become more popular in college football in the years to come, NFL scouts would scratch their heads when attempting to project a player's performance at the next level.

"I knew our defense was going to be great; I knew we had talent on offense," Walsh says. "I just didn't feel like it was going to be an enjoyable season for me."

Although they didn't follow their leader out the door, Walsh's skepticism was shared by his teammates on offense.

"Our offense [under Johnson and Stevens] was a professional offense," says wide receiver Randal Hill. "It could fit into any professional team. What Coach Erickson brought in was a damned good college offense. Yeah, it put up a lot of numbers. Yeah, it did well, and he's been very successful in the collegiate ranks. But what we had before then was a very successful professional offense."

New quarterback Craig Erickson's pedigree was promising. Because the Hurricanes had been so far ahead in games the previous two years, Erickson had seen plenty of action, throwing for nearly seven hundred yards and eight touchdowns to just two interceptions his freshman and sophomore seasons. In the first game of the 1989 season, at Wisconsin, Erickson threw four touchdown passes and the Hurricanes rolled 51–3. They continued to dominate through most of September, blowing out the Badgers, Cal, and Missouri to validate the No. 2 ranking that placed them behind only Notre Dame.

In the fourth game of the season, however, a 26–20 victory over Michigan State, Erickson broke a knuckle on his throwing hand. The brother of former Vinny Testaverde backup Geoff Torretta, redshirt freshman Gino Torretta, was thrown into the fire that afternoon and performed as well as could be expected, completing about half of his passes and helping the Hurricanes avert disaster.

Torretta's first start came the next week against Cincinnati, and it helped ease any doubts about the direction of the Miami offense without its starting quarterback. By halftime Torretta had thrown for 239 yards and three touchdowns. The Hurricanes won 56–0. For an encore, he threw for 468 yards the next game, a 48–16 dismantling of San Jose State.

Dennis Erickson may have changed Miami's offense, but he hadn't changed everything about the way the 'Canes played the game. After the game, San Jose State's Claude Gilbert fumed about Miami's taunting.

"It takes away from their greatness, that style," Gilbert said. "Some of our personal fouls were in retaliation, and I don't like that. But under the circumstances, to hell with it. I'm glad our guys fought them all the way."

"That was the nature of how we played," Erickson says. "It wasn't degrading anybody. That's what everybody said, but that wasn't what it was. They enjoyed playing. At times we went overboard, no question about it, but they just enjoyed playing."

With the way the offense was clicking, it seemed as if the Hurricanes wouldn't miss a beat during Craig Erickson's absence. On October 29 they traveled upstate to Tallahassee to face Florida State in the biggest college football game of the season to that point. And on that afternoon it all finally caught up to them. Torretta, a future Heisman Trophy winner, finally revealed what he actually was at that stage of his development: an overmatched first-year player. He threw four interceptions and Miami turned the ball over on five consecutive possessions, falling 24–10 with just four more regular-season games remaining.

After the way Jimmy Johnson's teams had manhandled the Seminoles in the previous few seasons, it was not a good loss for his replacement—a man that many Miami backers hadn't wanted hired in the first place—to absorb so early in his tenure.

"It wasn't pleasant after that game," Dennis Erickson says. "[But] I just coached. I didn't think about it like that. It wasn't like it is now. There weren't chat boards. There wasn't the Internet. I can't imagine what it would have been like now with all that crap, but it wasn't like that then. You didn't even think about it. You'd read the newspaper. They'd get on you a little bit, and then you just got ready to play the next game."

As they had the year before after losing to Notre Dame, the Hurricanes, with Craig Erickson recovered from his hand injury and back behind center, managed to plow through the distractions and entered the final week of the season ranked seventh in the nation, that loss to Florida State their only blemish. "The thing about that program, at that time, is there were a lot of guys who were mentally very tough and very strong," says Rob Chudzinski. "People talk about the talent that was at Miami at that time, and that was definitely the case. But you can't just win on talent alone. I think the mental toughness of those teams was really underrated at that time. We kept it together because that's what we do. There was no other choice."

A national championship was still a long shot, but Miami could begin to make its case when No. 1 came to town. All year long, the Hurricanes had kept one eye on the challenge immediately in front of them—and one eye on Notre Dame.

"We want Notre Dame to stay on top," defensive end Willis Peguese said. "We don't want anyone to knock them off but us. We want them to come down here ranked No. 1 with us No. 2 so it will be the biggest game of the season. In our hearts, we believe we are the best."

CHAPTER 13

Third and Forty-three

Why did a certain segment of the population, including a large percentage of men wearing orange and green in the mid- to late 1980s, have a visceral reaction of disgust when Notre Dame was the topic? This, from the pen of *Inside Sports* magazine's Brad Buchholz, may help to illustrate:

> College football *needs* Notre Dame, and the Irish have resurfaced just in time. In an era when the concepts of athletic excellence and academic integrity fit together like White Snake and Bing Crosby, there is no better time for major college football's most famous symbol of athletic integrity to be on top of the football polls.... Who knows? Perhaps Notre Dame's football resurgence will bring the academic ideal back into style. Perhaps integrity will be the game's next popular fad, like four-receiver sets or steroids.

In the early fall of 1989, the defending national champion Irish began the season at the top of both major wire service polls—which ensured a heavy dose of hyperbole so long as they could stay there—and fanned the flames of the burn in their rival camp down in Coral Gables. And Notre Dame, perhaps having outgrown the costume of the plucky underdog, was suddenly feeling the heat of being the hunted.

"I think there was a point in our senior year where, instead of being excited about wins, we just took a deep breath and said, 'Okay, we got that one, let's just move on to the next one,'" says Notre Dame offensive lineman Tim Grunhard. "I remember looking at the scoreboard in the middle of the third quarter and we'd be up, and I'd just be wishing it was the fourth quarter. It was just too much."

Meanwhile, the image of Notre Dame extolled by the preseason *Inside Sports* article was quickly fading. Before the rivalry game against USC, the Irish again brawled with an opponent while holding their ground near the stadium exit tunnel. Again, tough-guy upperclassman linebacker Ned Bolcar was in the middle of it.

"They came toward their locker room singing our fight song, mocking us," Zorich says. "Ned Bolcar said, 'Fuck them. They don't deserve to sing our fight song.'"

In its account of the USC game, *Sports Illustrated* wrote that the Irish under Lou Holtz were developing "a reputation for intimidation and hooliganism that used to be the hallmark of schools that most Notre Dame alumni regard with unabashed contempt." The writer cited, not just the Miami brawl and the recent one against the Trojans, but an early 1989 tussle with Michigan as well. The Irish, still on their Faust-era revenge tour, had brawled with each of their three major rivals in a one-year span. They had also—channeling Miami's Hurricanes, in a manner of speaking—somewhat marred their national title victory against West Virginia the year before with several late unsportsmanlike conduct penalties.

"*Sports Illustrated* said, 'This is the new Notre Dame, with thugs now fightin' everybody,'" says Zorich. "We had guys from Florida, guys from some really rough areas, who were coming in now and, yes, you still had some guys wearing coats and ties who were on the team. But then you've also got the guys who today would be wearing baggy pants with their hats turned the other way.

"I don't want to say we were thugs. We didn't have people walking around and beating people up on campus, but we were a different crowd than what people were used to."

———

Most coverage of Rice in the media as the season progressed conformed to a fairly narrow narrative: The senior QB had been the recipient of a lot of criticism, mostly related to his questionable passing skills, but he had proven all his critics wrong. The details, as documented through three seasons of accumulated statistics, mattered less than the fact that he was a *winner*.

In reality, overt criticism of Rice rarely came from the press but rather from fan letters published in places like fan magazine *Blue & Gold Illustrated* or the campus newspaper, the *Observer*. And, of course, from his coach. Throughout Rice's time in South Bend, Holtz had probably gotten in more public digs at his quarterback than the entire media combined. "I don't know if he'll ever be good enough to play on Sunday," Holtz had said as recently as late August of Rice's senior season. Further assessment came from others within the Notre Dame family. "I really wish that Tony would pass better," said John Lujack, Notre Dame's 1947 Heisman-winning quarterback. "I think the race is up for grabs, but it probably wouldn't be if Tony could just complete fifty percent of his passes."

By November, straw polls for the Heisman race were popping up. An ESPN fan call-in poll had West Virginia's Harris drawing 39 percent of the vote, with Rice languishing far behind in a tie for fourth with Indiana running back Anthony Thompson at 7 percent. That wasn't much of a fair fight, with Harris's Mountaineers appearing in prime time on the network that evening, but it was still a sign of how public opinion was shaping up.

Despite the pressure of defending a national championship, and a No. 1 ranking from the get-go, the Irish kept on winning in 1989. Notre Dame had won twenty-three consecutive games, and the Hurricanes, fully recovered from the earlier loss to Florida State, had revenge on their minds.

"Any year you don't play for a national championship at the University of Miami is a losing year," offensive tackle Mike Sullivan said. "Maybe we're a victim of our own success, but if we lose to Notre Dame, we'll be 9–2 in the regular season and that feels like failure. That kind of thing just doesn't happen around here."

A crowd of 81,634 filled the Orange Bowl, the largest in the fifty-plus-year history of the venue. Sellouts were no sure thing in Coral Gables—the week before, the building was only half full, with about forty-two thousand attending a dismantling of San Diego State—but there was no question of packing the seats for the No. 1–ranked Irish. Fans gathered inside the stadium well before kickoff and gained energy as the teams went through warm-ups, then headed to their locker rooms for final preparations.

"The OB was already up in age then," says Randy Bethel, a tight end on the '89 team. "You'd get in that locker room, and it almost sounded like the dadgum stadium was about to come down. I don't know if it was just that magnified, but it was crazy, man. It was deafening some-times to hear the intensity outside. Now, if you're a visitor and you hear that, and then you combine it with the fact that it's nighttime, it just went to another level then."

To accommodate the large crowd, Miami added 3,400 bleacher seats in one of the end zones, selling those out. The school also squeezed in individual seats on the ground around the perimeter of the stadium, behind the two teams. The result was an audience that was larger than any that had ever jammed the Orange Bowl to watch the NFL's Miami Dolphins play—larger even than the crowd that attended the 1976 Super Bowl between the Pittsburgh Steelers and Dallas Cowboys. And in a crowd that large, that frenzied, and that well-oiled after hours of draining beers in the parking lot—the game was being played in prime time to accommodate a huge television viewing audience—there was bound to be a handful of bad apples. Irish offensive lineman Justin Hall's family members, who flew to the game from Texas, were spit on as they tried to take their seats, and they were hardly the only Notre Dame supporters treated to that sort of greeting.

"That was the most vile, vicious venue for a college football game that I've ever been in," says Tim Prister, who covered the game for *Blue & Gold Illustrated*. "They weren't there for Miami. They weren't there just to see Miami win. They wanted blood from Notre Dame. There was a nastiness—I would even call it an evilness—in the crowd that night. You could cut it with a knife. You could feel it that night in the Orange Bowl."

So could the players.

The year before, the Irish had asserted themselves in the tunnel brawl before the game, the players shedding their reputation as meek Mass-goers and reviving the brawling, blue-collar Notre Dame of old. Given more than a year to deal with being punked on the road, first in pregame and then on the field, the Hurricanes were the ones motivated to reassert their manhood at the Orange Bowl.

"They came across our lines to start fighting us," Zorich says. "So we started to fight back, and Holtz literally jumped in the middle and said, 'No, no, we're not gonna do this, we're not gonna do this.'"

Holtz continued to admonish his team in the locker room. In South Bend the season before, the Notre Dame locker room had erupted in mayhem, with Holtz himself fueling the testosterone with a pregame speech for the ages. This time he explained that his players had to back off challenges like the one the Hurricanes had thrown down, and that the university's administration was bearing down on him about such incidents.

"He literally took the air out of everybody in that locker room," Zorich says. "The exact opposite of the year before. I'm not trying to say I was better than anybody else, but I was thinking, *Fuck that. This is a battle.* So I played my ass off, but one person can't win a game. He took all the gas out of us. They come out of the locker room pumped, hyped, ready to go. We're flat. We're playing afraid."

The eighty-one-thousand-plus reached an early crescendo as the ball was placed on the tee for Hurricanes kicker Carlos Huerta, and he responded by booting the ball well into the end zone. Irish game breaker Ismail harmlessly took a knee.

Rice took the first snap of the game and headed upfield through an extra-wide hole that coach Joe Moore's Notre Dame offensive line had blown into the stout Miami defensive front. By the time Rice was finally brought down, he had gained twelve yards and silenced the Orange Bowl crowd.

They wouldn't stay quiet for long.

The second play was a handoff to Ricky Watters. After his year in exile at receiver, Watters had started at tailback all season for the Irish. Although Notre Dame, with so many men sharing carries, didn't run the kind of offense that lent itself to monster seasons out of its running backs, Watters had been a force late in the season. He had run for 134 yards on just nine carries against Navy, then torched Penn State for 128 yards two weeks later. As they had in the previous play, Notre Dame's linemen blew open a hole on the left side of the Miami defense, and Watters headed that way. But Anthony Johnson, Notre Dame's fullback, darted into the space ahead of Watters with the job of knocking Miami middle linebacker Bernard "Tiger" Clark off his feet, or at the very least keeping him occupied long enough to let Watters past him. Instead, Clark swatted Johnson aside as if he were nothing more than a South Florida mosquito. Clark, who hadn't lost any of his balance while flicking Johnson away, plowed into Watters's legs as the tailback came following through, flipping him over and sending him headfirst into the turf. Watters went one way, the ball went another.

Officials ruled that the ground had caused the fumble—Notre Dame recovered anyway—but the tone was set. On the next play, a handoff to Ismail went nowhere. On third-and-eleven, Notre Dame attempted a play-action pass. Rice spotted Watters in the flat, but Clark was keeping pace with him. Forced to try to place the ball perfectly where Watters could make a play on it but the Miami linebacker Clark could not, Rice threw the ball into the ground a few yards out of his running back's reach. Which meant fourth down, which meant a Notre Dame punt, which meant pandemonium in the Orange Bowl.

Rice's incompletion ended Notre Dame's first offensive series with a whimper, but it was notable for what it indicated about his growth as a quarterback over his three years with the Irish. The Rice who took over for Terry Andrysiak in the middle of the 1987 season had been a raw talent with remarkable athletic ability, along with an iron will demonstrated by his season in Prop 48 exile. But his grasp of Holtz's offense was thin, and his field savvy almost nonexistent. In between flashes of brilliance in those early days, he did things like line up behind the guard instead of the center, or step out of bounds on fourth and everything. A lot of that was attributable to nerves, of course. Now, in the last regular-season game of the 1989 season, the lead author of Notre Dame's school record twenty-three-game winning streak was as calm, cool, and collected as they came.

Entering the Miami game, Rice was on the short list—along with Indiana's Anthony Thompson, Houston's Andre Ware, and West Virginia's Major Harris—of Heisman Trophy candidates. When he busted out for 141 yards on the ground against Penn State the week before the game at the Orange Bowl, he seized the race's momentum. The third-down incompletion wasn't the kind of play on which Heisman Trophies were won, but it certainly was the kind of play on which Heismans—and national championships—could be lost. By this game, his twenty-eighth start behind center at Notre Dame, Rice was very much a man aware of and at peace with his limitations as much as he was his strengths. Rice had worked hard on his accuracy over the years, and was much better at hitting his targets than he was when he arrived in South Bend, but trying to thread the needle with a Miami linebacker looming would probably not have been the prudent choice at that juncture of the game.

If only, for Notre Dame's sake, he could have shown that kind of patience all night.

Early in the second quarter, Miami led 10–0, and memories of the year before—not good ones—were about to be stirred for the Hurricanes and their faithful. On second-and-one from the Miami sixteen-yard line, Notre Dame running back Anthony Johnson found open field and headed toward the goal line. On his dive near the Hurricanes one, however, Miami defensive back Charles Pharms reached in and knocked the ball out of Johnson's grasp. The sequence was almost identical to the previous year's Cleveland Gary fumble, when officials had ruled a Notre Dame recovery. Superior replay angles at the Orange Bowl, however, showed this one to be even more definitive than the blurry, distant images of the Gary play. Johnson had clearly fumbled, the ball coming out before either knee or elbow made contact with the ground. When officials ruled instead that he was down, the Orange Bowl erupted in boos. It was first-and-goal, Notre Dame ball at the one-yard line.

On first down, Johnson was stuffed at the line of scrimmage for no gain.

On second down, Hurricanes tackle Willis Peguese blew up Irish offensive lineman Dean Brown, punishing Rice four yards behind the line of scrimmage.

Tired of trying to win the line of scrimmage against the brick wall that was the Miami front four, Holtz instead sent in a pass play. Rice's throw to a well-covered Watters fluttered harmlessly to the ground. Needing to get some points on the board, Holtz sent in placekicker Billy Hackett, who drilled his twenty-two-yard attempt. Eighty-thousand-plus Miami fans, feeling robbed of a chance at a shutout, again serenaded the officiating crew with lusty boos.

As his quarterback had done earlier by not forcing a pass into coverage, Holtz showed patience by electing to take the easy field goal rather than let the emotion of the moment lead him into an ill-conceived decision on fourth down. But also like Rice, Holtz carried with him a limited amount of patience.

A year before, when the two programs clashed at Notre Dame Stadium, Holtz had drilled into his team that any time the Hurricanes went for it on fourth down or resorted to any sort of gimmickry, it represented an act of desperation. The result was that even when Miami succeeded in such situations, the Irish picked up confidence and energy. This time, however, Notre Dame was the team giving off a desperate vibe with its in-game decisions. In the middle of the second quarter, the Irish drove the ball into Miami territory. Down 10–3, Notre Dame faced a fourth-and-one. Holtz elected to keep his offense on the field. Rice kept the ball and charged into the center of the mass of humanity at the line of scrimmage. Almost immediately, Bernard Clark burst through and popped him, sending Rice stumbling backward. But the Notre Dame quarterback's superior lower body strength and balance allowed him to remain on his feet, and he fell forward for the first down.

It was a temporary victory for the Notre Dame offensive line, but if the Irish were going to spend the evening playing with fire, they almost certainly were going to get burned. Three plays after Rice's plunge, Notre Dame again faced fourth-and-short, this time at the Miami thirty-four. Anthony Johnson took a handoff and threw himself into the teeth of the Hurricanes defense. Officials untangled the bodies and spotted the ball, calling on the chain gang to come out and measure. The nose of the ball sat inches from a first down, and Miami's defenders sprinted off the field in triumph.

"They expected our quickness," Russell Maryland said. "But expecting our quickness and doing something about it are two different things."

Lest anyone had forgotten, however, Notre Dame's defense wasn't too shabby, either. "We weren't 'overachievers,'" says Terrell. "We were somewhat PO'd because other teams looked at us like that and they thought that." Even during the early portion of the broadcast, CBS analyst Pat Haden had questioned whether Notre Dame linebacker Ned Bolcar, a slow-rolling tank on a field full of cheetahs, would have any sort of impact. He received his answer late in the first half. On a third-and-five play, Craig Erickson spotted his tight end crossing the field beyond the first down sticks. He threw his way, but the pass was a little behind Chudzinski, and Bolcar read it all the way. He intercepted the ball around midfield, then hurdled Erickson on his way to the end zone. None of the Miami cheetahs came close to tracking down the Notre Dame linebacker, who was supposedly too slow to compete in this game. The game was tied 10–10, and on the ensuing Miami possession the energized Irish defense held the Hurricanes to three and out deep in 'Canes territory.

On first down following a Miami punt, with about a minute to play, Notre Dame running back Rodney Culver ripped off a nine-yard run to advance into Miami territory. The jolt of Bolcar's interception return had apparently affected the personnel on both sidelines. At best, Notre Dame would cram the ball right down the Hurricanes' throats and head to the locker room with a 17–10 or 13–10 lead, pulsating with confidence. At worst the Irish would run out of time and head to intermission, pleased to have survived Miami's strong start.

But then Tony Rice ran out of patience.

From opening warm-ups onward, Miami's Clark, along with many of his teammates, had mercilessly badgered Irish tight end Derek Brown. For all of Notre Dame's real or perceived advantages in recruiting, Brown was the kind of player who wasn't supposed to end up in South Bend, at least prior to the Cerrato-Holtz revolution. *Parade* magazine had named the six-foot-seven-inch, 235-pound specimen its national player of the year following his senior season at Florida's Merritt Island High School. Hardly any prognosticators of note ranked Brown anywhere below the third-best player in America that fall. He seemed to be a lock to attend Miami, and only reinforced that suspicion after his visit to Coral Gables. "He was sitting in our locker room," says Clark, "talking about how excited he was about coming to Miami the next year. Then he commits to Notre Dame. So when I saw him at the game—*whoo!* I was kind of hot with Derek. I was, like, 'Bro, you're in for a long night. I cannot believe you embarrassed us the way you did.'"

All night against the run-heavy Irish, Clark had wreaked havoc near the line of scrimmage, helping to make the stout front four even more imposing. But now, remembering a Rice pass to Brown for a first down earlier in the quarter, he quickly lobbied Miami linebackers coach Tommy Tuberville in between plays.

"Coach, I can jump it," Clark said. "Let me jump it. I'm telling you, I can jump the play. I can read it. I see what's going on."

"Okay," Tuberville relented. "Do it one time. If it doesn't work, we're going back to playing it the other way."

As Clark suspected, Brown began cutting across the field on a cross route, and Rice looked his way. Clark lingered a step behind, by no means out of Rice's line of vision. But this time, instead of placing the ball where only his receiver could catch it, the Irish quarterback hung the pass in the air a split second too long. He had tried to make a pass he wasn't capable of making, and he paid for it. Clark jumped the route, just as he had said he would.

By the time Brown finally dragged him down, Clark had advanced the interception inside the Notre Dame ten-yard line.

"Did I ever want the end zone," Clark says. "You don't know how bad. I still hear about the fact that I didn't make it to the end zone."

The Orange Bowl shook once again as Miami's fans came to life. But it wasn't so loud that the players on the Hurricanes offense couldn't hear Craig Erickson on the sideline, exhorting them to capitalize on this unexpected turn of events.

"This cannot be a field goal!" he screamed.

Two plays later, with less than thirty seconds to play in the first half, Stephen McGuire slashed right through the Notre Dame defense for a six-yard touchdown. Miami led 17–10.

———

As dominant as the Hurricanes defense was, the game would long be remembered for an improbable play converted by the Miami offense.

Unlike some of his Miami teammates, who scoffed at Notre Dame's claim to college football royalty, Craig Erickson was deeply respectful of the sport's midwestern roots. His father had played quarterback at Northwestern for Ara Parseghian before Parseghian left Evanston for Notre Dame. While southern powerhouses descended on West Palm Beach's Cardinal Newman High School to woo him to their program,

Erickson reached out to Northwestern. The program was in the middle of twenty-three consecutive losing seasons at that point, and Erickson was mystified when his father's alma mater did not return his interest.

"They sent me back a note to send them a game film, which I did, and they never called me back," Erickson says. "My dad said, 'Well, it's pretty cold up there anyway.'"

There were also some gravitational forces pulling the Catholic schoolboy toward Notre Dame. Erickson's Hall of Fame high school football coach, Sam Budnyk, had grown up in northern Indiana, near Chicago, and graduated from Notre Dame. The connection had helped the Irish land two Cardinal Newman standouts during the Gerry Faust years, kicker John Carney and running back Alonzo Jefferson, a major recruit whose career was derailed by a knee injury. For Erickson, however, Miami was too much of a logical fit to turn down. The program was contending for national championships while cranking out Heisman Trophy candidates behind center, not to mention that it was close to home.

However, there would be one hurdle on the path to Coral Gables. After one season at Purdue, near his home in Indianapolis, cannon-armed quarterback Jeff George announced he would transfer because of a coaching change. Initially, with three years of eligibility remaining, George selected Miami. "I've watched him warm up," says Erickson, "and I've never, to this day, seen anybody throw the football like him." The specter of competing with George for the job, however, was not enough to frighten Erickson away from his commitment. He was hooked after visiting the locker room a few days before the infamous 1987 Fiesta Bowl against Penn State.

"I met Vinny Testaverde, he's in bare feet and a pair of shorts, and he's like five inches taller than I am," Erickson says. "I've never seen a bigger quarterback in my entire life. I was kind of intimidated. And then next to him is Alonzo Highsmith, and it was like Charles Atlas carrying the football. I had never seen a bigger person in my entire life. And he was funny. I thought he wanted me to suit up and go practice with him.

"Then Jerome Brown was over there, carrying on. I looked at these guys and said, *Holy shit, if I don't play with them, I'm going to have to play against them, and I really don't want to play against these guys.*"

Notre Dame didn't have a monopoly on selling education as part of its total recruiting package, and as Erickson and then Hurricanes offensive coordinator Gary Stevens walked through campus, Stevens talked up the university's rising academic reputation. Jeff George be damned, Erickson was sold. He officially signed a few weeks later, and in the end it was the superstar George, not the relative unknown Erickson, who backed off because of the uncertainty of a starting position. *Steve Walsh is the starting quarterback,* Jimmy Johnson explained, but then Dennis Erickson brought his new offense and Walsh left for the NFL and suddenly Erickson was the starter. The broken knuckle that sidelined him midseason finally ended his streak of good fortune, but as the second half began against the Irish, Erickson was in position to guide his team past the No. 1 team in the country and back into the national title hunt.

For a few plays it appeared that Notre Dame was the team that had come out of the locker room reenergized despite the deflating end of the first half. Clinging to a 17–10 lead, the Hurricanes were backed up deep in their own territory, at the seven-yard line. Miami had been moving the ball steadily on its opening drive of the half, converting once on third down and again on a gutsy fourth-and-one run that saw McGuire barely push past the sticks. But then they had begun to self-destruct. An unsportsmanlike conduct penalty away from the ball backed up Miami immediately after McGuire's first down around the Miami forty-one. On the next play, a pair of Notre Dame defensive linemen, Bryan Flannery and Eric Jones, quickly penetrated the Hurricanes offensive line and chased Erickson down, jarring the ball loose and sending it bounding deeper and deeper into Miami territory.

The sight of the ball rolling down the field was a terrifying one for the Hurricanes, as was the sight of the man chasing after it: Notre Dame pass rush specialist Devon McDonald. The Jamaican-born McDonald was six feet three, 237 pounds of chiseled muscle, and moved like a speedy wide receiver. The only thing that slowed him down at Notre Dame was a nagging knee injury, but rumbling after the loose football, McDonald looked perfectly healthy. A game-changing play was clearly afoot. But then, as McDonald puts it in his thick Caribbean accent: "I made a boo-boo."

In 1989, defensive players were not allowed to advance a fumble, a rule that would be changed three years later. But in the heat of the moment, McDonald forgot that. With at least a step on everyone else chasing the ball, instead of falling on it and setting up the Irish deep in Hurricanes territory, he instead chose to try to scoop it up and run with it. But he lost his balance while reaching down, and the ball instead fell into the arms of Miami offensive lineman Bobby Garcia at the three.

Second down and forty-eight.

"Every yard they get adds another yard to the punt," said Haden in the CBS booth.

On second down, McGuire gained five yards, advancing the ball to the seven.

Third and forty-three.

"What do you call here?" CBS's Brent Musburger asked his partner, laughing out loud at the lunacy.

Musburger wasn't the only person who thought the situation was impossible to convert, and most teams would have been content just to give their punter some breathing room or call another low-risk run or a dump-off pass. After all, the Irish had already returned one interception for a touchdown, and a year before had forced the Hurricanes into seven turnovers.

But these Hurricanes weren't known to take the safe way out.

"That just wasn't our attitude at the time," Dennis Erickson says. "We probably had the fastest receiver in the country. Even if they were playing off, we thought we'd have a chance. If it was incomplete, we'd punt it."

For all of its cocky flourishes, Miami's go-for-broke offensive philosophy was possible because of a dedication to the kind of dominant defense that was a shared characteristic of many of the most celebrated dynasties in football's blue-collar lore.

"Football is usually all about protecting the ball and avoiding turnovers and this and that," Craig Erickson says. "But when I played it was, 'We're gonna throw the ball deep, we're gonna throw the ball short, we're gonna throw it all over the field. We're gonna throw on first down, second down, we're gonna throw it from the one-yard line,' because our defenses were so strong that it didn't matter."

According to receiver Randal Hill, the 'Canes coaching staff did send in a more conservative play call. But the offensive skill players and

QB Erickson had developed a series of discreet hand signals to use when they noticed a potential soft spot in the way the opposing defense had aligned.

That was exactly what happened. McDonald had made Notre Dame's first mistake by not simply falling on the Erickson fumble. Alvarez and the Irish defensive staff made the second one by sending in a base package of four defensive backs, a strange decision a year after the Irish had confused the daylights out of the Hurricanes with a bevy of five- and six-defensive-back formations. Hill, for what it is worth, says that Notre Dame's alignment would have had little impact on the offense's decision to go for broke on the down.

"Regardless of what play was called, we were gonna do what we had to do," says Hill. "If it was a run play, we were gonna throw it deep to me. If it was a screen, we were gonna throw it deep to me. A lot of times, coaches like to call something that they feel they can just get better field position from and then punt the ball away. In my opinion, that's setting yourself up for failure. The bottom line is, make it work. We changed a lot of plays. That was Coach Erickson's first year and I think he was a good coach, and I think he knows what he's talking about, but we also showed him what we were all about."

Erickson dropped back again, this time receiving perfect protection, and spotted Hill beating a double team by cornerback Stan Smagala and safety Pat Terrell. He heaved the ball as hard and as far as he could and somehow Hill came down with it. First down, Hurricanes.

"I didn't even know where the sticks were," Hill says. "My thing was to catch the ball and secure the ball. Now Craig, he was one of those individuals, he always knew where the sticks were. He threw the ball right past the sticks, and I happened to catch the ball on the other side of the sticks."

From a sheer showman's standpoint, Hill was glad the play ended up as it did, with the throw netting precisely enough yards to keep the drive going.

"I could have caught the ball and kept running," Hill says, "but that wouldn't have been as climactic, as opposed to me catching the ball right at forty-four yards. We'll go down and score, which is no big deal, which is what we did."

When Doug Flutie connected with Gerard Phalen for a Boston Col-

lege touchdown at the end of the 1984 season, Miami purchased an un-
desired place in college football lore. When Hill came down with Erickson's heave, the Hurricanes finally produced their own toss-and-catch
for the perpetual highlight reels.

"It gets longer and longer all the time," Dennis Erickson says. "It's
gone to fifty as the story gets better and older. That obviously was a
huge play. We just called a streak and he just ran by the guy. That
changed the whole momentum of the game."

It was first-and-ten, and Miami's march continued. Before it was
over, the drive that included the improbable completion to Hill would
eat up ten minutes and forty-seven seconds of the third-quarter clock
and span twenty-two plays. "I'd say, 'Okay, we've got to stop them on this
play,' and they'd get another first down," said Notre Dame's Smagala. "It
happened over and over, and each time it happened, it would take a little something out of you."

On seven of those plays, the Hurricanes converted a third or fourth
down. That included the final play of the drive, a bullet to Daryl
Dawkins in the back of the end zone, his second touchdown of the
night, to put Miami ahead 24–10. "Ultimately," Chudzinski says, "I
think us being able to score on that drive broke their will in that game."

"Notre Dame back then was a lower grade of the University of
Miami," Hill says. "Those were the little golden boys, [but] they never
had the killer instinct like the University of Miami did. They were never
going to beat us. We were like master Jedis. There's no way a Jedi Master is going to lose. We had the Force. We had the Force that night."

———

In the long history of college football, there might be no defensive line
better than the one that suited up for the University of Miami in 1989.
While Hurricane quarterbacks had received a lot of the attention
through the years, the defensive linemen had become the heart and
soul of the program. In the 1980s, Lester Williams, Jerome Brown,
Daniel Stubbs, and Bill Hawkins all earned All-American recognition.
The mouthy Brown, in particular, was considered a founder of the "U"
aesthetic and perhaps its ultimate embodiment. To the outside world,
that meant Miami's notorious swagger. To insiders, it meant long

hours in the weight room and lengthy afternoons sweating in the blazing South Florida sun.

Miami's defensive linemen didn't always arrive in Coral Gables as can't-miss prospects. But those who wanted it the most usually developed into All-Americans. Cortez Kennedy, a tackle on the '89 line, played his first two seasons at Northwest Mississippi Junior College.

"When I first got there from junior college, I'll never forget working out, lifting weights in the weight room and I see Alonzo Highsmith and Jerome Brown," Kennedy says. "I'm, like, 'Wow, I just saw them on TV.' The first thing Jerome Brown said was 'Where's that fat little kid that's supposed to be like me?' Then he came up and gave me a hug."

After he accepted the job, Dennis Erickson grilled Jimmy Johnson about the players he was leaving behind: what he could expect, what buttons he might have to push. "Cortez Kennedy's name didn't even come up," Erickson said.

"When I came to Miami, nobody knew who I was, and I would see all these All-American football players walking around and I'd say to myself, *I'm going to be known and be a big star just like them*," Kennedy said. "[But] I was too fat to be a great player."

After spending that first year, 1988, mostly watching from the Hurricanes sidelines, desperation pushed Kennedy to a higher gear in anticipation of his senior season. The Miami media guide predicted that Kennedy "should see plenty of action as a back-up defensive tackle." Instead, he unseated All-American candidate Jimmie Jones for his starting spot, his development fueled by endless hills run in the summer heat and humidity with other, equally dedicated Hurricanes, past and present. "I didn't know when I first got to Miami that the guys worked that hard," Kennedy says. "[Former 'Canes linebacker Randy] Shannon and the guys said, 'Never quit. You might walk it, but never quit. We don't believe in letting anybody quit.'" A few months after the season, Kennedy's name would be called as the third overall pick in the NFL Draft.

He was hardly alone on the Miami line, however. Down the road, Chicago native Russell Maryland would do his line mate Kennedy two better and become the first overall selection in the NFL Draft. Maryland was one that got away from Notre Dame during the 1986 transition from Faust to Holtz, a local kid who was an excellent student and would have put wide grins on the faces of the Notre Dame admissions people. Defensive end Willis Peguese was a Miami native who had bided his time behind graduated All-American Bill Hawkins. The other end, Greg Mark, entered the 1989 season with nineteen career sacks, and added fourteen and a half more for good measure in the season's first ten games. The Miami line had allowed just four rushing touchdowns all season, and three of them had come against Florida State. "They were having to double-team Russell and Cortez and leave one guy on Greg Mark and Willis Peguese," says Maurice Crum, a linebacker who benefited from the attention paid to the 'Canes' fearsome front. "It was just free rein a lot of time for the linebackers to just roam and make plays. It was swarm, swarm, swarm. Everybody to the ball."

Against the Irish, the Miami front faced its biggest challenge to date. Since his arrival in 1986, Holtz had given the program a toughness transfusion. Nowhere was that more evident than on the offensive line, coached by old-fashioned Joe Moore.

Moore and Holtz seemed destined to coach on the same staff. Both came from blue-collar backgrounds in the Pennsylvania-Ohio rust belt. Both stood about five foot ten, 160 pounds. Neither let their small stature come between them and knocking the snot out of somebody, whether that meant literally on a football field or figuratively, as in dressing down a player when a soft, nurturing hand no longer seemed to be an option.

Growing up in Pittsburgh, Moore had been exposed to sports by his father, John Lawrence "Dinty" Moore. Although Dinty Moore never coached on a high level, he did have one claim to fame: He had managed the great shortstop Honus Wagner on a semipro team after Wagner's Hall of Fame career with the Pittsburgh Pirates ended. Joe left Pennsylvania after high school on a football scholarship to the University of Tennessee, where he was a quarterback. But the culture shock was too great, and he left after a year to join the military. After two years in the service, he resurfaced on the Penn State campus as a running back. He would never again leave the game.

Moore spent seventeen seasons as a high school football coach in Pennsylvania until receiving his big break, an offer to join the staff at Pitt in time for the 1977 season. Jackie Sherrill, the Pitt head coach at the time, was looking for a Pennsylvania high school coach for his staff, for recruiting purposes. Moore's long track record of success made him a prime candidate, although the decision wasn't easy. Coaching at Upper St. Clair High School may not have made Joe and Fran Moore rich and would never have made Joe famous outside the insular circle of Pennsylvania high school football, but it provided a stable salary and the chance to throw down some roots. College coaches were notoriously transient, and that kind of lifestyle was much easier to face at age twenty-five than it was on the other side of forty. Despite the potential pitfalls, however, Moore decided to take the risk and join the staff at Pitt, where he would remain for nearly a decade, regularly churning out NFL stalwarts.

Moore was not on Lou Holtz's coaching staff during Holtz's first two seasons at Notre Dame. But after the 1987 season, the Notre Dame coach was searching for someone to coach tackles and tight ends, and Holtz placed a call to Sherrill, whose Texas A&M team had just flattened Holtz's Irish in the Cotton Bowl.

"He can coach offense, defense, the line—you name it," Sherrill said of his former assistant, who was by then coaching at Temple. "If you have a chance to hire him, do it."

The interview, a meeting between two headstrong coaches with exceedingly specific philosophies about how offensive line fundamentals should be taught, went as well as could be expected: They disagreed about how certain blocking techniques and schemes should be executed, Moore didn't back down, and Holtz went ahead and hired him anyway. However, Holtz did put forward a caveat: "If they don't work," Holtz said, referring to Moore's methods, "we'll change it to my way."

Moore's antiquated methods—for example, the Irish didn't use blocking sleds under his guidance, instead beating on each other all week—and his grizzled, lived-in appearance earned him the immediate respect of his players, some of whom towered over him by six inches or more and outweighed him by 150 pounds. "Joe Moore was willing to stand up and be accounted for," Holtz says.

"He looked like a mechanic, like a guy you want to change your spark plugs," Grunhard says. "He would smoke a pack of cigarettes during practice—menthol cigarettes—and suck on menthol cough drops. He always had fresh breath, but there was always smoke coming out of that mouth—in a lot of different ways."

"Joe Moore was an old-school coach who believed that football was a game of wills," says Notre Dame tight end Rod West. "His idea was: You give me a guy who is tough as nails and you give me a guy with suspect character and great skills, and my guy who is tough as nails will knock the living shit out of him every time."

At the Orange Bowl, however, the tough-as-nails Irish line wasn't beating the shit out of anyone. The Irish entered the game hoping to complete their first back-to-back undefeated national championship seasons since Knute Rockne roamed the sideline. They would leave with their first loss since the 1987 Cotton Bowl.

The Hurricanes tacked on a late field goal to make the final 27–10. The lasting image of the victory was the long third-down completion to Hill, but the real star was the Hurricanes defense. Miami had ended the season by going fourteen consecutive quarters without allowing their opponents an offensive touchdown. After surrendering 220 rushing yards to Florida State, the Hurricanes had closed the season by allowing 79 to East Carolina, 28 to Pittsburgh, 18 to San Diego State, and now 136 to Notre Dame and Moore's vaunted offensive line. Even that number seemed inflated, though, considering the way the game had gone. In the first half the Hurricanes had stuffed Anthony Johnson and Rice at the goal line, inside the one. They stopped Johnson short on fourth down later in the half.

"The key to our success was the way we shut down Tony Rice," Greg Mark said. "We took their leader out of the game, and when you do that, all you have is a bunch of chickens running around with their heads cut off."

In 1994, the *Miami Herald* broke a story alleging that former Miami players who had gone on to the NFL would provide money from a pot—bounties, essentially—for big hits and plays during key games. Sourced to former players Randy Bethel and Brett Perriman (Perriman would recant almost immediately after), among others, one of the most specific allegations in the piece was that Hurricanes celebrity booster Luther Campbell, lead singer of the rap group 2 Live Crew, offered $1,500 to whoever could knock Rice out of the contest and $1,000 if someone could dispose of Rocket Ismail (the injuries had to come on clean hits—the 'Canes weren't completely without ethics).

The notion fed into Miami's reputation as the bad boys of college football, but it was, according to Greg Mark, greatly exaggerated: By 1989, stars from each side of the rivalry had bonded over their shared experiences, and any threats sent Rice's way were meant in jest. Even the *Herald* article containing the story about alleged bounties against Notre Dame refers only to "whisper(s)" circulating among current players along the sideline before the game after they had all witnessed a huddle between Campbell and some former Hurricanes, suggesting at least the possibility that the Rice and Ismail bounty dollar figures were the stuff of instant urban legend.

(Bernard Clark did admit—unapologetically—that he was compensated handsomely by Campbell for his thirteen tackles: "He gave it to me in a big wad and I spent it," he said. "I didn't see anything wrong with it. And I still don't." Receiver Darryl Dawkins, on the other hand, vehemently denied receiving a penny from Campbell or anyone else despite two touchdowns.)

"We had fun with it," Mark says of the back-and-forth with Rice and the Irish players. "I had [Rice's] phone number and we would call him up and tell him about what we were gonna do to him. We'd call him up while we were watching film on each other and say, 'What happened here? What was that deal?' Ragging on each other, basically. Just being playful. Hit lists, things of that nature? No, there was no type of hit list at all."

Regardless of whether or not a hit list existed, the game had a profound effect on the national rankings. Just a few weeks after seemingly bowing out, the Hurricanes, scheduled to play Alabama in the Sugar Bowl, were right back in the national championship picture. But they would need some help from Notre Dame, who, despite the loss, didn't consider themselves out of the race, either.

PART THREE

The Changing Landscape

CHAPTER 14

Controversy All Around

On October 21, a few weeks before the loss at the Orange Bowl, Notre Dame had defeated Southern California 28–24. The victory was the program's nineteenth straight overall, dating back to the 1987 season Cotton Bowl. The Irish were ranked first in the nation. They were the toast of the sport. Maybe William Beauchamp felt a little bit cocky that week. He, along with everyone else at Notre Dame, certainly had a right to be. But did the university vice president have a right to set in motion all that was to come? That question is central to a debate that exploded in the action's immediate aftermath and would rage for decades. Well into the future, whenever the evolution of the sport was discussed—from the massive and sometimes rancorous conference realignment of the 1990s to the eruption of nationally televised games through the 2000s and beyond—the University of Notre Dame's wheeling and dealing after the 1989 season would stand out as the crucial turning point.

It began innocently enough, with a letter. Three days after the Irish victory over the Trojans, Beauchamp penned some thoughts to Chuck Neinas, then executive director of the College Football Association. The CFA, which included all of the major football-playing schools not in the Big Ten or Pac-10 conferences (which had their own television deals), was in the process of renegotiating its national television deal with CBS that was set to expire after the 1990 season. The organization had been formed in 1977 and really consolidated its power in 1984 after successful legal challenges to the stranglehold the NCAA maintained on television rights. The CFA was an all-for-one, one-for-all collective that increased the schools' bargaining power with the networks by allowing them to negotiate as a single bloc.

From the time of its formation, Notre Dame had taken on a key leadership role within the organization. Beauchamp's predecessor in the vice president's office, Edmund Joyce, had been one of its founding members in 1977. Beauchamp had taken over for Joyce at Notre Dame in 1987, with Reverend "Monk" Malloy simultaneously replacing long-time university president Theodore Hesburgh. Neinas called Joyce the "moral conscience" of the CFA. Beauchamp, in his short time, had picked up where Joyce had left off, serving as the secretary-treasurer of the organization—"the best one we ever had," according to Neinas—as well as occupying a key role on the powerful collective's Television Negotiating Committee.

In October, the CFA agreed in principle to a $29-million-a-year secondary-rights deal with cable network ESPN. Without knowing how the rest of the deal would shake out, however, Beauchamp declined to finalize Notre Dame's commitment.

"I know that you have been anxious to receive from Notre Dame its commitment to participate in the ESPN package for the 1991 through 1994 football seasons," Beauchamp wrote. "We are not willing to make an absolute commitment to participate at this time."

Nor, Beauchamp indicated, would the school commit just yet to the bigger deal that would be coming down the pipe, probably sometime in the next couple months. That would be the network television contract to replace the existing one with CBS.

"It seemed to me that you would sign your primary deal first before you would sign your ESPN deal. But they didn't," says Beauchamp. "I just said that this doesn't seem right, to lock ourselves into this commitment to ESPN before we see what the total package is going to be. It didn't make sense to me."

Beauchamp's reservations had deep roots in the barnstorming template for Notre Dame football established by Knute Rockne so many decades before. Notre Dame was *in* South Bend, but it was not *of* South Bend. It was located in the Midwest but possessed a fan base that reached from coast to coast. It was truly a national program.

It was all by design. Once upon a time, Rockne had packed his boys on trains and sent them rolling to all corners of the map. Showcasing his teams nationally generated a loyal base of Catholic "subway alums" all over the United States in the 1920s, in time transforming the University of Notre Dame from small regional school to national athletic powerhouse. What barnstorming around the continent was to the 1920s, nationally televised games were to the 1980s. And the way Notre Dame saw it, a new CFA contract, if not executed to its benefit, could put Notre Dame's national exposure in peril. ABC already owned the rights to Big Ten and Pac-10 games. If the network were also to secure the CFA contract, it would own the broadcast rights to more games than it could possibly showcase every Saturday. The obvious solution: massive regionalization. Broadcast the Notre Dame-Purdue game to the West Coast? Not if, say, Oregon and Arizona were locking horns at the same time.

Even Lou Holtz, who constantly had to battle his belief that a fiery head coach could guide any collection of players, ability be damned, to a successful season, had come to realize that talent was the lifeblood of a program. Besides, Holtz had been around long enough and had certainly coached in enough places to understand that by 1989 the nation's top talent didn't often crawl out of the Midwest—not the way it had in Leahy's day and Parseghian's day and even Faust's day. It certainly didn't emerge very often from Indiana.

"Chuck," Beauchamp continued in his letter, "we will simply not lock ourselves into a position that in the end might be harmful to our best interests without having all the facts before us."

At the same time, Beauchamp said he "fully expected" his school to be a part of any new television agreement. After all, CBS still had the right of first refusal on the next college football contract. As long as the network met the CFA's asking price, the congestion of games that would result from an ABC deal would not be an issue.

————

While Notre Dame and Miami may have been the nation's two marquee teams in 1989, the University of Colorado just went out and won game after game—and, along the way, the hearts of college football fans. Before the 1989 season, former Colorado quarterback Sal Aunese had died of cancer, and his teammates dedicated the season to his memory. In particular, they used a written message from him, scrawled just days before his death, to fuel their Saturday efforts: *Strive only for victory each time we play.*

When the Irish were picked to play the No. 1–ranked Buffaloes in the Orange Bowl game following the '89 regular season, the script seemed ready-made for a Colorado victory. The Irish, after all, had struggled miserably in their recent trips to the stadium, all of them made to play Miami. The opponent wouldn't be the Hurricanes this time, but the memories in the stadium haunted Notre Dame just the same.

On top of all that, there was some sentiment that the Irish had recently lost their swagger. Before the Miami loss, the entire Hurricanes team had left their sideline and stood on the field, taunting the Irish. Holtz had warned his men that they couldn't get into any more fights, and the Irish had backed off. In the wake of the incident, and the subsequent meltdown on the field, some had taken to calling Notre Dame the "Flinching" Irish.

"I don't know," linebacker Ned Bolcar mused afterward. "Maybe we should have gone out and thrown some punches."

Even so, Colorado coach Bill McCartney wasn't anticipating a dejected Notre Dame team to gift wrap a national title for his upstarts. "They're warriors," he said of the Irish at a bowl week press conference. "When you knock a warrior down, he gets up. Notre Dame recruits those type of kids."

And what kind of kids did Colorado recruit? Even with national championship implications of some immediacy, the Orange Bowl lacked the panache of a Notre Dame–Miami matchup. But CATHOLICS vs. CONVICTS T-shirts, redesigned to incorporate the Buffaloes' black-and-gold color scheme, would not have been out of place.

In 1984, McCartney's third season in the Rockies, the Buffaloes had finished 1–10 and the team's leading wide receiver, Loy Alexander, had fumed. "We've got enough altar boys," he said. "We need some athletes." Consider it done. In the ensuing years, the Colorado program had improved steadily, making regular postseason appearances, albeit in lower-tier games. All the while, Buffalo players became more and more familiar to Boulder area law enforcement. In a three-year span beginning in February of 1986, more than two dozen players were arrested. The various charges ran the continuum of abhorrent, testosterone-fueled antisocial behavior. "Back off," running back J. J. Flannigan had allegedly said to a man intervening in an argument between him and his girlfriend, "or I'll get my nine-millimeter and put you six-foot under." Charges were dropped in that incident, but a few months later Flannigan pled no contest to a separate third-degree assault charge. Just weeks before the 1989 season, former Colorado linebacker Miles Kusayanagi pleaded guilty to charges that he was the infamous "Duct-Tape Rapist" who had terrorized university women.

Things were bad enough as they were, with the program eventually requiring players to attend a ninety-minute date-rape seminar. McCartney's tone deafness made them worse. In a comment that would echo years later in much-publicized comments by Buffs coach Gary Barnett about former Colorado female kicker Katie Hnida, McCartney decided to put his legal expertise on display to rationalize the alleged actions of one of his many hooligans. Big mistake.

"Rape by definition," he explained, "is a violent act, an act whereby there's real physical violence involved. And so I don't think that's what we're talking about here."

The specific incident that McCartney referred to had led to charges of sexual assault and burglary against a freshman player. According to Boulder police, the player had broken into a dorm room shared by two women at 2 a.m. one evening, then bit one of them on the neck and raped her after his advance was rejected.

McCartney's comment induced Boulder district attorney Alex Hunter to retort, "It's obvious to me that one more spot in that date-rape seminar should be reserved for the football coach." (McCartney had boasted another time, "You'll notice that we haven't had anybody shoot anybody.")

And yet, after all that, the Buffaloes still entered the Orange Bowl as enormous sentimental favorites in the matchup with America's Team. Yes, the Buffaloes were ranked No. 1. Yes, they were unbeaten and untied. But they were still viewed as the plucky underdog. Under Holtz, the Irish had long since abdicated that role, its last vestiges dissolving in that moment when Pat Terrell batted down Steve Walsh's two-point conversion heave in the end zone a season before.

Until 1989, the Buffaloes had won only two championships of any sort since World War II, both of them Big Eight conference titles. Even more than that, however, the ordeal of former quarterback Aunese made the Buffaloes a story for people to get behind. In the off-season

Aunese had been diagnosed with inoperable stomach and lung cancer. Before the season, he showed up at a Colorado practice. Hooked to an oxygen mask, he tried to address his teammates before finally giving up and retreating to the car that had driven him to the practice field. Aunese succumbed to his disease about a month into the season, and his death cut deeply. McCartney ended months of gossipy speculation by acknowledging at his former QB's memorial service that Aunese was indeed the father of McCartney's four-month-old grandchild. And finally, posthumously, Aunese was able to deliver the message to his teammates that he had struggled to get out during that emotional visit in the late summer.

Bring home the Orange Bowl, he had written in a letter left behind.

Because Colorado had become such a heartwarming story, comments Holtz made to his team at a practice in Miami became big news. Colorado, Holtz told his men, "[has] been living a lie all year."

The speech had been caught on camera by a Denver television station, NBC affiliate KCNC. Holtz's words were actually fairly standard, vanilla motivational stuff. But they took on a life of their own for a couple of reasons. By 1989, Holtz's reputation for denigrating his own team and talking up the opponent was well known. So the KCNC cameras had, in a small way, raised the curtain on a hypocrite. However, there were also insinuations in various news accounts that the "living a lie" comment had been some sort of reference to Colorado's use of Aunese's death as motivation. The full context of Holtz's words made it clear that the accusation wasn't anywhere close to the truth: He was speaking mostly about Colorado's schedule and how the Buffaloes offense had yet to face a defense like the one the Irish would send onto the field. But once a story gets rolling, little things like context and perspective become secondary. And yet, while the press frothed, the Colorado camp mostly shrugged.

"It doesn't anger me at all," Colorado linebacker Alfred Williams said. "It sounds just like what a coach would say to his team." McCartney told reporters that he was not offended and that Holtz's apology was unnecessary.

"From what I've been able to gather," McCartney said, "he was not saying those things for anyone other than his squad. He should have been granted privacy to talk to his squad."

That KCNC was filming during an open portion of Notre Dame's practice, when cameras were permitted to roll and reporters were allowed to scribble at will, hardly mattered in this repositioning of the "controversy." Holtz picked up the ball McCartney had left for him and charged full steam ahead with it.

"When I made those comments," he whined, "never in my wildest dreams did I think that they would be made public. It was not a press conference. It was in our practice. I had no idea they were there."

Then, as if the Irish needed any more reasons to tank in a bowl game for the second time in three appearances under Holtz, there was the potential distraction brewing around the rapid disintegration of the coaching staff. Defensive line coach John Palermo had accepted the head coaching job at Austin Peay State University. Running backs coach Jim Strong was heading to UNLV to take over that program. The biggest potential loss, however, was the team's beloved defensive coordinator, Barry Alvarez.

As the head coach of one of the top programs in the country, Holtz realized that his assistant coaches would become hot commodities as head coaching positions opened. So, in the first meeting with his coaches prior to Orange Bowl preparation and practices, he ticked off the list of openings and asked which coaches had been contacted by which schools.

"Rutgers?" Holtz asked.

Alvarez raised his hand.

"Pittsburgh?"

Alvarez again raised his hand.

"Wisconsin?"

Alvarez again.

A few days later Wisconsin athletic director Pat Richter flew into South Bend to conduct a formal interview of the Irish defensive coordinator. Alvarez wasn't the only candidate: Also high on his list were Michigan defensive coordinator Lloyd Carr and Ohio State offensive coordinator Jim Colletto. He also harbored a pie-in-the-sky hope of luring West Virginia head coach Don Nehlen to Madison.

Richter's search dragged on through Notre Dame's bowl preparation, and on December 30, two nights before the game, Alvarez called Madison to speak to Richter.

"If you're going to hire me, you need to hire me tomorrow," said Alvarez, who thought that his presence at one of the day's two marquee bowl games would be a recruiting boon on his new job. "We can make a big splash that will help us in recruiting."

The next day, Richter called the hotel where Notre Dame was staying to offer Alvarez the job. He accepted. But even with one foot already out the door, Alvarez had one more contribution to make to Notre Dame.

"You've got to set our guys loose," Alvarez told Holtz. "You can't let our guys sit there like martyrs before the game."

In his pregame speech before his team faced Colorado, Holtz apologized to his team for asking them to stand down against the Hurricanes a few weeks earlier.

"I allowed it to happen," he said as the room grew quiet. "I put the handcuffs on you guys. As of right now, I am sticking to this promise: We will never be intimidated. We will never back down from anyone. I'm taking the handcuffs off."

The room erupted, and the Irish went out and played inspired football, defeating the nation's No. 1-ranked team and America's sentimental favorite 21–6. Rice and Rocket Ismail were fantastic, especially in the second half, but really it was the Irish defense that spurred the victory, stonewalling the Buffs until the Irish offense found its groove in the third and fourth quarters and pulled away.

"Colorado was an unbelievable team," says Tim Grunhard, a starting offensive lineman on the '89 Irish. "They were, lights out, the best team in the nation that year, and we just kicked the crap out of them up and down the field."

Inside the Orange Bowl, as Notre Dame's lead grew, Miami fans in the crowd kept close track of what the Hurricanes were doing in New Orleans at the Sugar Bowl, where they were building a lead in an eventual 33–25 victory over Alabama. They cheered with equal passion for the Irish, whom they needed to knock off the No. 1 Buffaloes to give their Hurricanes a shot at a title.

When the day began, five teams still had a shot at the national championship. By the time the games were over, two were left: Notre Dame and Miami.

Having noticed the Miami fans uncharacteristically rooting on the Irish, Irish tailback Ricky Watters said afterward, "Wouldn't it be funny if they root for us and we still get the national championship? Then they'll be sad for another year."

With Colorado disposed of, all Notre Dame could do was wait on the voters.

The Irish felt they had a legitimate case. According to the NCAA's strength-of-schedule ratings, Notre Dame had taken on the nation's most difficult slate. They had played nine bowl teams and defeated eight of them. Notre Dame defeated the champions of the Big 10 (Michigan), the Pac-10 (Southern California), the Big Eight (Colorado), and the ACC (Virginia). Miami, in contrast, had played the nation's twenty-ninth most difficult schedule. However, the Hurricanes had beaten the Irish head-to-head, and they had done it in the season's final regular-season game. The game wasn't the blowout that the 27–10 final score indicated, but a 17-point deficit was a 17-point deficit.

Holtz, who had spent most of the season pooh-poohing his team publicly, altered his approach as he tried to send his message to voters.

"We were No. 1 for eleven weeks and we came back and beat the No. 1 team by fifteen points," Holtz said. "Golly, how can you pick anybody else? If you have the best record against the toughest schedule, the case rests."

———

In South Bend on the morning of January 2, a haggard-looking Holtz stepped onto the podium and faced a room full of reporters. He asked for a glass of water, then slammed down two Excedrin capsules in an effort to stave off a growing headache.

All season, Holtz and his team had denied that another national championship was foremost on their minds. But hours earlier, voters from both major polls announced their respective champions. The wait had taken its toll, but now it had ended.

In the Associated Press poll, thirty-nine of the nation's writers granted the Hurricanes their No. 1 vote. Nineteen of them selected Notre Dame. In the final tally, Miami edged Notre Dame 1,474 points to 1,452, the second-closest margin since the AP first instituted a post-bowl poll following the 1968 season.

The coaches voted even more decisively against Holtz and the Irish.

Not only did Miami beat out Notre Dame for No. 1, but the coaches also gave Florida State a razor-thin advantage over the Irish (661 points to 660 points) for the runner-up spot.

"We played everybody at an emotional peak, everybody was sky high," Holtz said. "You can justify why Miami won it, but you can't justify why we didn't. We played the toughest. We had the best record. We were No. 1 every week but one, and we came back and beat No. 1 quite decisively.

"I feel exceptionally bad for our athletes," he added. "I wear my feelings very poorly. Had I heard this news earlier, maybe I could have hid my feelings. I think today sums up this whole year. Another disappointment."

In Coral Gables, the Hurricanes reveled over defeating their archrival for the second time in just a few months. The disappointment of 1988 had stayed with the Hurricanes for a year, then even longer as they sweated out the final vote. They had lost their coach. They had lost to Florida State. Now, finally, they could exhale.

"Lou," Miami safety Charles Pharms said, sending a gleeful message to his program's biggest nemesis, "relax, calm down. Go back to South Bend and be happy you finished No. 2."

———

In the spring, former Prop 48 and near academic casualty Tony Rice graduated from Notre Dame. It was the end of a long journey and a redemptive moment for the quarterback and for Holtz, who had staked his reputation with the school's administration on a young man he had believed in.

But for Rice, the triumphant moment of picking up his degree was tempered by another event that spring: the NFL Draft. Because of his lack of accuracy and his awkward mechanics, NFL teams considered converting Rice to defensive back. He certainly had the strength to play safety in the league. But the Chicago Bears timed him at a pedestrian 4.84 in the forty-yard dash, a shock to anyone who had seen him outrun fleet-footed defenders for three years at Notre Dame. "Just couldn't run on the turf," Rice lamented. "Just not my day for running." Rice had cried when he called his mother after feeling overwhelmed his first year at Notre Dame; he cried again when his name wasn't one of the 331 called on draft day.

"How is [Jeff] George worth $15 million and Rice not one bent penny?" *Indianapolis Star* columnist Phil Richards raged.

Rice's career had ended without a second national championship. Without the Heisman. Without a place at the highest level of the sport.

In this darkest of moments, however, true Irish believers could take solace in the famous line from the school's fight song. "Old Notre Dame will win overall," it went, and it was about to be proven true in a way that would rattle the college football world to its very core and change Notre Dame's reputation forever.

CHAPTER 15

"One Word. Greed."

Dick Rosenthal was the kind of man who seemed to have been born to lead the Notre Dame athletic department. It just took him a while, his attention preoccupied by a successful first career, to find his way to that role.

Like Notre Dame president Reverend Edward A. "Monk" Malloy, Rosenthal was a former Notre Dame basketball player. A high school All-American at William C. McBride High School in St. Louis, Rosenthal matriculated to Notre Dame afterward, declaring a major in finance and also joining the Irish baseball team. But it was the basketball court where he excelled. A six-foot-five-inch, 210-pound post player, Rosenthal started three years at Notre Dame, from 1951–52 through 1953–54, and the team improved from 16–10 to 19–5 to 22–3 during his time there. He thrived in Notre Dame's biggest games, scoring 25 points and pulling down fifteen rebounds in a 1954 NCAA Tournament victory over defending champion Indiana. He even scored the winning basket in the 65–64 upset. In that same March tournament, he poured in 31 points against Loyola-Chicago. "Rosey was possessed," teammate Jack Stephens would later say of that virtuoso performance.

Upon graduation, Rosenthal was named the top scholar-athlete in his senior class. He then spent two seasons with the Fort Wayne Pistons of the National Basketball Association. An academic standout with both a sports and finance background, decades later Rosenthal would have been a prime candidate to soar up the collegiate athletic administration or professional sports front-office ladder. But his was a different time, and instead of athletics Rosenthal went into banking. By the time he was hired to replace Gene Corrigan as Notre Dame's athletic director in 1987, Rosenthal had already spent twenty-five years as the chief executive officer of a highly successful South Bend bank.

"Athletics as business is important today," Beauchamp said upon making the hire, "and Dick Rosenthal has the business background."

———

By late 1989, Notre Dame and broadcasting were hardly newlyweds.

The first Notre Dame football game to be broadcast on the radio, a homecoming contest against Indiana University, was carried on South Bend's WGAZ on November 4, 1922. Just days earlier, October 28, a game between Princeton and the University of Chicago, in Chicago, had been broadcast on New York station WEAF. The Irish were not the first college football team to have their game broadcast over the airwaves, but they didn't miss out on the distinction by much.

Television began arriving on the American media scene in the 1940s, just as Notre Dame football was peaking under head coach Frank Leahy. The university signed a groundbreaking exclusive contract with the DuMont Television Network, an upstart that was trying to compete with NBC, CBS, and ABC to broadcast its home games for $2,500 apiece beginning with the end of the 1948 season. In 1950, DuMont bid $185,000 to again beat out the bigger networks for the exclusive rights to Notre Dame football in South Bend. Notre Dame football broadcasts would also include *Behind the Gridiron*, a thirty-minute segment extolling the academic virtues of the school, hosted by the president and vice president of the university.

At the time that Notre Dame was capitalizing on the new medium to fill the university's piggy bank and expand the exposure of its football program, much of the rest of college football was moving in the opposite direction. Concerns were rampant during the era that television exposure would harm attendance at games and ultimately be the financial downfall of the sport, and the idea of Notre Dame, with its enormous national following, being shown every week in markets around the country was a positively frightful prospect for the rest of the nation. The Big Ten banned its members from broadcasting games on television in 1950. Citing statistics that seemed to show attendance at games was adversely affected in markets where televised games were available, the NCAA's member schools then voted 161–7 to restrict schools to broadcasting under the NCAA's severely limited schedule. Teams could follow the rules or face serious repercussions, including possible expulsion from the organization.

For a while Notre Dame considered legal action against the NCAA, on the grounds that the restrictions were unconstitutional. But the university, along with fellow renegade University of Pennsylvania, eventually gave in, and for decades afterward the NCAA kept the availability of televised games limited. Even this wasn't such an awful thing for Notre Dame: A member of college football's royalty, they were always guaranteed television time each season.

The growth of cable television in the 1980s again tempted Notre Dame to go its own way. In 1984, Atlanta-based superstation WTBS approached Notre Dame about leaving the CFA and selling the network its home broadcasting rights.

"It was a lot of money," said then Notre Dame athletic director Gene Corrigan. "A lot of money. They wanted to do every one of our games. They said they were going to make us America's team. I remember telling the guy I thought we already were America's team."

Enticing as such an offer was, the administration decided that it wasn't the time. In 1984, Georgia and Oklahoma won a landmark Supreme Court case against the NCAA, finally wresting broadcast control away from the governing body and into the hands of its members. But at that point Notre Dame didn't want to break its affiliation with the association. And besides, as much of an emerging force as cable television was during that time, it was still a long way from matching the reach of the networks. In 1984, 43.7 million U.S. households subscribed to cable television, which marked more than a twofold increase in just five years. But it remained an emerging technology and would have represented quite a risk for Notre Dame during a time period when the football program had long since abandoned any cutting-edge tendencies.

While the university maintained its leadership role in the CFA for the time being, however, groundwork was already being laid for the day when circumstances would suggest Notre Dame take the leap. Ken Schanzer, an executive vice president at NBC Sports under head honcho Dick Ebersol, began forming relationships in South Bend under the prior Notre Dame administration, growing particularly close to former athletic director Corrigan. NBC broadcast some Irish basketball games, and Schanzer attended football games at Notre Dame Stadium several times as a friend of the university, nudging his friends occasionally about the idea of a football marriage between the two entities. "I always said, kiddingly or not, if you guys ever wanted to come alone, I'll do it," Schanzer said. "I said that repeatedly, without having any inkling that it would happen."

During negotiations in the fall of 1989 and spilling over into the early winter of 1990, members of the CFA, along with executives at CBS and ABC, operated under the assumption that Notre Dame would be a committed member of whatever deal was eventually worked out. Beauchamp's letter, sent in October, seemed hardly to have made a ripple.

"We were watching the SEC," said Len DeLuca, a bigwig at CBS Sports. "There was never a negotiation they didn't like to dance from."

In fact, a few years before, Notre Dame had coaxed that league into the existing CFA television agreement when it had considered exiting. In the 1989–90 negotiations, the first shoe dropped when CBS declined to renew its existing contract for the CFA's asking price of $40 million a year. Subsequently, NBC also walked away, leaving ABC as the only remaining interested network. ABC owned ESPN, which had already acquired the secondary rights to the CFA television deal. With ABC's Big Ten and Pac-10 contract still in place for several more seasons, locking up the CFA would give the network control over the broadcast rights to every college football game that mattered. Under the prior contract, CBS had shown about seventeen games per season, leaving the other networks to bid on games not shown on that network. The CBS broadcasts had been truly national: With the Big Ten and Pac-10 rights belonging elsewhere, there just weren't enough marquee games to roll out a full regional slate à la the NFL. An ABC–ESPN monopoly, however, would change the dynamics. With every big game under its purview, ABC planned to televise about fifty games a season, regionalizing contests to maximize the viewing audience in every market. Bidding only against itself, ABC paid $42 million a year for the rights, a good-faith offer that was $2 million above the CFA's asking price. In all, the ABC–ESPN deal was for $350 million over five years. Confident that all sixty-four teams were on board, the parties announced the terms in January.

The day the deal was announced, Notre Dame's Rosenthal happened to be in New York City, meeting with NBC's Schanzer about Notre Dame basketball on the network. During their meeting, Rosenthal expressed displeasure at the thought of regionalization. After he left, Schanzer immediately made a beeline for the office of his boss, NBC Sports president Dick Ebersol. "I might be crazy," Schanzer said. "[But] I just sat there and talked to Dick Rosenthal and I'm not altogether positive that we couldn't work some magic."

The details of the timeline are important, because they mean the difference between savvy business acumen on the part of the Notre Dame administration and clearly unethical behavior.

In his role on the negotiating committee, Notre Dame's Beauchamp sat in almost every second of the contract talks and was privy to every contour of the negotiations and eventual deal in principle. Had he been speaking on the side with Schanzer and NBC during that period, it would have been a violation of standard business ethics on a grand scale.

"The classic fox in the classic henhouse," authors Don Yaeger and Douglas S. Looney would term it in their 1993 book *Under the Tarnished Dome: How Notre Dame Betrayed Its Ideals for Football Glory*, a bestseller highly critical of the Holtz era of Irish football.

However, Beauchamp and Notre Dame have always maintained that it did not go down that way.

"That is absolute, unadulterated garbage," Schanzer said.

"What surprised me, quite frankly," says Beauchamp, "was the misinformation that got out and what people accused us of that was totally untrue."

According to the narrative told by Notre Dame and NBC, the first time the subject was even broached was the day after the CFA deal with ABC was announced, when Schanzer called Rosenthal and asked if they could legally engage in talks about a possible exclusive-rights deal. Also, as blindsided as the CFA member schools, along with ABC and ESPN, would feel in the aftermath of what was about to go down, Beauchamp had always left the door open a crack. There had been his October letter, of course, along with subtle signs during the negotiations that Notre Dame was not all in until the ink was dry. "Beauchamp was being a little reticent in the meetings," Len DeLuca would later recall.

In late January, NBC and Notre Dame executives met in secret in South Bend to advance negotiations. When a deal seemed imminent, the university's administrators contacted NCAA executive director Dick Schultz, who extended his blessing. Schultz, in his previous role as commissioner of the Atlantic Coast Conference, had led his league to stay out of the CFA deal for a year in 1985. The most awkward step in the process came in early February, when Beauchamp and Rosenthal had to tell CFA head Chuck Neinas about what was developing. Neinas lived in Colorado and thought the pair were coming out to ski, as they had done in the past. Oblivious, he even suggested a resort where everyone could meet. Instead, they met at the airport, where the Notre Dame administrators filled Neinas in on what was about to happen. "He was furious," said Beauchamp. Said Neinas: "They didn't have any difficulty interpreting my reaction."

Although Notre Dame increased its monetary take several times over and above what it would have cleared in the CFA deal, Beauchamp and Rosenthal have always maintained that the original NBC contract, estimated at about $40 million over five years, was not about money. The price of a package, Schanzer has maintained, was not discussed at the first meeting. Since Notre Dame never breathed a word of the deal to CBS, the university's story has merit. After all, it could easily have started a bidding war between the two networks. Money, says Beauchamp, was secondary to the fear that regionalization would marginalize Notre Dame as a Midwest school and athletic program.

"It was almost better for us not to be on at all than for us to be on regionally," Beauchamp says. "I would have to answer all these letters: 'How come my cousin in Podunk, Iowa, can get the Notre Dame game and I can't get it in New York City?' As a national school, it didn't help us to get put on regionally. It was more problematic than not being on at all."

Holtz had no official say in the television deal, as it was a business matter, but he was consulted informally. Savvy as he was about the recruiting advantages a national television deal would proffer, he also warned that such an action could trigger a national backlash against Notre Dame. He wasn't the only one who anticipated the possibility.

"I said from the very beginning," says Beauchamp, "when the overture was made and we were considering it, I said to our president and I said to the chairman of our board, 'We are going to be accused of being greedy. You just need to know that.'"

As the talks between the university and the network became more intense, Rosenthal gathered the athletic department in a meeting room and asked for input on what might be some of the pros and cons of such a deal. Roger Valdiserri, the school's retired longtime sports information director, raised his hand.

"Have you thought about the adverse reaction nationally that we are going to get?" Valdiserri asked. He also raised the possibility of schools boycotting the Irish. Valdiserri's concerns proved to be prophetic: Within days, the University of Kansas canceled a two-game home-and-home men's basketball series.

Although schools didn't back out of playing the Irish in football—playing Notre Dame was about the best national platform a school could obtain for its program—the reaction to the news was swift and almost universally negative.

"Notre Dame has vacated its leadership role," said Arkansas athletic director Frank Broyles, the man who once hired (and fired) Lou Holtz and alienated Jimmy Johnson. "This is greed."

"Ultimate greed," said Vince Dooley, Georgia athletic director.

Holtz may have been the king of the one-line zinger, but his school's new television contract gave one of his coaching rivals, Penn State's Joe Paterno, the opportunity to let loose a golden one of his own.

"It's been a fun year for all of us," Paterno said. "We got to see Notre Dame go from an academic institute to a banking institute."

But the statement by Dooley rankled Notre Dame's administration the most.

"One word," Colorado State athletic director Oval Jaynes steamed. "Greed."

"I'm thinking, 'Georgia?'" says Beauchamp. "'You're the ones who brought the lawsuit against the NCAA to make this possible because you wanted to have your own ability to do this.' Notre Dame's 'sin'—quote, unquote—is we were the first ones to do it."

The way the deal was structured, Notre Dame's opponents, which still included Penn State, would also receive a financial payout from NBC for playing in South Bend. So certainly the charge of hypocrisy, a criticism born of the television deal and still levied almost reflexively at Notre Dame to this day, could also apply to the school's miffed peers, who weren't exactly lining up to give back their piece of the pie. Ironically enough, Penn State had come to NBC a few years before to attempt to negotiate a similar deal, as had Oklahoma and Miami. But Miami, somewhere along the line, made a business misstep that Notre Dame, guided by an athletic director with a banking background and a savvy priest as president who sported both a law degree and an MBA, avoided. Miami signed away its rights to the CFA. Notre Dame's participation was always voluntary, making threats of legal action in the wake of the NBC deal empty bluster.

Despite all of that, however, when it came to the NBC contract, in February of 1990 there was only one school taking the heat.

"By putting their name on the dotted line," wrote *Chicago Sun-Times* columnist Terry Boers, "Rosenthal and friends have exposed themselves for what they really are—a gaggle of greedy, money-grubbing backstabbers. This deal, which calls for every Irish home football game to be televised nationally, should serve as yet another example Notre Dame is no different, no better, than any other major college power."

"On and off the field, Notre Dame's holy water image finally has been muddled," wrote Norman Chad of the *National Sports Daily*.

"Notre Dame's place in college football is unparalleled," opined Blaine Newman of the *Seattle Times*. "So, now, is the gall and the greed."

Although they were relatively scarce, some media members were at least a little more understanding.

"In truth," *Sports Illustrated*'s William F. Reed wrote, "many of the schools making the most noise are no doubt jealous and would have done the same thing if they had had the chance."

"The Irish deliver numbers," wrote Bob Ryan, the *Boston Globe* columnist. "You put a Notre Dame game on and people will watch. For every two or three people cheering, there will be at least one throwing shoes at the set, but who cares? Ratings are ratings. They don't come in positive and negative."

Ryan had a point. Six times during the 1989 regular season, the Irish had gone head-to-head nationally against a televised game on another network. They had won the battle all six times, and rarely had the fight for eyeballs been close. The opener against Michigan, shown on ABC, drew a 10.5 rating. The other game in the time slot, between Illinois and Colorado, drew a 2.8 rating on CBS. Even college football's most storied programs and its most revered rivalries didn't stand a chance. On November 18, the Irish and Penn State clashed on CBS. The game was watched by twice as many viewers as the Southern California–UCLA game on ABC at the same time. Sure, that was a regional matchup, but ABC had tried to remedy that by beaming the Indiana-Illinois game to portions of the heartland. That did nothing to narrow the viewing gap.

If Miami was Notre Dame's only real competition on the field in 1988 and 1989, a pack of aging quipsters, also located in Miami, seemed to be the program's only fair competition in the Nielsens. On November 25, the Irish loss to the Hurricanes drew an astronomical 14.9 rating. But, alas, it was smoked that night by NBC's sitcom *The Golden Girls*, which logged a 20.4. Still, the football game did clobber ABC's lineup of *Mr. Belvedere*, *Living Dolls*, and *Columbo*.

Ironically, Notre Dame's Beauchamp says he saw the NBC deal as an opportunity to preserve tradition, not undermine it.

"We didn't like playing games at night and all different times of the day," Beauchamp says. "And then they eventually went to Thursday games and Friday games. We didn't want to get involved with that. It totally disrupts the campus. It's the same reason why, when we renovated the stadium, we didn't put luxury boxes in. To us, that is not college football. College football is Saturday afternoons in a [traditional] stadium, and that's always been Notre Dame."

————

All rhetoric aside, Notre Dame's television contract snapped Joe Paterno to attention. For decades, the Nittany Lions had been the East's answer to Notre Dame, a proudly independent football powerhouse that stood alone and seemed like it would always do so. Penn State was a member of the Atlantic 10 Conference in every sport but football. Notre Dame's NBC contract was the first note of a song that suggested a game of musical chairs had begun. For all its success, including the national title won in the Fiesta Bowl against the Hurricanes just a few seasons prior, Penn State didn't want to be the last program left standing.

"I've been concerned about two or three schools getting together and doing something like Notre Dame did," Paterno said. "We were afraid we might be left out of some arrangements that would be put together by other people."

In early June of 1990, just a few months after Notre Dame had reestablished its independent identity by spurning the CFA for NBC, the university presidents of the Big Ten Conference—referring to themselves with the regal moniker the "Council of Ten"—voted to extend an invitation to Penn State. The decision wasn't unanimous. The current ten members had been together for about four decades, since Michigan State had joined the league in its last expansion way back in 1950, and were set in their ways. This time around, Michigan State was one of three schools to oppose the expansion. Michigan and Indiana were the others.

"Not one athletic director was consulted on this matter," Michigan athletic director and longtime coach Bo Schembechler groused. "How can they do that?"

Soon enough, Schembechler and other old schoolers would be able to see for themselves that moves like Penn State's entry into the Big Ten, a geographic head-scratcher at the moment, were simply inevitable. Florida State, another remaining independent powerhouse, would join the Atlantic Coast Conference soon afterward. South Carolina, also independent, would be joining the Southeastern Conference. And those were only the first winds of change to blow as the era of the independent flickered rapidly.

As complicated and confusing as some of the business dealings between schools, conferences, and, of course, television networks could be, the path of the dominoes, falling at a breakneck pace, is not that difficult to trace if one takes a long view. After the 1985 season, a well-traveled football coach named Lou Holtz took over the tradition-rich but floundering football program at the University of Notre Dame. In his first year, Holtz had the Fighting Irish competing with the big boys once again, just a few months after a humiliating 58–7 loss to the reviled Miami Hurricanes. A year after that, 1987, Holtz had the program back in a major New Year's Day bowl game, the Cotton Bowl. The next season the Irish were champions once again, the signature win during that season a controversial 31–30 heart-stopper against Miami at Notre Dame Stadium.

A year later, one of those two programs, a tenured member of the college football establishment with some long dormant rebellious tendencies, would be secure enough in its autonomy to declare complete independence from the rest of the college football world.

The other, the sport's proudest, mouthiest renegade, would find itself suddenly and ironically no longer willing or able to go it on its own.

One of the reasons that Jimmy Johnson had left Oklahoma State back in 1984 for Miami was because in the Big Eight, a definite pecking order had developed over the years. Every season, heavyweights Nebraska and Oklahoma battled it out for league supremacy, while the other six schools were left to play for pride. In 1976, a few seasons before Johnson's arrival, Oklahoma State actually won its first conference title in fifty years, sharing it with Oklahoma. Even in their moment of triumph, the Cowboys had to share the stage with their big brother up the road.

The same was true in some of the other major conferences. Ohio State and Michigan, for example, usually battled for the Rose Bowl berth in the Big Ten in their late-November matchup. Sure, you'd have a Purdue or Michigan State rise up from time to time and reach Pasadena, but it was rare that anybody bucked decades-long trends that had developed in America's major football conferences.

In the late 1970s, Miami was floundering as a program. But Miami was also an independent, unaffiliated with any existing league. And as such, when Howard Schnellenberger arrived to coach the Hurricanes beginning in 1979, he saw unlimited room for growth. Miami wasn't weighed down by the perception of a conference pecking order. With scholarship reductions and the easing of television restrictions changing the college football landscape, the program could climb as high as university support, changing state demographics, and the ingenuity of its ambitious new coach could take it.

"I did not come here to waste my time," Schnellenberger said in one of his first meetings with his Miami assistant coaches. "I could've stayed in the National Football League for years and years. But I came here to win a national title."

Coaching a private school playing in a warm climate in an NFL sta-dium with a wealth of talent ripe for the plucking in its own backyard, Schnellenberger thought he could build the "USC of the South" in Coral Gables.

Unburdened by an inflexible conference calendar, Schnellenberger, could tailor his program's schedule to its advantage. Schnellenberger viewed schedules in terms of "A" games, "B" games, and "C" games. The "A" games were games against opponents that his Hurricanes would likely lose to. The "B" games were the swing matchups: contests against comparable programs that could go either way, depending on the year. And the "C" games were games that Miami, in most years, should have won. Schnellenberger thought a perfect schedule would include a pair of "A" games, a pair of "C" games, and a whole batch of "B" games.

Playing a group of perennial powers certainly had its advantages, most of all exposure. But it also trapped Miami in a cycle of never-ending .500-or-worse campaigns. By the time Miami won the 1983 na-tional championship, Schnellenberger had worked to remove Alabama, Syracuse, and Penn State from the schedule. The strategy worked. The Hurricanes had just enough fuel left in the tank by season's end to squeak by Florida State 17–16 in the final regular season game and then defeat Nebraska 31–30 in the Orange Bowl.

Schnellenberger believes that the meteoric ascent would never have been possible had Miami played in a conference in the early 1980s.

"There were too many things that would have had to have fallen per-fectly for us," he says.

By 1990, however, college football was changing yet again.

Penn State, the proud, longtime independent, made the Big Ten an eleven-team league. Other independent powers began to scramble for conference homes as well: West Virginia, South Carolina, Florida State, and others.

Right before Christmas, Miami athletic director Sam Jankovich re-signed to become the chief executive officer of the New England Patri-ots. He used the press conference pulpit to blast away at what he perceived as raging hypocrisy in college sports, particularly the puri-tanical expectations placed on big-time football schools.

"We say it's not big business," Jankovich said, "we say we don't have to win, but at the collegiate level, a program such as ours, you have to win and it is big business. At least in the professional ranks you know what the ground rules are from Day 1."

It was a rant that the administration at the University of Notre Dame could certainly appreciate. After all, it had been just a few months since the Irish were lambasted nationally for their lucrative new contract with NBC. Now one of the leaders at Notre Dame's most heated football combatant was saying what Notre Dame could not—at least, not without inspiring another round of bloviation about how greedy Notre Dame had lost its way.

Jankovich's exit left Miami's conference aspirations in some degree of limbo. With great awareness of the value of his school's football program to the league's credibility, Jankovich had driven a hard bargain in negotiations with the Big East, even though he realized that the Hurricanes needed a conference home in the blossoming new era as badly as those conferences needed them. At the same time, Jankovich felt that Miami, like Notre Dame, was a national program and needed to schedule accordingly. He desired a six-team football conference, with Miami, West Virginia, and Rutgers serving as the flagship members. The Hurricanes, Jankovich felt strongly, should not lock themselves into any more than five league games a year. That would leave room for a smart mix of tomato cans and heavyweights.

It was a creative way to think about things, but ultimately untenable at that moment in the sport's history. Soon enough, the Hurricanes were a full-fledged member of the fully formed Big East football conference. For years Miami had postured as the sport's consummate rebel, but now money had spoken. And loudly. When all was said and done, only Notre Dame stood alone.

CHAPTER 16

Crisis Coach

Recalling the series' humble beginnings, when Notre Dame used Miami as little more than a punching bag every fall, the media, teams, and public became nostalgic about the end of the rivalry as the 1990 contest approached.

The contract between the schools was expiring and would not be renewed. Miami wanted to continue the series, but the Irish had turned the Hurricanes down. Not once, but twice. First, the Irish said that they were overscheduled through 2004 as they pursued a desire to play road games in new markets. At a mutual press conference with Miami athletic director Sam Jankovich in the summer of 1990, Notre Dame athletic director Dick Rosenthal said that if a spot opened up on Notre Dame's schedule, he would certainly give Miami a call. Soon afterward, Penn State pulled out of its contract with Notre Dame because of its commitment to the Big Ten. But Notre Dame turned to Florida State to fill the slots instead of Miami, even though Jankovich offered to play one game in South Bend and one game at a neutral site.

Notre Dame–Miami was destined to be a relic of the 1980s, as anchored in its time as Cyndi Lauper and *The Breakfast Club.*

"It is the best rivalry in college football," Dennis Erickson lamented. "Two of the best teams in the country playing each other. You just hate to see a rivalry like that end. It's the kind of rivalry that keeps college football alive."

Notre Dame's players were equally disappointed.

"You have two teams that have an undying desire to be No. 1," linebacker Andre Jones said. "I personally feel this series should go on."

T-shirts flying off the rack around the Notre Dame campus billed the meeting as CATHOLICS VS. CONVICTS III—THE FINAL WAR. Notre Dame officially banned the shirts, but that didn't stop two student entrepreneurs from grossing $120,000 on their sale.

"What began as a beach party for the Irish," one sportswriter mused in the days leading up to the game, "ends Saturday in the Final War."

That vibe, particularly from the fans of each team, was the major reason the Notre Dame administration chose to let the contract expire at its conclusion rather than order up another few seasons of guaranteed ratings bonanzas. Administrators like William Beauchamp and Dick Rosenthal didn't like the turn the South Bend campus took when the Hurricanes came to town, and they certainly didn't enjoy the atmosphere at the Orange Bowl when the Irish were the visitors.

"This rivalry is a little bigger than it should be," Rosenthal said.

"In the end," says Beauchamp, "it had gotten to the point where *rivalry* was no longer the right word. It was almost to the point that it was a war. We didn't think it was a particularly healthy environment for either school."

There has also always been speculation that Notre Dame, witnessing the Hurricanes' growing reputation for shenanigans on the field and off, no longer wished to associate with them as an opponent, lest it be viewed as giving its tacit approval to the way Miami comported itself. On one hand, considering that Notre Dame had just inked the controversial deal with NBC that made it another sort of villain in the narrative of college football—a far more dangerous one, in many people's eyes, than the fatigue-wearing, touchdown-celebrating 'Canes—that sort of snobbery can be viewed as more hypocrisy from the university. On the other hand, considering the long string of self-induced public relations nightmares the 'Canes would suffer in short order, a move for that reason by the Notre Dame administration seems in hindsight to have been prescient.

"Obviously, Notre Dame wants to be participating with schools that participate in intercollegiate athletics at a high level, and at a level that is something we want to be proud of to participate in," says Beauchamp. "We're not saying every school has to be Notre Dame, and we would expect that not every school would be interested in being what Notre Dame is. But I think when Notre Dame sets up their schedule, a number of factors come into play, and one of them, yes, is that we want to play schools that we feel comfortable playing."

A desperation attached to both teams that had been missing in previous seasons, when both rampaged through the early portions of their schedules on the way to their meeting.

The Hurricanes, who had begun the 1990 campaign ranked No. 1, had suffered a shocking early-season setback, perhaps their most surprising defeat since the Sugar Bowl blowout against Tennessee in Jimmy Johnson's first season. For years, a power struggle between the football program and university president Tad Foote had been brewing, with Foote embarrassed by the antics of the players and the 'Canes feeling misunderstood. But before 1990 the message was clear: Tone it down. Foote announced during the season that he would end athletic dormitories on campus. A lifeless Miami bunch fell to BYU and eventual Heisman Trophy winner Ty Detmer to begin the season. "I have never seen a quarterback better than on that day," says Hurricanes defensive lineman Marty Golloher. "We dislocated both of his arms. He still kept bringing it."

The BYU defense was equally formidable.

"They had a good game film on us and they exposed some stuff," says Miami quarterback Craig Erickson. "They had a couple good blitzes for us that we didn't adjust to. I think nine out of ten times we would have had our way with them. But they outplayed us, outcoached us, outeverythinged us. Outquarterbacked us.

"We knew they were a tough team: good, hard-headed guys," he explains. "And they were. They're mean. BYU players, those Mormons, those guys will bite you and claw you. They're tough. Ty is one of the nicest guys in the world, but he's one of the best athletes you'll ever meet in your life. They had our number that night. They had some things we couldn't block. They had three guys coming at me all night. It was not one of our better performances, that's for sure."

The loss was devastating to everyone in the 'Cane family, past and present. Former Hurricane Michael Irvin, for example, was absolutely incensed.

"This ain't right," he said in a phone call to wide receiver Lamar Thomas. "Somebody makes a big play and you guys don't do anything?"

Irvin's reaction was tame compared to those of some other former

Hurricanes. Former All-American wide receiver Brett Perriman, a New Orleans Saint, flew from New Orleans to Miami just to corner some current players at the student union and read them the riot act. Bernard Clark, who had spearheaded the 1989 victory over the Irish, videotaped a tirade directed at the current players, repeatedly telling them they were a "fucking embarrassment," and sent it to Erickson to show them.

Something surely clicked. Next up was Cal, and Miami turned into the old Miami again. The Hurricanes defeated the Golden Bears 52–24, with Miami's players prancing and exalting after every play they made. From there the talented Hurricanes continued to win games, winning four in a row, including a victory over Florida State, leading into the game in South Bend. The week before the Notre Dame trip, the Hurricanes hosted Kansas. Thirty minutes before the game, in a virtual repeat of the scene at Notre Dame Stadium two years before, the 'Canes stormed through the Jayhawks' pregame lines, instigating a near brawl in which punches were thrown.

Equilibrium was restored, with Miami back in the national title hunt. But they clung to it precariously: No team had ever won the national title with two losses.

———————

It was, without a doubt, the last thing that Florida interim coach Gary Darnell needed.

Inexcusable, he thought. Inexcusable that his players wouldn't know better. "We're not allowed imperfections," he explained in a press conference.

In mid-October 1989, in the middle of routine morning workouts, Darnell received a phone call from his boss, University of Florida athletic director Bill Arnsparger.

"Gary," Arnsparger said, "I need to see you."

From the tone, Darnell assumed that Arnsparger wasn't thinking late brunch; perhaps a friendly game of racquetball to follow. Like most college football teams, every day the Gators walked past a sign posted in the training room: DO NOT GAMBLE. There was no fine print, no exceptions granted. This rule was ironclad, the consequences potentially devastating. And the Florida coaches didn't merely leave it up to a training room sign to deliver the message. They invited police officers in every year to speak to the team about gambling.

And yet...

It didn't seem like a huge deal at the time. Gators quarterback Kyle Morris knew some guys in a fraternity at the University of Georgia, and they had a house bookie. Morris started placing some small bets, as did his backup, freshman quarterback Shane Matthews. And then another guy. And another. They weren't shaving points. They weren't even betting on Florida games or providing information to professional gamblers or oddsmakers. But, again, no exceptions.

"The total bets were no more, altogether, than about $35," Darnell says. "But because they were calling back to this fraternity in Georgia, in Athens, using interstate telephone lines, that's a felony. I get called in and have five of my quarterbacks being Mirandized by the FBI. I thought, *Well, this is really something.*"

Ultimately, the players were not indicted, although they were suspended for the rest of the season, forcing Darnell to dip deep, deep into his quarterback depth chart. It was a mess, but in actuality it was pretty much par for the course for Darnell and the Florida program in the fall of 1989. Like most career coaches, the forty-year-old native Arkansan had taken all the requisite steps on the journey to what he hoped would be a head coaching position somewhere, sometime. Graduate assistant at Oklahoma State. Position coach at SMU and North Carolina. Defensive coordinator at Kansas State, Wake Forest, and, finally, Florida. As dominant as his Florida defenses had been, he seemed a lock to snag a head coaching job very soon. But he figured it would happen the traditional way. An interview after the season. A follow-up. An offer.

Instead, Darnell had been thrust into the interim role in Gainesville under the black cloud of scandal. Head coach Galen Hall was under NCAA investigation, suspected of slipping a player some money to make child-support payments, along with paying unauthorized, under-the-table salary supplements to a couple of his assistants. Florida, already dealing with a drug scandal in its men's basketball program, fired Hall in midseason and elevated Darnell to the interim head coaching role.

Florida's scandal could not have been timed more poorly. Just a couple of years before, the NCAA had come down hard on SMU for major violations, imposing the so-called death penalty on the program for the 1987 and 1988 seasons. And so the media was on the lookout for the next program to head to "death row," the fact of which all but tied the noose around the Gators' necks in the fall of 1989. Some of Darnell's coaching colleagues were of no particular help, either.

"Gambling is something that can ruin college athletics," LSU coach Mike Archer said after that story came to light. "I think in the long run, it will."

Not that Darnell had time to worry about what the NCAA might or might not decide at an undetermined future date. He had a season to hold together, and it always seemed like something was going haywire on him.

"I said, 'Well, where's so-and-so?'" Darnell says, remembering one practice when a key player was unexpectedly absent. "And they said, 'Well, Coach, he's not gonna be here.' I said, 'What?' They said, 'Well, they just hauled him off in a straitjacket.' I said, 'Oooh, this is not good.'"

The Gators went 3–4 under Darnell, a more-than-respectable showing under the circumstances. Arnsparger even seriously considered elevating him to the permanent head coaching position until a Florida legend, former Heisman Trophy winner Steve Spurrier, decided to take the job. However, Darnell's crisis-a-minute experience had not been without its benefits: It proved to be good preparation for the future.

Good preparation for life under Lou Holtz, who hired Darnell to replace Barry Alvarez after the latter left Notre Dame for Wisconsin after the 1989 season.

"He was a crisis coach," Darnell says. "He fed off of creating chaos."

Soon enough, the Irish would have a real crisis to deal with, not just one concocted by their head coach as a way of keeping his team and staff on their toes. After they started fast and some other teams, including Miami, faltered, the Irish took their place as the nation's No. 1 team and seemed to have a clear path to another national title run.

Then Stanford came to town.

In a performance that harkened back to the Faust days, Notre Dame, which had already logged victories over highly ranked Michigan State and Michigan to begin the season, turned in a stinker of epic proportions. Notre Dame led at halftime 24–7 but had no answer in the second half for Stanford's offensive cast, including running back "Touchdown" Tommy Vardell, quarterback Jason Palumbis (twenty-six-of-thirty-four passing), and receiver Ed McCaffrey (111 yards receiving). When Vardell plunged across the goal line with less than a minute to play, the Cardinals, who had come into South Bend with a 1–3 record, left with a shocking 36–31 victory.

"I don't know if I've ever been in a loss this difficult," Holtz said afterward.

Shocking as the defeat was, considering that a Holtz-coached Notre Dame team had yet to lay an egg on a Saturday through his first four-plus seasons, with the possible exception of the '89 game at the Orange Bowl, it was inevitable that it would happen at some point. "It's hard to do that week after week," says former *Blue & Gold Illustrated* beat writer Tim Prister, "especially when you run a program the way Holtz did, where he always had his players on edge."

On a practical scale, Darnell's attacking defense just wasn't meshing with Notre Dame's personnel, which he was finding—despite the up-grades under Holtz through the recruiting process—could not move the way his teams had at Florida.

"As a defensive lineman, he tried to get us up the field a little bit more, not reading as much as Alvarez did," says Bob Dahl, a starting defensive tackle in 1990. "I don't think it worked out so well."

With a hellacious schedule still to play and the Irish in danger of falling out of the national title hunt earlier than they had since Holtz's first season, Holtz took the defensive play calls away from his first-year defensive coordinator and star off-season hire.

"You have to believe so strongly in what you're doing that you're say-ing, 'I'm going to insist you do it my way and if it doesn't work, I'll take blame for it.' So many people don't want to do that," says Holtz.

"A lot of people got complacent," Zorich says. "You can't afford to be complacent when your only shot is the national championship. What Holtz did in '88 and '89 was remarkable. But he even feels he got complacent because he wanted to maintain, he didn't want to exceed.

"I'm not saying it was his fault we lost, but it was an overall attitude that *Maybe we really are that good.* After that game, I didn't speak to the media. Roger Valdiserri came up to me and said, 'Who the fuck do you think you are? You lose one game and you can't talk to the media?' It was an eye-opening experience for me."

———

A few days before Notre Dame was to host Miami in 1990, memories of the last few years emerged with great clarity.

Sure, there were great games and great moments in the contests between the two teams—everything from Miami's failed 2-point conversion attempt at Notre Dame Stadium to the third-and-forty-three the 'Canes had converted to reassert their dominance in the rivalry—and over the sport as a whole. But where the public was concerned, those things took a backseat to the more pressing issue: Were the Irish and Hurricanes going to brawl again?

As thrilling as the previous two meetings had been, they had been marred by pregame incidents. Or, depending on your perspective, elevated by them. There was the brawl in the tunnel before Notre Dame's victory in 1988. Then, a year later, Miami taunted the Irish mercilessly at the Orange Bowl before kickoff. Only Notre Dame's restraint—at Holtz's command—prevented another melee.

Now the two programs were set to meet again. Early in the week, Holtz and Hurricanes coach Dennis Erickson arranged a telephone "summit," an attempt to maintain an uneasy peace. Holtz pledged that he would resign as Notre Dame's coach if his players were involved in another such incident. At the same time, he said that he understood that it was the price he would be willing to pay if the Hurricanes came into Notre Dame Stadium and acted as the aggressor. After being intimidated right out of the game the year before, the Irish couldn't afford to surrender their edge yet again, not against their biggest rival in the biggest game of the year. Not even if it meant losing their coach.

"Sometimes," Holtz said, "you just have to take a stand. You just have to defend yourself. There comes a time when you just have to say enough is enough. You aren't just going to keep backing up."

Notre Dame's players embraced the possibility of meeting the Hurricanes head-on should something develop. Holtz had a camera installed in the tunnel to record evidence in case anything should develop.

"If somebody comes after us," quarterback Rick Mirer said, "we're going to defend ourselves."

"I'm not backing down from anybody," tight end Derek Brown added.

"We don't want to have a fight—period," Notre Dame linebacker Scott Kowalkowski assured. "But that's not to say we're going to back down."

It was all idle chatter, however. The most important result of the telephone summit between the two head coaches was the careful stage-managing of the pregame logistics. Participants were welcome to boast all they wanted during the week. They were not getting anywhere near each other until kickoff on Saturday afternoon, even if they wanted to.

———

The Miami team that was coming to town was averaging 37.2 points per game and throwing for 306 yards a game, fourth best in the country. Led by All-American defensive tackle Russell Maryland, the Hurricanes were allowing only sixty-two rushing yards a game. The BYU game was well in Miami's rearview mirror, and the Hurricanes seemed to have adjusted to behaving themselves during games.

Miami coach Dennis Erickson, on the other hand, had not yet adjusted to the constant strain of coaching in a pressure cooker like Miami. Erickson had been able to recover quickly from the Florida State loss in his first season, guiding his team back on track while blocking out the criticism from outside the program. That was more difficult after BYU. Letters poured into the football office. Weeks after the loss, Erickson still woke up sweating at night, overcome by fear of failure. "I'm obsessed with winning," he explained. By Notre Dame week, the second-year coach had lost twenty pounds since the start of the season, barely a month before. Erickson's immune system was shot, and in the days before facing the Irish he developed fever blisters around his mouth.

Even so, things looked better for him than for his rival.

Despite all the pregame rhetoric about not backing down, things just didn't look promising for the Irish. Notre Dame was led by Rick Mirer, a sophomore quarterback, who would have to try to figure out an elite Miami defense that even Tony Rice, a perfect fit for Holtz's system and an experienced starter, struggled against the year before. Then again, things hadn't looked promising two years before, either, but the Irish held on in the game's waning seconds to upset the No. 1–ranked Hurricanes. The prospects had also seemed bleak a few months before, when they rebounded from a deflating defeat to Miami to dominate Colorado in the Orange Bowl.

"Miracles still happen," Holtz said. "And they happen in our stadium more than some others."

Holtz believed the Irish had some combination of God and luck on their side. More important, they had Rocket Ismail, who had become a national phenomenon in 1989. In an early-season showdown against Michigan, the earliest in a season that the No. 1 and No. 2 teams in the nation had ever met on the field, Ismail returned two kickoffs for a touchdown: It had been decades since Bo Schembechler's Wolverines had even allowed one kick return for a score. The cover of *Sports Illustrated* that week had featured Ismail on the cover, along with a lengthy profile inside and the game story documenting his heroics against Michigan. Suddenly, everyone in America knew about "The Rocket."

For Raghib himself, it was too much, too soon.

"His freshman year, he was very outgoing and really seemed to enjoy it," says John Heisler, Notre Dame's longtime sports information director. "There was a novelty to it all back then. I think somehow the Michigan game his sophomore year seemed to change things. He became such a big name so quickly because of what he did on the field, I think he honestly felt that he was receiving too much of the publicity. He didn't feel like that was the kind of thing that was supposed to happen to you as a sophomore. You weren't supposed to be the star of the show."

The spotlight grew even brighter as he entered his junior year the clear front-runner for the Heisman Trophy. Heisler and his staff struggled to get the reticent superstar to fulfill even the most mundane, unintrusive press obligations. Reporters who covered the Irish in the era recall finding out on different occasions that Rocket had folded his five-foot-ten-inch frame under a laundry cart to escape detection while in the presence of the media.

"There was no hiding who he was," Heisler says. "He wasn't just one of the guys anymore."

In 1990, realizing that Miami would try to blanket his best player in coverage, Holtz came up with a plan: He would line Rocket up in the backfield. At first, the idea chafed Ismail. A reluctant superstar, he worried that his coach had an ulterior motive.

"You're not doing this because of the Heisman stuff?" Ismail asked Holtz. Holtz said, "No, it's in our best interests."

Ismail reminded Holtz that there were plenty of tailbacks on Notre Dame's roster who were more than capable of carrying the football. But Holtz wasn't in the mood for a debate. "I'm the coach," Holtz answered.

Before he would be unleashed as a running back, however, Ismail would beat Miami in a more familiar way. In the first quarter, Miami led 10–3. Following his team's touchdown, Hurricanes kicker Carlos Huerta sent a kick spiraling down the middle of the field, right into Ismail's waiting arms.

"My first thought was why did he do that?" Ismail would later say.

"They were arrogant enough to kick off to him," Holtz says. "Some people are arrogant enough to say, 'Okay,' and they were."

Ismail gathered the ball in at the Notre Dame six-yard line. A moment later he was gone, with only Huerta to beat. The kicker never had a chance. The ninety-four-yard touchdown tied the game just seconds after Miami had taken the lead.

The Rocket had given Notre Dame the early momentum. But whether he would be around at the finish line was another matter. In the second quarter, Ismail saw what he believed was a Miami defender out of the corner of his eye. He turned to block the Hurricane but ended up throwing his body into nothing but thin air. He realized he was dehydrated and damned near hallucinating. Quickly, the Notre Dame sideline staff inserted a saline IV. At halftime, Ismail received another fluid IV.

It worked. Ismail rushed for seventy-five of his 108 yards in the second half. For the game, he had 268 total yards, his career high. In Notre Dame's biggest rivalry, perhaps its most exciting player of all time had come up huge.

And yet, despite the efforts of the flashiest player in college football, the final battle between the two top programs in the game was anything but flashy.

For a decade, save for the epic 1988 victory, the Irish offense had been unable to solve the Miami defense. This time around the Irish moved the ball but found difficulty, as always, finishing drives against Hurricane defenders. Rick Mirer, the new Notre Dame quarterback, was only a specter of the passer who would go on to become the second overall selection in the NFL Draft two years later. At one point early in the game, Mirer was a lousy one-for-five for thirteen yards passing. He largely avoided big mistakes, but he wouldn't be the one to make a difference in this game.

It would be an unknown Notre Dame special teamer who would rise to Miami's challenge.

The year before, Miami's all-time great defense had stopped the Irish cold, ruining any chance of Holtz's team completing a second consecutive unbeaten national championship season. This time, utilizing Ismail along with more conventional back Rodney Culver, who carried the ball twenty-one times, Notre Dame moved the ball seemingly at will against the Hurricanes. The nation's best rushing defense, however, seemed to reappear every time Notre Dame drove inside the red zone.

It was there that Mirer's inexperience was costly as the one-dimensional offense struggled on a short field. The Irish also missed Rice, a quarterback who could make things happen with his legs.

In the first quarter Notre Dame drove inside the Miami ten but had to call on placekicker Craig Hentrich to finish off the drive.

"I remember the first field goal opportunity I had was fairly close," Hentrich says. "I hit it right down the middle and just got confidence from there on in."

Confidence was indeed something Hentrich had in spades, even in the face of such an enormous game. In his media guide bio, he said that others found him "lazy, indifferent and nonchalant." In response to "The most amazing thing I've ever seen on a football field is..." he wrote: "The Miami Hurricane cheerleaders." On competing in the game of the year: "You just stay away from the hype and the TV and the players," Hentrich says. "The goalposts didn't narrow because this was a big game. You just go out there and do it."

That early Irish drive was a harbinger of things to come. In the second quarter Notre Dame continued to move the ball, and continued to grind to a halt when the end zone was within striking distance. But then came Hentrich, hitting two more field goals in the second quarter, from forty-four and thirty-four yards, and Notre Dame went into intermission trailing just 17–16. Like the season before, the Irish trailed, but this felt different: The game was in South Bend, the offense was moving the ball, and there were no big Miami plays or Notre Dame flubs in the closing minutes to take the wind out of Notre Dame's sails.

———

Soon after arriving as Notre Dame's new defensive coordinator, Gary Darnell had recognized that Holtz was a coach who thrived on crisis. And Holtz had elevated the defense's difficulties to that level leading into the final battle with Miami by essentially stripping Darnell's authority from him and instituting a scheme that largely tracked the one that Alvarez had run before his exit.

The payoff would come in the third quarter. The Hurricanes received the second-half kickoff but quickly punted. Notre Dame's defense was on a mission. "We knew this was it," said All-American linebacker Michael Stonebreaker, a holdover from the '88 national title team. "This is why we were recruited, why we work out, and why we play football—to play games like this." Miami's next drive ended when Notre Dame linebacker Scott Kowalkowski forced a fumble deep in 'Canes territory. A few plays later Hentrich's fourth field goal of the game gave the Irish a 19–17 advantage. His fifth, later in the quarter, established a new Notre Dame single-game record and put his team ahead 22–17.

Meanwhile, the defense continued to respond to its head coach. Two years before, in the 1988 Notre Dame victory in South Bend, South Florida native Pat Terrell had made the game's biggest play, batting down the Miami 2-point conversion to seal the victory for the Irish. In 1990, an effort by another Floridian would give Notre Dame's victories some symmetry. Greg Davis, a product of Hollywood, Florida, intercepted a Craig Erickson pass early in the second quarter. Then, in the fourth quarter, he forced a fumble at the Notre Dame two, keeping the Hurricanes out of the end zone on what would turn out to be their final possession. The plays by Davis were indicative of the kind of effort the previously maligned Notre Dame defense was able to produce throughout the afternoon against one of the most innovative and explosive offenses in college football. And after the final one, the Notre Dame offense finally completed a drive, with Mirer connecting with Culver on a play that Holtz had drawn up at the breakfast table earlier in the day. The score gave Notre Dame a 29–20 advantage, and there it would remain.

Although the offense got bogged down in the red zone, Joe Moore's offensive linemen earned some redemption after being thoroughly dominated at the Orange Bowl a year before, doing more than their part to contribute to the victory. The Irish rushed for nearly three hundred yards against the nation's top-ranked defense, setting Hentrich up again and again to chip-shot the 'Canes into submission. Just a few weeks removed from an unconscionable loss to Stanford, Notre Dame was right back in the national title picture. Miami, meanwhile, was out of the national title picture because of the loss, the earliest that had happened in many years.

Notre Dame had struck the perfect balance between old-time football, grinding out yards on the ground before handing over things to the kicker, and new-time flash, with Rocket Ismail's return the only touchdown for the Irish until the late score to finally put the game out of reach.

"What can you say about the Rocket?" Dennis Erickson said after the game. "You work against it all week in practice, you know what to do. Then you get in the game, he gets the ball...and he's gone."

Was it as epic as the victory two years before? It would be hard to say so, as that earlier game had been infused with the subtext of the 1985 blowout, the last demon the rejuvenated program had to exorcise. Neither did it have the same feeling as the 1989 contest, which took place at season's end and served as a quasi–playoff game. But as this was the last meeting between the teams, there was something extremely satisfying about gaining the last word, considering where the program had been just five years before. After the victory, Notre Dame's players and fans celebrated on the turf of Notre Dame Stadium, repeating the scene from two years earlier, when a victory over Miami carried the Irish to the national championship.

But even as the celebration raged, others were saddened. They knew they had just witnessed the end of something wonderful, an altogether accidental rivalry that had blossomed into the most eagerly anticipated Saturday of each year.

"Shirt drawers are going to be a lot thinner now that it is over," *Chicago Tribune* columnist Bernie Lincicome lamented, "and college football is going to be a lot duller."

Notre Dame fans remember it as perhaps the worst day of their fandom.

Chris Zorich remembers it as the worst day of his life.

There would be no storybook ending to the 1990 season for the Irish, no repeat of their rampage to the national championship after the 1988 victory over the Hurricanes. After retaking the No. 1 spot in the polls, the Irish fell late in the season at home to Penn State. However, they were still able to secure an Orange Bowl invitation, a date with No. 1–ranked Colorado. It was unlikely that Notre Dame, with two losses, would leapfrog the teams ahead of them to claim at least a share of the national title. But the Irish could certainly play spoiler.

Zorich was dominant against the No. 1–ranked Buffaloes, helping the Notre Dame defense hold its opponent to just 10 points going into the final minute of the game. Colorado led 10–9, then punted the ball back to the Irish with about a minute to play. But Colorado coach Bill McCartney did not learn from Dennis Erickson's mistake earlier in the season. Instead of punting the ball out of bounds, Colorado punter Tom Rouen booted the ball forty-four yards down the middle of the field, right into Ismail's waiting arms at the nine-yard line.

Ninety-one yards later, it appeared that the Irish had spoiled Colorado's national title hopes, and the Rocket had provided a video clip that might supplant Flutie's throw against Miami as the ultimate highlight.

If only.

Instead, the play was called back because of a clip by Notre Dame's Greg Davis. Colorado won the game and shared the national title with Georgia Tech.

Zorich, named Notre Dame's most valuable player in the game, called his mother afterward to lament the loss.

"You played so well, though," she said.

"Yeah, Mom, but we lost."

"But you were all over the place," Zora Zorich countered. "I was so proud of you. You played great."

"Yeah, Mom, I did play great, didn't I?" Zorich finally said, checking over his shoulder to make sure no teammates heard him.

A major academic risk from the inner city, Zorich had been driven by one thought: to succeed at Notre Dame, through his early struggles in the classroom as well as on the football field, and to lift his mother out of poverty on the South Side. In the aftermath of the Orange Bowl loss, Zorich was disappointed that his college career, in which he would be twice honored as a consensus All-American, was over. But at least, with the NFL on the horizon, he would be able to finally help his mother financially.

The day after the Orange Bowl, he arrived back home in Chicago, ready to talk to his mother about the exciting times ahead, including graduation in a few months followed by a pro career. But the conversation never happened. Zora Zorich lay dead in the apartment, having finally succumbed to the health problems that had plagued her for so long.

"I think I was in shock for a while," Zorich says. "But I had a great support system. All the guys on the team came to Chicago for the funeral. The whole team was there. When I came back to school, people started to ask me, 'Why are you in school? Your mom just died.' I said, 'My mom would kick my ass if I took a semester off.' There's no way, anywhere, that I could have let something like that happen."

The death of his mother was devastating for Zorich, but it didn't deter him. After being drafted in the second round by the Chicago Bears, he set up the Christopher Zorich Foundation in Chicago, using his celebrity to help other impoverished children out of the Chicago slums. He played for seven years in the NFL, earning a Pro Bowl invitation after the 1993 season. But Zorich wasn't done with his education. After football, the man who once scored a 740 on the SAT and two Ds in his first semester at Notre Dame applied to Notre Dame Law School.

He was admitted, graduating three years later. However, after working at a law firm for a couple of years, he left to join the athletic administration staff at Notre Dame. Today he works as a student-athlete welfare coordinator in the department, and dreams of running his own athletic department someday as athletic director. He is still very active in his charitable foundation.

And of course Zorich is not the only person for whom life did not end when Notre Dame–Miami did.

Gerry Faust didn't stay unemployed for very long after his resignation/firing at Notre Dame. Faust was hired as the head coach at the University of Akron soon afterward, giving him the opportunity to coach another Division I-A program and also to settle back in Ohio. Although he will always be most associated with his five years at Notre Dame, Faust would coach at Akron almost twice as long. He was fired after the 1994 season, during which his Zips went 1–10. Faust's Akron teams compiled an overall record of 73-79-4. He never coached again, but has been far from a recluse in retirement. Faust still attends most home games at Notre Dame, sitting in the press box and mingling with fans and reporters. During his own ultimately failed tenure, former Irish head coach Charlie Weis invited Faust back to be the keynote speaker at the team's year-end banquet.

Greeted by the same kind of skepticism that had dominated his arrival at Miami, Jimmy Johnson went to work in the coaching position with the Dallas Cowboys that he had been hired for amid controversy. Johnson's first Dallas team finished 1–15, seeming to verify people's suspicions that he was in over his head. But in the meantime, with the football world ready to write him off as a college-to-pro bust, Johnson pulled off one of the biggest heists in NFL history, inducing the Minnesota Vikings to surrender a slew of early-round draft picks in exchange for running back Herschel Walker, Dallas's one recognizable star. Johnson used the draft selections to build the nucleus of a true NFL dynasty: quarterback Troy Aikman, running back Emmitt Smith, and wide receiver Michael Irvin, Johnson's volatile former 'Cane, whom the Cowboys had nearly given up on by the time Johnson arrived. The Cowboys improved steadily in Johnson's first few seasons, then in 1992 and 1993 won back-to-back Super Bowls over former Miami quarterback Jim Kelly and the Buffalo Bills.

Despite their success, Johnson's Cowboys were as apt to make head-lines for the wrong reasons away from the field as for anything they did on the field. Hailed as college cronies when Johnson was hired, Jerry Jones and Johnson suffered a professional falling-out, which eventually led to Johnson's exit after the second Super Bowl victory. He was re-placed by his old boss at the University of Oklahoma, Barry Switzer. Johnson resurfaced three years later as the head coach of the Miami Dolphins, but he could not replicate his success in his previous two stops. Johnson's Miami teams lost all three playoff games they played, including a humiliating 62–7 defeat against the Jacksonville Jaguars in the final game Johnson would ever coach at the end of the 1999 season. He currently works as one of Fox's NFL studio analysts.

Though drafted in the supplemental draft by Johnson, Steve Walsh was unable to beat out Troy Aikman for the starting job in Dallas. He was traded to the New Orleans Saints after the season, beginning a career as an NFL journeyman. Walsh was the starting quarterback for two playoff teams, the 1990 Saints and the 1994 Chicago Bears. Walsh's Bears, coached by former Miami defensive coordinator Dave Wannstedt, defeated the Minnesota Vikings 35–18 in the wild-card round of the 1994 playoffs before falling the next week to the San Francisco 49ers. He retired after the 1999 season, when he backed up Peyton Manning in Indianapolis. In 2009, after several years in the business world, Walsh got back into the game as the head coach at West Palm Beach, Florida's, Cardinal Newman High School.

Tony Rice's pro career was even less successful than Walsh's. After Rice went undrafted by the NFL, he knocked around some other pro leagues for a while, including the Canadian, World, and Arena Football Leagues. Rice's pursuit of a pro football career would end in 1992 as backup in the Arena League to someone named Mike Pile. He eventu-ally would move on to other areas of his life, including fatherhood and success in business.

After the Miami dynasty began to crumble under its own weight, Dennis Erickson bolted for the NFL's Seattle Seahawks in time for the 1995 season. However, his days of tormenting Notre Dame did not end with the 1989 season finale victory over the Irish. One of Erickson's first moves as Seahawks coach was to bench former overall No. 2 draft pick Rick Mirer, who had quarterbacked the Irish to a victory over

Erickson's 'Canes in the 1990 final showdown, in favor of John Friesz, whom he had once recruited to the University of Idaho. Erickson struggled in both his NFL stops, with the Seahawks and San Francisco 49ers. In 1999, Erickson took over at Oregon State, recruiting from junior college wide receivers Chad Johnson and T. J. Houshmandzadeh. The pair ran roughshod over Notre Dame in the Fiesta Bowl after the 2000 season, a 41–9 victory for Oregon State. Erickson became the head coach of Arizona State in 2007, tying USC for the Pac-10 conference title in his first season. However, by Erickson's third campaign the Sun Devils had dropped to 4–8 overall and ninth place in the Pac-10.

Cleveland Gary, the Miami fullback who famously fumbled—or didn't—near the goal line in 1988, spent six seasons in the NFL, rushing for a league-leading fourteen touchdowns for the Los Angeles Rams in 1990. He rushed for a career-high 1,125 yards in 1992. Today, Gary is the owner of several businesses, including the Internet-based Black Shopping Channel.

Vinny Cerrato, Holtz's ace recruiting coordinator, left his mentor's side after the 1990 season to take a job in the player personnel department of the San Francisco 49ers as the director of college scouting. In that role, he drafted two Notre Dame players, Ricky Watters and Bryant Young, who would contribute to the team's trouncing of the San Diego Chargers in Super Bowl XXIX. Cerrato eventually worked his way up the NFL front-office ladder, becoming the Washington Redskins' vice president for football operations—essentially the franchise's general manager—in 2002. Cerrato was fired during the 2009 season, in the midst of a 4–12 season.

Miami receiver Randal Hill, who hauled in the forty-four-yard catch that buried Notre Dame in 1989, never became the NFL star that many projected him to be. After being selected in the first round by the hometown Miami Dolphins in 1991, Hill's best season came in 1992, when he caught fifty-eight passes for 861 yards for the then Phoenix Cardinals. Hill provided perhaps the consummate highlight for Miami detractors after the 1991 season, running through the end zone and into the tunnel after a touchdown in the Cotton Bowl against Texas, then coming out and pantomiming six-shooters using his hands and fingers. Today, Hill works as an agent in the United States Department of Homeland Security in Florida.

A potential first overall selection in the NFL Draft after his Notre Dame career, Rocket Ismail instead took the road less traveled, signing for millions with the Canadian Football League's Toronto Argonauts. He eventually joined the NFL, putting together back-to-back thousand-yard receiving seasons with the Carolina Panthers and Dallas Cowboys in the late 1990s. Rocket Ismail played nine seasons in the NFL but never returned a punt or kickoff for a touchdown. By 2009 he was attempting to recover financially after the loss of hundreds of thousands, perhaps millions of dollars from bad business investments.

Lou Holtz was able to make one more real run at a national championship at Notre Dame, and falling short was even more painful than the 1989 runner-up finish to the Hurricanes. Late in the 1993 season, the No. 2-ranked Irish knocked off No. 1-ranked Florida State in a matchup of unbeatens widely dubbed "The Game of the Century." With just one game to play, Notre Dame's path to the national title seemed clear. The Irish had only Boston College to beat in the regular season and Texas A&M in a bowl game.

Instead, the emotionally spent Irish fell to the Eagles, and controversial votes by both polls after the 1993 season gave the national title to Florida State.

Holtz left Notre Dame after the 1996 season, then came out of retirement a few years later to take the job at the University of South Carolina. His first team at South Carolina in 1999 went 0–11. But Holtz showed soon after that he had not lost his touch when it came to reviving downtrodden programs, guiding the Gamecocks to an 8-4 record in 2000 and a 9-3 record in 2001, along with back-to-back bowl victories. Unfortunately for Holtz, however, his tenure at South Carolina was marred by a brawl in his final game, the Gamecocks' rivalry showdown against Clemson. And much more so than the brawl against the Hurricanes in 1988, the South Carolina–Clemson brawl was an embarrassment for both schools. Holtz, who had already announced his retirement, and the university said they would decline any bowl invitations as a self-sanction. Holtz has not coached since, and today is visible as one of the primary college football studio hosts on ESPN. During the 2008 season, the twentieth anniversary of his only national championship at the school, Notre Dame unveiled a statue of Holtz inside the Notre Dame Stadium concourse. He was enshrined in the College

Football Hall of Fame one year later. In the spring of that year, Holtz coached a team of former Notre Dame players against a Japanese all-star team. During a tryout for the exhibition, Holtz was asked what advice he would give coaches considering a daunting challenge.

"There are," he said, "no good jobs."

———

It didn't last. It couldn't.

In the 1970s and '80s, major changes in the landscape of college football created the circumstances that enabled the University of Miami to rise from obscurity into the dominant program of the decade. But those circumstances, which fostered parity that the sport had never experienced, also ensured that a decades' long dynasty wouldn't last—*couldn't* last—by 1990.

An early indication of that came at BYU in early 1990, when quarterback Ty Detmer humbled the Hurricanes. The beginning of the end, however, came after the regular season, at the Cotton Bowl. In the early 1980s, the Hurricanes were a national darling as they rose from nowhere to upset Nebraska in the Orange Bowl following the 1983 season. Even when they stomped on Gerry Faust's Notre Dame Fighting Irish, drawing Ara Parseghian's rage, at the end of the 1985 season, there was a sense that someone new and fresh had put an entitled member of the establishment in its place. However, in Dallas in early 1991, the number of Miami's defenders had long since dwindled.

The Hurricanes picked up three consecutive unsportsmanlike conduct penalties early on against No. 3-ranked Texas. They rolled up sixteen penalties overall for 202 yards. They danced. They taunted. And they steamrolled the Texas Longhorns 46–3. But this time hardly anyone enjoyed the spectacle. "Sooner or later, the street would take over," columnist Will McDonough wrote in the *Boston Globe*, lamenting how the 'Canes were "dancing like fools every time they scored a touchdown."

In a few short years, public sentiment had largely turned violently against the Hurricanes. Erickson's 'Canes had few defenders. *New York Times* columnist William C. Rhoden was one of them:

I loved the Miami performance. Loved it probably for all the wrong reasons. Love it in part because of the contradictions it represented: White universities embraced this Faustian pact two decades earlier when they began bringing black athletes to their campuses by the truckloads. They wanted black muscle but not the attendant zeal and style. They somehow thought these athletes would all arrive at their campuses as sanitized as Jackie Robinson. They pretended that these athletes weren't going to arrive with their own baggage, baggage that a history of living in a white supremacist country had helped to pack.

If, however, the reaction to Miami's Cotton Bowl victory was simply evidence that the nation misunderstood the Hurricanes, even their staunchest defenders couldn't rationalize what happened a few years later. In 1993, student adviser Anthony Russell pleaded guilty to falsifying more than ninety federal Pell Grant student aid forms for players, defrauding the government out of $220,000. Miami team chaplain Leo Armbrust, at Miami since the early years of the Schnellenberger era, had been a longtime defender of the program. Sure, he figured the program gave off a renegade vibe from time to time, but that wasn't always a bad thing.

Now even he began to lose faith. In the mid-1980s, Florida State lineman Pablo Lopez, a Miami native, was shot and killed. However, draconian NCAA restrictions kept his Seminole teammates stranded in Tallahassee, as the school was not permitted to foot the bill for their trip to his funeral. In their place, dozens of Miami players showed up to support Lopez's family and friends. But even underreported gestures like that couldn't make up for some of what the Miami program had become. The reaction to military fatigues had been overblown; the reaction to a wide-scale federal aid fraud was appropriate. "We had to take a look at every aspect of what we were doing," says Armbrust. In 1995, *Sports Illustrated* wrote a devastating critique of the program, framed as an open letter to university president Tad Foote. The cover that week, in large letters against a plain green background: *Why the University of Miami should drop football.*

Inertia kept things afloat for a while. The Hurricanes rebounded from the losses at BYU and Notre Dame to win the 1991 national championship, going undefeated. But the next year the pack began to overtake them. With a second straight national title on the line, the Hurricanes fell 34–13 to Alabama in the Sugar Bowl, reminiscent of the 1985 loss to Tennessee in the same building. The next season the Hurricanes fell 29–0 to Arizona in the Fiesta Bowl. For all intents and purposes, the swagger was gone. Sanctions imposed after the Pell Grant scandal saddled the program in the 1990s, and by 1997 the Hurricanes had fallen to 5–6, their worst mark since the late 1970s.

Things weren't so great at Notre Dame, either.

Holtz, who had a history of bringing programs up to speed in a hurry before eventually wearing out his welcome, kept the Irish near the top for a few more years. In 1993, the unbeaten and second-ranked Fighting Irish welcomed No. 1–ranked Florida State to South Bend late in the year, and Notre Dame won the contest they called the "Game of the Century." But unlike the 1988 victory over the Hurricanes—recalled so fondly largely because that team was able to complete the task and win out for the national championship—the victory over the Seminoles remains marred by what came after. The following week, in the final game of the regular season, the Irish fell behind by a large margin early in the fourth quarter before storming back to take a late lead against Boston College. But as time expired, BC kicker David Gordon split the uprights to give the Eagles the victory.

After the season and an Irish victory over Texas A&M in the Cotton Bowl, voters in both polls selected Florida State their national champion. For the second time in Holtz's tenure, the Irish felt robbed of at least a portion of the national championship. They have not come close to another national title since. It is fair to say that Notre Dame has not recovered since.

But that hasn't meant the Irish have been out of the news. The 1993 season was played under the cloud of a bestselling book about Holtz's program released that fall: *Under the Tarnished Dome* by Don Yaeger and Douglas S. Looney. It included accusations of player abuse, rampant steroid use, and corner cutting, academic and otherwise, on Holtz's watch. Notre Dame and Holtz largely ignored the accusations in the book, but from a public relations point of view it dealt a blow to the program's reputation. To those who had railed against the NBC contract a few years before, this was poetic justice—and perhaps a confirmation of what they already suspected. From those detractors throughout the 1990s, the program would turn out to be the gift that kept on giving. Although Notre Dame's malfeasance never rose to the level of Miami's, it earned a slap from the NCAA in the late nineties. Kim Dunbar, who qualified as a booster because she had paid an entry fee into the school's Quarterback Club, was found to have showered a dozen Irish players with gifts and travel from 1993 to 1998. Making the story even more salacious, Dunbar had provided the funds from a stash of more than $1 million she had embezzled from a former employer. Then former offensive line coach Joe Moore sued the school and won for age discrimination after his dismissal under Holtz successor Bob Davie, adding one more link to the disastrous chain of events.

Apart, Notre Dame and Miami could not chart the future course of college football the way they had in those brilliant years together. But the legacy of the series remains. By the late 1990s, the powers that be had created the Bowl Championship Series, ensuring that at the conclusion of each season, No. 1 and No. 2 would be able to settle their differences on the field. What seemed like a perfect solution in theory has not worked out so well in practice. Twice, in 1997 and 2003, Associated Press voters and the BCS standings differed, resulting in the kind of split national title that the system was created to prevent. Perhaps most troubling, the haves of the college football world have used the system to permanently sequester themselves from the have-nots. Several times, unbeaten teams, including a Utah team in 2009 that clobbered a 12–1 Alabama squad in the Sugar Bowl, have been frozen out of the national title hunt because the system is engineered that way. In 2009, TCU and Boise State both finished the season unbeaten and qualified for BCS bowl berths. Rather than giving them a crack at an SEC or Big Ten team, the powers that be pitted the pair against each other in the Fiesta Bowl. What the current system has done, essentially, is choke off any route for another Miami to rise from the pack to challenge the established order. And the game is poorer for it.

Cleveland Gary's fumble at the goal line was emblematic of an era in which the feet and eyes of officials were no longer keeping up with the pace of the game. With television replay technology improving by the year, it was only a matter of time before the sport adopted some sort of replay review to ensure that its mistakes were quickly corrected and that national titles did not come down to blown calls. That happened in the 2000s. The recruiting frenzy begun by Vinny Cerrato and fueled by excited Notre Dame fans—as well as those in the Big Ten and Southeastern Conference, equally rabid—has become a full-blown industry unto itself, with two national Internet networks updating player decision-making practically in real time (the old warhorses Tom Lemming and Allen Wallace continue to plug away as well). As of 2010, Notre Dame remains on NBC. And the contract has remained true to Beauchamp and Rosenthal's ideal. No night games (with the exception of a 2009 neutral site contest in San Antonio). No weekdays. And, most important of all, Notre Dame remains college football's only major independent, free from the shackles of conference affiliation. Miami, meanwhile, now plays in the Atlantic Coast Conference.

In many ways, college football is a better sport than it was from 1985 through 1990. There are more games on television. More teams with a shot at the big-money bowls. Less mistakes by officials and pollsters. For sheer fun, however, it will always be difficult for it to match that period: when two perfect rivals, representing college football's storied past and its rapidly changing present, met each year for the soul of the sport.

ACKNOWLEDGMENTS

A few years ago, I wrote my first book, a biography of semi-obscure but eminently fascinating (at least to me) 1920s baseball Hall of Famer Edgar Charles "Sam" Rice. While I certainly could not have pulled it off without the assistance of a few key people, the nature of the book meant that most of the work was between me, a couple of useful libraries, and the search for needles in the haystack of old newspaper articles preserved on microfilm and PDFs. I had read plenty of other books in which authors went on for multiple pages thanking all those whom they could not have done it without, and as I whipped out my skimpy thank-yous, I wondered why it so often seemed to take a village for everybody else.

I'm not wondering anymore.

First of all, thanks go to my agent at Venture Literary, Frank Scatoni, as well as my editor, Mark Tavani, and the rest of the people at ESPN Books. I approached Frank with several seeds of ideas for books, and he believed in the Notre Dame–Miami idea from day one. With his attention to detail in shaping the lengthy proposal and his diligence in finding a publisher, Frank believed in getting the story to print as much as I did. As far as ESPN Books goes, there is an old maxim among authors that the smaller the ball, the better chance you have of finding someone to get behind your project. Instead of buying into that, ESPN has been willing to tap into America's obvious passion for college football and bring it to the printed page. Mark and the rest of the staff at ESPN Books were enthusiastic from the outset, helping to shape the narrative into something far more focused than I had presented.

Any book I have ever come across that has Notre Dame football as its subject is universally breathless in its appreciation for the university's sports information staff. This book will not be an exception. John Heisler, the longtime director of the department, was helpful both in sharing his own memories of the era as well as sharing contact information of Irish players from the Holtz era. The files kept by the staff are exhaustively maintained and meticulously organized. Specifically, thanks go to Carol Copley and Susan McGonigal for tracking down phone numbers, photos, clips, and whatever else I asked for.

I would like to, of course, thank the former coaches of both programs for taking time to share their memories of those years. Dennis Erickson returned my phone call within the hour in the middle of recruiting season. Lou Holtz took time out of a busy schedule on a weekend back in South Bend to talk with me. Gerry Faust was completely willing to talk about the worst night and week of his career in coaching, which didn't surprise me whatsoever considering the pretty much universal experience that others have had dealing with him. Howard Schnellenberger—like Erickson, still actively leading a Division I-A program—shared his memories. So did Dave Wannstedt. The programs and the now dormant rivalry, of course, would not be what they are without the quarterback legacies at each school. And this book would not have been possible without the contributions of Tony Rice, Steve Walsh, Craig Erickson, Rick Mirer, and Steve Beuerlein. So many people agreed to give up their time freely to be interviewed, more than one hundred when it was all said and done. Every single one of them contributed something valuable to the finished product. They included Frank Stams, Wes Pritchett, Ned Bolcar, Rex Kerns, Barry Alvarez, John Krimm, Bob Crable, Mark Green, Mark Bavaro, Dean Masztak, Devon McDonald, Bernard "Tiger" Clark, Steve Kim, Scott Kowalkowski, Leon Searcy, Lindsay Knapp, Mike Kovaleski, Justin Hall, D'Juan Francisco, Byron Spruell, Doug Browne, Jim Martz, Tom Hanrahan, Pat Eilers, Randy Bethel, Cortez Kennedy, Marty Golloher, Dan Sileo, Mel Campbell, Jason Hicks, Rick Antle, Dave Stewart, Chuck Hirschman, Chuck Lanza, Chuck Killian, George Streeter, Shannon Crowell, Chuck Heater, Brian White, Dwayne McMullen, Joel Williams, Jason Budroni, Andre Jones, Steve Alaniz, Rod West, Erik Simien, Bob Dahl, Tom Freeman, Tom Lemming, Vinny Cerrato, Ted Gradel, Allen Wallace, Joe Allen, Paul Gullifor, Tim Grunhard, Gary Darnell, Tony Yelovich, Corny Southall, Timm Rosenbach, Steve Lawrence, Steve Broussard, Rob Chudzinski,

Andy Heck, Pat Terrell, Bob Bratkowski, Mike Sullivan, Greg Cote, Todd Lyght, Kris Haines, Mike Azer, Maurice Crum, Greg Mark, Craig Hentrich, William Beauchamp, Vince Phelan, Randal Hill, Scott Provin, Carlos Huerta, Marc Trestman, Chris Zorich, Leo Armbrust, Tim Prister, Rich Dalrymple, Joe Montgomery, Michael Sloan, Darryl Dickey, Charlie Adams, and Matt Patchan.

I am grateful to Bob Wieneke, Eric Hansen, Bill Bilinski, and Al Lesar at the sports staff of the *South Bend Tribune*, where I formerly worked covering Notre Dame football, not just for their friendship but for their resources, including a stack of Notre Dame media guides that they will no doubt enjoy having back. Jim Martz, perhaps the preeminent historian regarding Miami Hurricanes football, was kind enough to trust me with his media guide collection as well. It was absolutely invaluable. Sports information staffs around the country sprang to action almost any time I asked, usually out of the blue, including Pete Clawson, Rob Turner, and Bobby Dwyer at William & Mary; Steve McClain at the University of Florida; Tyler Dunkel at New Mexico State University; and Bill Stevens at Washington State. Michael Preston, media director of the Notre Dame–Japan Bowl, was able to get Lou Holtz and me in the same room together, enduring my e-mails and phone calls even though there was little I could do to assist him in promoting his game, which he knew. Bill Johnson of the San Diego Chargers was a huge help, as was Dave Pearson of the Seattle Seahawks and Robbie Bohren of the Tennessee Titans. North of the border, a thank-you is extended to Eric Forest of the Montreal Alouettes. Also: Tony Petrocelli of the Gateway Sports Hall of Fame and John Furey and Sharon Hill at the University of Portland. And, of course, the media members. My friends for life from the Notre Dame beat deserve special thanks, some just for their reassurance every step of the way: Brian Hamilton of the *Chicago Tribune*; Michael Rothstein, formerly of the *Fort Wayne Journal-Gazette*; Pete Sampson, Tim Prister, Jake Brown, and Jack Freeman of Irish Illustrated; Steve Wiltfong of Irish Eyes; Ben Ford of the *Elkhart Truth*; and John Walters of AOL Fanhouse. Neil Hayes of the *Chicago Sun-Times* deserves special thanks: He helped me get the project started, most importantly sharing his agent's contact information with me, something that isn't done lightly in this business. Also in the media: Adam Gorney of Rivals.com; Jeff Pearlman of SI.com; Teddy

Greenstein of the *Chicago Tribune*; Jim Carty, formerly of the *Ann Arbor News*; Susan Degnan of the *Miami Herald*; and Adam Rittenberg of ESPN.com.

Finally, it is customary for authors to thank their significant others upon completion of a project. To those outside this business, it probably seems like a nice gesture. It is more than that. I shudder when I think of what my wife, Kelley, endured during the course of this writing. While I was married to the book, we moved twice within a few months, then welcomed our first child, Ben, into our lives. I have a lot of time to make up, that's for sure. No more book projects for... for at least a few weeks.

SOURCES

During the course of researching this work, nothing was more valuable than the recollections of the approximately one hundred people who were interviewed personally by the author. At the same time, participants, historians, and journalists who had written about the two programs in the past left a terrific road map. A few sources were particularly valuable. Jimmy Johnson and Lou Holtz both wrote wonderfully thoughtful and candid autobiographies that helped fill in the gaps in their past, as well as taking readers behind the scenes during key moments of their tenures. Keith Dunnavant's work, *The Fifty-Year Seduction*, and Pete Gullifor's *The Fighting Irish on the Air* were both extremely helpful in allowing me to understand the pervasive impact that television and broadcasting have had on the college game. Marvin Dunn's brilliant work on the city of Miami's sordid history helped place the Hurricanes rise in the social context of its time. Writers at the Notre Dame *Scholastic* helped do the same for that program. Bruce Feldman's *'Cane Mutiny* is a wonderful romp through the rise from the ashes of the Miami program—and, for the purposes of this work, quite informative. *Under the Tarnished Dome*, a critical look at Notre Dame football by two *Sports Illustrated* writers in the early 1990s, has gotten a bad rap from Irish fans because of its obvious point of view, but if one can overlook the tone, which isn't easy, it also filled in many of the gaps in Holtz's background in impressive detail. Journalists from *Sports Illustrated*; the *Chicago Tribune*; the *South Bend Tribune*; and the *Miami Herald* left behind a treasure trove of hard-nosed, informative coverage. Media guides from both universities were an invaluable source of background and vital but hard-to-track-down facts. Sitting down and watching the important games ensured that part of the storytelling was accurate.

ARTICLES

Adams, Charlie. "The Chris Zorich Story." NCSA College Athletic Scholarships Blog, Feb. 3, 2009.

Buchholz, Brad. "Wake Up the Echoes." *Inside Sports*, Sept. 1989.

Ellenport, Craig. "The Rocket Man." *Sport*, Nov. 1990.

Kelleher, Ted. "Has Notre Dame Overcome?" *Scholastic*, Nov. 26, 1985.

Kelly, Jason. "Zorich Back as the Mentor He Never Had." *Notre Dame Magazine*, Autumn 2008.

Looney, Douglas S. "Deep in Hot Water in Stillwater." *Sports Illustrated*, July 3, 1978.

Looney, Douglas S. "Hard Man, Soft Heart." *Sports Illustrated*, Oct. 1, 1990.

Looney, Douglas S. "The Luck of the Irish." *Sports Illustrated*, Oct. 30, 1989.

Looney, Douglas S. "Time to Wake Up the Echoes." *Sports Illustrated*, Dec. 9, 1985.

Murphy, Austin. "Clip off the Old Block." *Sports Illustrated*, Jan. 14, 1991.

Murphy, Austin. "No. 1. No More." *Sports Illustrated*, Dec. 4, 1989.

Newman, Bruce. "This Is for You, Sal." *Sports Illustrated*, Oct. 9, 1989.

Reed, William F. "We're Notre Dame and You're Not." *Sports Illustrated*, Feb. 19, 1990.

Reilly, Rick. "What Price Glory?" *Sports Illustrated*, Feb. 27, 1989.

Reynolds, Cathyann. "Opening the Door: Black Admissions at ND." *Scholastic*, Nov. 26, 1985.

Sullivan, Robert. "Time to Play Foote Ball?" *Sports Illustrated*, Dec. 21, 1987.

Villano, Jaclyn. "Hall Portrait: Grace." *Notre Dame Magazine*, Autumn 2006.

Wiley, Ralph. "The Light and the Lightning." *Sports Illustrated*, Sept. 25, 1989.

Wolff, Alexander. "Broken Beyond Repair: An Open Letter to the President of Miami Urges Him to Dismantle His Vaunted Football Program to Salvage His School's Reputation." *Sports Illustrated*, June 12, 1995.

BOOKS

Alvarez, Barry. *Don't Flinch: Barry Alvarez, The Autobiography*. Champaign, IL: KCI Sports, 2006.

Bilinski, Bill. *Champions: Lou Holtz's Fighting Irish*. South Bend, IN: Diamond Communications, 1990.

Coffey, Michael. *Echoes on the Hardwood: 100 Seasons of Notre Dame Men's Basketball*. Lanham, MD: Taylor Trade Publishing, 2004.

Delsohn, Steve. *Talking Irish: The Oral History of Notre Dame Football*. New York: Perennial, 1998.

Dressman, Denny. *Gerry Faust: Notre Dame's Man in Motion*. Cincinnati: A. S. Barnes, 1981.

Dunn, Marvin. *Black Miami in the Twentieth Century*. Gainesville, FL: University Press of Florida, 1997.

Dunn, Marvin, and Bruce Porter. *The Miami Riot of 1980*. Lexington, MA: D. C. Heath, 1984.

Dunnavant, Keith. *The Fifty-Year Seduction: How Television Manipulated College Football, from the Birth of the Modern NCAA to the Creation of the BCS*. New York: Thomas Dunne, 2004.

Faust, Gerry, and Steve Love. *The Golden Dream*. Champaign, IL: Sagamore Publishing, 1997.

Feldman, Bruce. *'Cane Mutiny*. New York: New American Library, 2005.

Gullifor, Paul E. *The Fighting Irish on the Air*. South Bend, IN: Diamond Communications, 2001.

Holtz, Lou (with John Heisler). *The Fighting Spirit: A Championship Season at Notre Dame*. New York: Simon & Schuster, 1989.

Holtz, Lou. *Winning Every Day: The Game Plan for Success*. New York: Harper-Business, 1997.

Holtz, Lou. *Wins, Losses, and Lessons*. New York: William Morrow, 2006.

Johnson, Jimmy (with Ed Hinton). *Turning the Thing Around: My Life in Football*. New York: Hyperion, 1993.

Jones, Pat (with Jimmie Trammell). *Tales from Oklahoma State Football*. Champaign, IL: Sports Publishing, 2007.

Kelly, Jim (with Vic Carrucci). *Armed and Dangerous*. New York: Doubleday, 1992.

Lieberman, Richard. *Personal Foul: Coach Joe Moore v. The University of Notre Dame*. Chicago: Academy Chicago Publishers, 2001.

Mandel, Stewart. *Bowls, Polls & Tattered Souls*. Hoboken, N.J.: John Wiley, 2007.

Martz, Jim. *Hurricane Watch*. Huntsville, AL: Strode Publishers, 1981.

Martz, Jim. *Tales from the Miami Hurricanes Sideline*. Champaign, IL: Sports Publishing, 2004.

Missanelli, M. G. *The Perfect Season*. University Park, PA: Pennsylvania State University Press, 2007.

Pearlman, Jeff. *Boys Will Be Boys: The Glory Days and Party Nights of the Dallas Cowboys Dynasty*. New York: HarperCollins, 2008.

Rhoden, William C. *Forty Million Dollar Slaves*. New York: Three Rivers Press, 2007.

Sack, Allen L. *Counterfeit Amateurs*. University Park, PA: Pennsylvania State University Press, 2008.

Sperber, Murray. *Shake Down the Thunder*. New York: Henry Holt, 1993.

Watters, Ricky. *For Who for What*. Danville, CA: Tigero Books, 2002.

Yaeger, Don, and Douglas S. Looney. *Under the Tarnished Dome*. New York: Simon & Schuster, 1993.

NEWSPAPERS

The Atlanta Journal-Constitution

Blue & Gold Illustrated

Boca Raton News

The Boston Globe

Chicago Sun-Times

Chicago Tribune

Colorado Springs Gazette Telegraph

Daily Oklahoman

The Denver Post

Eugene Register-Guard

Fort Lauderdale Sun-Sentinel

Fort Wayne Journal-Gazette

Gary Post-Tribune

Indianapolis Star

Los Angeles Times

Louisville Courier-Journal

The Miami Herald

Minneapolis *Star-Tribune*

The New York Times

Orlando Sentinel

Pittsburgh Post-Gazette

St. Petersburg Times

Seattle Post-Intelligencer

The Seattle Times

South Bend Tribune

Spartansburg Herald-Journal

The Tampa Tribune

The Washington Post

ABOUT THE AUTHOR

JEFF CARROLL is a freelance writer for the *South Bend Tribune* and the *Times* of northwest Indiana. His work has been honored seventeen times by various professional organizations, including the Indiana Society of Professional Journalists, the Associated Press Sports Editors, and the Illinois and Indiana state press associations. He lives in the Chicago area with his family.

ABOUT THE TYPE

The text of this book was set in Legacy, a typeface family designed by Ronald Arnholm and issued in digital form by ITC in 1992. Both its serifed and unserifed versions are based on an original type created by the French punchcutter Nicholas Jenson in the late fifteenth century. While Legacy tends to differ from Jenson's original in its proportions, it maintains much of the latter's characteristic modulations in stroke.